To Speak for the People

To Speak for the People

Public Opinion and the Problem of Legitimacy in the French Revolution

Jon Cowans

Routledge
New York   London

Published in 2001 by

Routledge
29 West 35th Street
New York, NY 10001

Published in Great Britain by

Routledge
11 New Fetter Lane
London EC4P 4EE

Routledge is an imprint of the Taylor & Francis Group.

Library of Congress Cataloging-in-Publication Data
Cowans, Jon.
    To speak for the people : public opinion and the problem of legitimacy
in the French Revolution / Jon Cowans.
        p.   cm.
    Includes bibliographical references and index.
    ISBN 0-415-92971-7   —   ISBN 0-415-92972-5 (pbk.)
    1. Public opinion —France —History —18th century.
    2. Legitimacy of governments —France —History —18th century.
    3. France —History —Revolution, 1789–1799.   I. Title.
    HN44.P8 C69   2001
    303.3'8'094409033— dc21   00-045730

Contents

Acknowledgments

I would very much like to thank those who have helped me along the way. First mention must go to Keith Baker, whose ongoing support has allowed me to get to this point, and with whom I have had the pleasure of many fascinating conversations about history, France, public opinion, academic life, and other subjects. Special thanks also go to Mary Louise Roberts, Paul Jankowski, and Daniel Gordon, who have taught me much about history and have been enormously helpful and supportive over the years. For comments on the manuscript, I would like to thank Keith Baker, Daniel Gordon, Darline Levy, Gail Bossenga, and Jeremy Popkin, and for comments on an article-length version, I wish to thank the members of the New York Area French History Seminar and its chairman, Gene Lebovics. I am also deeply grateful to my colleagues Beryl Satter, Clement Price, and Gabor Vermes for their support. The entire publication process has been remarkably smooth and easy thanks to the truly expert work of Brendan O' Malley, Nicole Ellis, and everyone at Routledge. I would especially like to thank my wife Traci for her years of love, support, wise advice, and computer help, as well as her patience with my weekend work and general domestic clutter. Finally, I wish to thank my parents for their love and support and for teaching me the most important things I have ever learned.

Introduction

❦

Public opinion has been such a ubiquitous part of life for so long that it can be hard to imagine a time when its meaning was just beginning to take shape. Unfortunately, historians have helped create an impression of the concept's timelessness by using the term in studies of countless periods and places without examining its origins or its historically changing meanings. Such usage seems to suggest both that public opinion has always meant more or less what it means today, in an era of mass literacy, universal suffrage, and opinion polling, and that the opinions of the citizenry have always played more or less the same role as they do today. And as historians have repeatedly spoken of "public opinion," "the public," and "the people" as living, breathing entities imposing their will on political leaders, they have reified those abstractions in ways not unlike those of the historical actors they are analyzing. If we are to understand the historical origins and development of democracy, we will need to think much more critically about concepts such as public opinion.

Fortunately, in recent years several important works on eighteenth-century France have begun to cast new light on the topic, not only clarifying public opinion's historical origins and meaning in eighteenth-century France, but also offering a trove of ideas and approaches that may prove useful to historians in other fields. In his 1962 work, *The Structural Transformation of the Public Sphere*, Jürgen Habermas argued that the term first arose around 1750 in France before quickly spreading throughout Europe.[1] Whereas the older term, "opinion," he wrote, had connoted uncertainty and a kind of unreliable social reputation based in prejudice, the new term was meant to describe something rational, reliable, and enlightened. In accounting for the rise of this new concept, Habermas pointed to the growth of commercial capitalism in early modern Europe, which gradually promoted more and more traffic in information and ideas across greater distances. As private citizens increasingly discussed matters of general concern through the press and through face-to-face meetings in new arenas such as salons and cafés, they began to form a common judgment they dubbed "public opinion." In the case of France, absolutism's censorship and repression forced private citizens meeting in the public sphere to avoid political issues at first, but those citizens slowly sharpened their critical faculties, and the reasoned consensus they produced through their public deliberations eventually laid the foundations for a truly political public opinion to begin flourishing in 1789. Inspired by this Enlightenment concept of public opinion, Habermas proposes a far more demanding definition than historians and others usually use, as he insists that the term only be applied to the product of rational-critical deliberation in a public sphere open to all regardless of personal status, and not to the irrational and unreflective result of coercion or manipulation. Although historians of France have certainly disputed many details of Habermas's historical descriptions, his theoretical ideas and his broad account of the rise of public opinion have proved immensely influential since the translation of *The Structural Transformation* into French in 1978 and into English in 1989.[2]

Taking a very different approach to the subject, Keith Baker, in works such as his 1990 essay "Public Opinion as Political Invention," sets aside the traditional idea of public opinion as a more-or-less measurable sociological phenomenon and a collective judgment with which governments and others must contend, viewing it instead as a political construct that orators use to secure authority.[3] In the case of eighteenth-century France, Baker argues that the concept emerged as a new means of claiming political authority and challenging absolutism, and he adds that royal ministers themselves inadvertently promoted the concept by joining the debate with their challengers and issuing their own readings of public opinion. So whereas historians have often dismissed politicians' uses of the term as too biased and imprecise to serve as reliable evidence of public opinion, Baker urges scholars to view that rhetoric not as a distorting lens but as an important object of historical analysis. And whereas historians have traditionally defined public opinion as the sum of people's opinions on a given issue, Baker holds that such thoughts and expressions constitute "a kind of perpetual noise in the system" with no political consequences until someone characterizes or articulates them, turning a babble of voices into an intelligible message.[4] In this view, public opinion is more a rhetorical device intended to create political authority than a preexisting sociological reality that imposes itself on political leaders.

Baker makes a compelling point, for although a social pattern of opinions that no one perceives or represents would make a very poor basis of anyone's authority, one can indeed derive power from a representation of opinions that people find credible, regardless of its actual correspondence to any measurable current of opinion. In other words, in the politics of public opinion, there can be a politically consequential representation without any corresponding reality, but there cannot be a politically consequential reality without any representation of it. Few historians, however, have fully appreciated these points, and the entire realm of representations of public opinion has remained largely unexplored historical terrain. For historians, whose studies of public opinion have often involved seeking to debunk or confirm historical figures' claims about public opinion by researching what ordinary people were really thinking—combing through archives in search of new information on a notoriously elusive subject—the idea of viewing public opinion as a rhetorical device calls for new methods that focus more on speech within the arenas of political power than on the opinions of the millions located outside those arenas.

This characterization of public opinion as a rhetorical device has certainly not gone unchallenged. Mona Ozouf, having found certain social groups who used the term regularly, insists that "public opinion was a concrete reality" in eighteenth-century France, and Habermas warns of "the danger of an overculturalized view of history, where the hard facts of institutions or economic imperatives and of social and political struggles are then too easily assimilated into fights over symbolic meanings."[5] Similarly, Sarah Maza writes that before public communications reached a critical mass in the 1770s, public opinion was "still mostly a rhetorical entity," a statement that follows the traditional view that what is rhetorical is not real.[6] To view public opinion as a rhetorical device, however, one need not deny that real people have real opinions or that the rhetoric of public opinion functions within a social environment deserving analysis; instead one can simply argue, as Baker does, that people's opinions and public declarations would remain noise without some unifying act of representation. Baker, it should be noted, does not reject the value of studying social institutions and practices, writing that he focuses on rhetoric "without denying the importance" of the socioeconomic changes Habermas outlines.[7] The two views, in short, need not be considered mutually exclusive, for part of what gave claims about public opinion credibility in eighteenth-century France was both their relevance to the social struggles of the time and people's awareness of the unprecedented amount of public discussion taking place. In other words, if one views rhetoric as an act involving not two parties (an orator and a listener) but rather three (an orator, a listener, and some broader public of which the orator and listener are aware) then one can see public opinion as a rhetorical device necessarily functioning within a specific social environment, an outlook that draws upon both Habermas's and Baker's contributions.

As useful as this literature on public opinion in eighteenth-century France has been, however, it has primarily examined the period from roughly 1750 to 1789, that is, from the rise of public opinion through the first months of the Revolution. In *The Structural Transformation*, for example, Habermas wrote at length on the rise of public opinion before 1789 but said very little about the Revolution itself. Similarly, Baker's essay, "Public Opinion as Political Invention," Mona Ozouf's "'Public Opinion' at the End of the Old Regime," Arlette Farge's *Subversive Words: Public Opinion in Eighteenth-Century France*, and other highly instructive works by Sarah Maza, Dena Goodman, Daniel Gordon, and David Bell also concentrate almost entirely on the years leading up to 1789.[8] Offering somewhat fuller treatment of the Revolution is J. A. W. Gunn's *Queen of the World*, which devotes one and a half of its ten chapters to the Revolution, but although those passages offer many useful comments, they still leave ample room for further exploration.[9] As for historical dictionaries, neither the 1973 *Dictionary of the History of Ideas* nor the 1989 *Dictionnaire historique de la Révolution Française* contains any entry at all on public opinion.[10] The 1988 *Critical Dictionary of the French Revolution* does contain an essay by Ozouf on "the public spirit," but in devoting a mere nine pages to both public opinion and the public spirit from 1750 through 1815, it can do little more than sketch out a few important themes.[11] Finally, although François Furet's *Interpreting the French Revolution* is certainly a landmark work on revolutionary political culture, it contains only a few comments on the concept of public opinion.[12] We have, in short, no book-length study of public opinion in the French Revolution.

This book seeks to address that problem, examining the historical development of the concept of public opinion in France from 1789 to 1799. While not rejecting the value of the older project of seeking to demonstrate what vast numbers of people thought about given issues, this study primarily pursues the idea of public opinion as a rhetorical device intended to secure authority and legitimacy for ideas, leaders, and policies. Although concentrating primarily on revolutionary language, however, it will show how the social struggles of the time shaped that language, and it will also assess certain patterns of opinion outside the main arenas of power. Regarding the analysis of political rhetoric, it must be noted that once the Revolution began, the term "public opinion" soon merged with an array of formerly separate terms such as "the general will" and "the people's opinion," so this study will analyze uses of the entire range of terms used to invoke authority from the same basic source. By examining the use of these terms in a series of key moments, this study will try to answer the following questions: How did various people at the time define public opinion? How and why were definitions changing? How did people believe public opinion was formed, or should be formed? How did people portray its internal composition, its "texture"? Whose opinions were and were not considered legitimate components of public opinion? How did others react to invocations of public opinion, and what did it take for these invocations to be convincing? What role did people believe public opinion should have in the new political order?

In order to answer these questions, this study examines public debate using several sources, the most important of which are transcripts of the proceedings of the various incarnations of the National Assembly.[13] Those debates constitute a valuable source for this study not only because of the importance of the decisions made there, but also because of the relatively broad range of views articulated in those arenas during much of the Revolution. Moreover, records of those debates offer a rare opportunity to assess the reception of political rhetoric by examining both the speeches that reply to previous speakers' arguments and the references to applause, heckling, and other interruptions by rival deputies and spectators in the galleries. Also consulted are the minutes from the Paris Jacobin Club, which offer another record of lively political debate, albeit within a narrower political spectrum.[14] Finally, the study samples public debate outside those arenas by examining letters and petitions sent to the National Assembly, as well as various contemporary books, pamphlets, and newspaper articles reflecting a broad range of opinions.

Given that this study examines the rhetoric of revolutionary orators throughout the entire decade from 1789 to 1799, space would not permit a full discussion of the historical context of each remark or speech cited. This study's choice of methods is not meant to deny the value of contextual analysis, but simply to take a different approach to the study of revolutionary rhetoric—one seeking patterns in the usage and interpretation of crucial terms and the problems that surrounded their use. Nor is this study's focus on rhetoric and its reception intended to deny the importance of the social and economic issues that long dominated the historiography of the Revolution. Although the historiographical debates of the last several decades have at times given the impression that one must choose between a "social" interpretation of the Revolution and one that examines political culture, ideas, and language, the logic of scholarly combat has probably led historians to make those two approaches seem more mutually exclusive than they need be. Therefore, the decision to focus on political culture—and to treat public opinion as a rhetorical device wielded by contenders for power rather than a measurable sociological force automatically produced by socioeconomic phenomena and imposed upon political actors—should not be viewed as a call for historians of the Revolution to disregard socioeconomic issues. Far from implying that general histories of the Revolution need only draw upon works on political culture, this study offers its conclusions in the hopes that those writing overall interpretations of the Revolution will consider them alongside the findings of works based on other approaches.

Some may object to this study's focus on Paris and on elite opinion. The choice of sources, however, is not meant to deny that significant debates took place in countless sites throughout revolutionary France among people who never rose to national prominence. Nor is it meant to deny that the powerful often lost control of a given political situation, as many an example from the Revolution demonstrates. Instead, this focus simply reflects the definition of public opinion outlined above, as well as a regrettable need to be selective when confronting the almost incomprehensibly large body of words the Revolution produced. If others find value in the questions raised and the ideas and methods used here, perhaps they will choose to undertake similar studies focusing on speech in other arenas.

Although this study's main goal is to analyze the politics of public opinion, it will also use the conclusions of that analysis to cast light on the broader problem of revolutionary France's chronic crisis of political legitimacy. Indeed those two topics are closely intertwined, for just as one cannot fully understand revolutionary France's search for a legitimate political order without a clear view of the politics of public opinion, one also cannot understand the importance of the politics of public opinion at that time without noting the extent to which the fragile legitimacy of France's formal political institutions deepened the need for legitimation by public opinion. Discussing this close connection between formal and informal modes of legitimation in the Revolution, Furet wrote that the weakness of France's formal institutions caused a drift "toward the unconditional triumph of rule by opinion."[15] Furet was certainly right to emphasize this relationship, but this book will argue that because of profound confusion and disagreement over terms such as "public opinion" and "the people" throughout the entire Revolution, it is better to speak of the failure than the triumph of rule by opinion. This study, then, has two closely related primary goals: to examine the politics of public opinion in the Revolution and to analyze the country's ongoing legitimacy crisis, paying particular attention to the role that the politics of public opinion played in that crisis.

Before 1789 claims about public opinion in France were made within the context of a system of royal sovereignty, and although those two forms of authority had many similarities, they remained clearly separate and competing powers at that time. It is not surprising, then, that the declaration of national sovereignty in 1789 quickly brought dramatic changes in ideas about the nature and political role of public opinion, for from that moment on, as we will see, the concepts of public opinion and the will of the sovereign became conflated. What is more surprising, however, is the degree of confusion and discord that continued to surround the doctrine of national (or popular) sovereignty despite nearly every orator's repeated declarations of support for this vital article of revolutionary faith. In short, analyzing public opinion in the Revolution requires paying close attention to competing visions and interpretations of sovereignty, so the examination of each period will begin with a look at the ways in which the French imagined the new sovereign, its qualities, and its relationship to public opinion.

Finally, because nearly everyone recognized that this new sovereign could not govern directly in a country as large as France, it is equally crucial to examine the revolutionaries' ideas about political representation. How an orator envisioned public opinion's relationship to the country's political authorities, for example, depended heavily on how that speaker conceived of the proper relationship between representatives and the represented, just as people's ideas about the proper relationship between representatives and the represented rested in large part on their convictions about the role public opinion ought to play in the new order. Therefore, in addition to examining prevailing notions of sovereignty, this study will identify some of the theories and practices of political representation that helped structure the politics of public opinion. It will also show the damage that enthusiastic assertions of public opinion's unlimited rights did to the authority and legitimacy of the country's elected representatives—including assertions that those representatives themselves made.

The first chapter will offer a brief summary of the existing historical literature on the concept of public opinion in France before 1789. That literature, however, rarely discusses contemporary views of "the people"—a group that

nearly every prerevolutionary writer agreed had little to do with public opinion — but because many of the French began to identify the people's opinion
with public opinion in 1789, it is important to have some sense of prerevolutionary perceptions of the people; therefore, in addition to summarizing recent works on the concept of public opinion before 1789, the first chapter will
briefly survey prevailing perceptions and definitions of the people in that period. The subsequent five chapters will then pursue the book's central questions over four periods: from May 1789 to the fall of the monarchy in 1792
(chapters II and III); from the fall of the monarchy in August 1792 to the fall
of the Girondins in June 1793 (chapter IV); the year of Jacobin rule and the
Terror (chapter V); and from the end of the Terror to Napoleon's coup d'état
in November 1799 (chapter VI). The analysis of each of those four periods
will begin with a discussion of sovereignty and representation, will then examine the politics of public opinion, and will close by assessing the problem
of legitimacy and public opinion's role within it.

I

Public Opinion and the People in Prerevolutionary France

For years, Western civilization textbooks have told us that the modern era began with the French Revolution. Yet if the advent of modernity is marked in part by a transition from royal absolutism to the politics of public opinion, then the many works on public opinion in prerevolutionary France that have appeared in recent years suggest that France's transition to modernity began well before 1789. If one compares the country's political culture and practices under Louis XIV with those of the 1780s, it becomes clear that something fundamental had changed by the latter period, as both the challengers and the defenders of the existing order had begun to pose their political claims by invoking a force that was essentially unknown — and completely without political legitimacy — under the Sun King. So although France officially remained an absolutist monarchy under Louis XVI, in certain ways the political beliefs and rhetorical practices of that era have more in common with our own than with those of the time of Louis XIV.

Paradoxically, however, the same historians who have traditionally viewed the French Revolution as the dawn of the modern era have also assumed that public opinion had existed for centuries, so those who have argued that public opinion only originated in the eighteenth century have been engaged in revisionism. As examples of the traditional outlook, one could cite — in addition to countless works that make passing references to public opinion in ancient, medieval, and early modern times — Bernard Faÿ's *Naissance d'un monstre: l'opinion publique*, which recounts the history of public opinion's role in French politics beginning in the early Middle Ages, or

Joseph Klaits's 1976 study of public opinion under Louis XIV.[1] More recently, scholars deliberately seeking the origins of the concept and the term "public opinion" have endorsed the idea that public opinion existed long before the eighteenth century. A team of researchers under Elisabeth Noelle-Neumann's direction sought early uses of the term in works from several European countries; those researchers found passages outlining something like public opinion in works by Shakespeare and Machiavelli, and they even found the term *opinion publique* in a work by Montaigne in the late 1500s. Defining public opinion as "an anonymous court passing judgments . . . by which reputations were created or destroyed," Noelle-Neumann portrayed a force with both social and political implications, and she cited Machiavelli as one early writer who realized "that a ruler or a future king must pay attention to the opinion of his environment."[2] Even more recently, J. A. W. Gunn contended that public opinion existed as far back as the Renaissance, writing that in traditional European monarchies, "the opinions that the people entertained of their ruler formed no small part of the authority that the king could exercise."[3]

The works by Noelle-Neumann and Gunn perhaps call into question claims that the term "public opinion" originated in the middle of the eighteenth century, but Noelle-Neumann's team did not actually find the term "public opinion" in Shakespeare and Machiavelli, and many of the earlier references Gunn cites are actually to *l'opinion*, a term he admits was not synonymous with *l'opinion publique* before the latter term appeared.[4] Also, despite occasional sightings of the phrase "public opinion" in obscure texts from the sixteenth and seventeenth centuries, those who see the concept emerging in the eighteenth century have in mind a very specific definition that had been unknown before then. Those scholars do not deny that people had always cared about their reputations or that rulers had long been concerned about the obedience of the governed, but they insist that when eighteenth-century publicists began using the term *opinion publique*, they were referring not simply to any kind of collective judgment with which governments or individuals might have to cope, but rather to a rational consensus formed through public deliberation, and a kind of irresistible and infallible tribunal to which all could appeal publicly, even in matters of state.[5] So although texts written before the end of Louis XIV's reign in 1715 do occasionally refer to the power that the sense of the community can have, the specific concept that arose after that date involved something quite different.

Although not completely unknown in earlier times, the notion of public opinion's irresistible power was a crucial part of eighteenth-century perceptions. In the words of Louis XVI's minister of finance, Jacques Necker, public opinion "reigns over all minds, and princes themselves respect it if they are not carried away by excessive passions; some cope with it voluntarily, because of their desire for public favor; while others, less docile, nevertheless submit to it without realizing it, through the influence of those who surround them."[6] Of course earlier notions of opinion had also emphasized its power, but the idea that public opinion could legitimately dictate even to kings was hardly an idea familiar to the France of Louis XIV. Indeed although Gunn criticizes Habermas's claim that public opinion only emerged in the middle of the eighteenth century, he essentially accepts one of Habermas's main arguments when he acknowledges that before 1750 the term had little role in politics and "was most often confined to issues where taste and conventional morality were involved."[7]

An even more profound change was the new sense that public opinion was a rational and necessarily positive force. Arguing that public opinion arose only when "the progress of enlightenment brought the governed closer to those who governed them," Necker wrote that it "opposes obstacles to abuses of authority in France."[8] He also distinguished between "ephemeral movements," which rulers should ignore, and public opinion, "which is slow to form, and whose judgments must be awaited patiently."[9] Inspired in part by Necker, Jacques Peuchet, editor of the 1789 *Encyclopédie méthodique*, called public opinion a "great means of civilization" that had arisen only "since the reign of reason in Europe."[10] For Peuchet, this "social product of our century" could be expected to produce "the most salutary effects for the improvement of morals and the progress of reason," and in calling it "the weapon that an enlightened people oppose *en masse* to the precipitous actions of an ambitious minister or a misguided administration," he contrasted an enlightened force and the mere product of rumor and gossip.[11] So whereas Machiavelli believed that opinion *could* constrain rulers' actions, perceptions of a rational, reliable, and enlightened force led eighteenth-century writers to argue that it *should* do so. Of course concerns about public opinion's rationality were still heard; in his 1786 essay on Turgot, for example, Condorcet contrasted "the general wish" with "public opinion," calling the latter "less constant, but also less tranquil, often just as powerful, sometimes harmful, and always dangerous."[12] Nevertheless, allusions to public opinion as a rational and positive force were becoming remarkably common by this time.

A third key difference between eighteenth-century perceptions of public opinion and previous concepts had to do with its formation process. Whereas reputations had traditionally been formed through gossip, rumors, and other small-scale, face-to-face communications, the formation of public opinion in the eighteenth century took place in more public arenas and relied much more on the press. As Habermas and others have shown, the new concept arose out of a network of relatively new (or newly transformed) social and intellectual institutions such as the salons, academies, and cafés, in which a larger and more diverse population than ever created an integrated Republic of Letters.[13] In this view, when the term public opinion came into wide use after 1750, it had a specific meaning unlike any previous term, so that to speak of public opinion before that time would be to project later conceptions onto previous eras. In short, the concept of public opinion that Habermas and others outlined was invented in the middle decades of the eighteenth century.

As for explanations of public opinion's emergence, Habermas's emphasis on the growth of capitalism and the consequent development of the press and various social institutions such as salons, cafés, and clubs has had a mixed reception among historians. Few have embraced Habermas's economistic explanations, but a remarkable number have taken up his interest in the social institutions, using many of his ideas as they explore subjects such as changing forms of communication, norms of sociability, and the egalitarian spirit that figured so prominently in the formation of public opinion.[14] Others, however, have sought public opinion's historical origins in areas Habermas did not examine, particularly the politics of the absolutist system, whose decline created a vacuum that the politics of public opinion arose to fill. Of course some of the reasons for the Crown's difficulties have long been familiar, but in recent years historians have added new material to the picture of a declining order. Dale Van Kley and Jeffrey Merrick, for example, have each shown how religious conflicts helped undermine belief in divine right, and several historians, drawing on Tocqueville's portrait of a centralizing monarchy, have argued that absolutism, which had been justified by the need for a sovereign to unify a disjointed collection of orders, estates, and corporations, undermined its own foundations by eroding privileges and weakening the regulations that supported those groups' existence and status. In Furet's words, "the political *ancien régime* had died before it was struck down," and to some extent historians have ruled that death a suicide.[15]

In that same vein, several scholars have argued that the monarchy inadvertently promoted the rise of a politics of public opinion. Habermas notes that royal authorities helped develop the institutions of France's public sphere by using newspapers to address their subjects directly and publicly, and as David Bell points out, it was the Crown that founded France's first newspaper.[16] Similarly, Baker observes that early in the century the Crown chose to defend its foreign policy before an international audience, and he adds that in its struggles with the parlements in the 1770s the Crown, reluctant to let the magistrates' arguments go unanswered, denounced them publicly, thus unwittingly helping to publicize them.[17] Others have shown how divisions within the Court led rival factions to plead their case before the public, both in cultural debates, as Thomas Crow has shown, and in political matters such as the Maupeou crisis,* in which, as Sarah Maza writes, "factions of courtiers and ministers hired their own pamphleteers to rebut the arguments of their adversaries."[18] Some of these officials who helped promote a public politics were men such as Necker, who was sympathetic to Enlightenment thinking, but even committed absolutists often found themselves unable to resist speaking publicly and invoking public opinion.[19]

Although these studies of absolutism's decline have helped clarify public opinion's origins, a few qualifications are in order. For one, the picture of a centralizing monarchy homogenizing society and removing intermediary corporations is only partly true, as several recent works have shown a complex pattern of a monarchy both weakening and strengthening corporate privileges.[20] As for the argument that the collapse of absolutism contributed to the rise of a new public politics, it is important to specify that it was only support for the monarchy's absolutist version that was collapsing. For while many began to challenge absolutism in the final prerevolutionary decades, France had but a handful of republicans before 1789, and most malcontents attacked the King's ministers and courtiers rather than the monarch himself, much less the idea of monarchy. And as for the Crown's inadvertent promotion of the politics of public opinion, it may be true that royal ministers would have been wiser to resist the temptation to rebut opponents' descriptions of public opinion, but it is not hard to understand why they acted as they did.

Part of what made such forays into the politics of public opinion so dangerous to absolutism was the specific French conception of public opinion as an all-powerful force, which could hardly coexist with any other.[21] Of course the idea of any similarity between these two powers might seem surprising at first. Whereas absolutism, for example, rested on the will of the sovereign, public opinion invoked the reason of the public; whereas absolutism defended privilege and hierarchy, public opinion stood for merit and some measure of equality; and whereas absolutism relied on secrecy, public opinion demanded publicity. Yet as historians have noted, believers in both systems envisioned a

---

* In the Maupeou crisis of 1771, the King's chancellor, R.-N.-C.-A. de Maupeou, shut down the rebellious Parlement of Paris, provoking a major political controversy.

unitary, indivisible power, and despite an apparent distinction between the rationalism of public opinion and the voluntarism of absolutism, theorists of absolutism such as Jacques-Bénigne Bossuet had argued that rationality was one of royal authority's essential characteristics.[22] Even more significantly, the language of public opinion made frequent use of royal metaphors, as in Necker's reference to public opinion issuing its judgments "as if atop a throne," and the many allusions to public opinion as "queen of the world."[23] In Furet's words, the new concept of public opinion "transferred the features of royal sovereignty to a new authority, also unique, which was an exact copy of the monarchic idea."[24] Public opinion, then, was in large part an offspring of absolutism, but if the child resembled its progenitor, the two had little chance of living together harmoniously under one roof.

The increasingly frequent invocation of public opinion in the late eighteenth century eventually raised the question of exactly whose opinions counted as part of this new force. Orators often avoided the question altogether, making no attempt to specify whose opinions they were describing, and when they used the word "public" as an adjective rather than a noun—as in terms such as *l'opinion publique, l'esprit public,* and *la voix publique*—they evoked a disembodied, abstract phenomenon independent of any individual's perceptions, much like reason or truth. Indeed for those who considered public opinion to be nothing less than reason or truth, the definition of "evidence" that François Quesnay wrote for the *Encyclopédie*—"a certainty that is by itself so clear and manifest that the mind cannot refuse it"—could also apply to public opinion.[25] In this outlook, it would hardly matter whether specific individuals actually held the opinion in question, for those who did not were simply in error and would rally to it once it was presented clearly to them.

Not everyone took this view, however, and those who spoke of "the public" rather than "public opinion" could not help raising the question of that entity's social composition. Of course not everyone using or hearing the term gave the question much thought, but Ozouf reports that Beaumarchais believed "the public to be a fiction that did not hold up under examination," and Dena Goodman reminds us that Mercier also questioned the fiction of the public.[26] In Baker's words, "One can understand the conflicts of the pre-Revolution as a series of struggles to fix the sociological referent of the concept in favor of one or another competing group."[27] The group most commonly associated with the public consisted of the enlightened and the educated; Condorcet, for example, wrote that "in the long run the opinion of enlightened men forms public opinion," and the writer Claude-François

Adriend Lezay-Marnézia specified that it was "philosophical writers" who formed public opinion.[28] For Condorcet, however, the public also comprised groups such as courtiers, financiers, and currency traders, and his disgust with opposition to Turgot's economic reforms led him to charge that even men of letters might not be particularly enlightened.[29] Yet if disagreements arose over which individuals were truly enlightened, practically everyone agreed that the public did not include what d'Alembert called the "blind and noisy multitude," and what Condorcet called "the most stupid and miserable part of the people"; indeed Condorcet, among others, distinguished very clearly between public opinion and popular opinion, calling the latter "the fantasy of an ignorant multitude."[30] Reflecting this reluctance to include the multitude, Necker made it clear that when kings sought to explain their motives, they were not "seeking to win votes," and he even wondered whether public opinion could exist in a republic, where "the influence of eloquence" would mislead the unenlightened.[31]

Unfortunately, as Habermas noted, to exclude anyone deliberately from the public raised problems for a concept based on values of publicity, openness, and universality. Because full participation in the public sphere required literacy and education, which in turn required a certain amount of wealth, it might have seemed possible to have a public sphere that was open in theory but restrictive in practice, but if passive means of exclusion worked well enough with the very poor, Daniel Roche and others have shown that many artisans, shopkeepers, and the like could read, and many of them frequented the cafés and other public places where newspapers were read aloud and discussed.[32] For those horrified at such popular participation (or at the whole idea of public opinion), there might seem to be little difference between "the public" and "the people." In 1781, for example, Foreign Minister Vergennes warned that Necker's *compte rendu* is, in the last resort, a pure appeal to the people, the pernicious effects of which for the monarchy cannot yet be appreciated or foreseen."[33] And whereas most educated observers abhorred the idea of opening public discussion to the semiliterate, not everyone felt this way. One writer who deliberately addressed as wide an audience as possible was Guillaume-Joseph Saige, who in 1775 took up the struggle against absolutism by writing a *Catéchisme du citoyen* that put complex political arguments into simple question-and-answer form; as one observer said, the work "puts within the grasp of the most simple and inept a doctrine that *L'esprit des lois* and *Le contrat social* have clouded in a metaphysics very difficult to understand."[34] Maza also reports that in 1786 the advocate-general of the Paris Parlement described public opinion as "the result of general suffrage" and "a voice composed of all voices."[35] Almost from its inception, then, the term "public opinion" was marked by tensions between desires for a selective and enlightened public and perceptions of a rather different reality.

Before 1789 membership in the public and the content of its opinions remained ill-defined for various reasons. One was largely practical, for as Daniel Gordon points out, "there were no instruments for measuring what a large group of people actually thought about any particular issue."[36] Of course Enlightenment beliefs in the self-evident nature of truth and the willingness of reasonable minds to accept it must have made elaborate methods for ascertaining opinions seem unnecessary, an attitude that brings to mind Tocqueville's famous complaint about political naïvety in prerevolutionary France.[37] Perhaps an even greater reason for this lack of interest in examining the public's composition and the distribution of opinions had to do with deeply rooted French fears of political division. In part because of memories of the religious wars and political rebellions of previous centuries—events that helped produce absolutism in the first place—the French of the eighteenth century had developed what Ozouf calls "a religion of unity."[38] In a political culture so sensitive to discord, trying to decide whose opinions should count and to document the distribution of opinions might have seemed an unacceptably dangerous project. Finally, the notion of the public could remain vague because of public opinion's lack of any formal role in the absolutist system, which ultimately made it possible to leave such troubling questions unsettled.

The events of the late 1780s, however, led the invention of public opinion to move, as inventions generally do, from a stage of initial conceptualization to one of practical refinement. As the government's financial and political problems deepened, assertions of public opinion's authority proliferated, but before the French could turn an abstract concept into a real power they had to answer some of the hard questions they had so far managed to leave unresolved. It soon became clear that whatever merits there might be to shifting the basis of power from birth to enlightenment, or from the King to "the public," doing so meant placing power on a far more nebulous, unverifiable, and problematic foundation. Physiocrats and philosophes, that is, might believe that even many wealthy men lacked the enlightenment necessary to help form public opinion or make political decisions, but how could they convince them of that? Men of wealth in turn might believe that women or artisans and shopkeepers lacked enlightenment, but how could they convince them of that?

A crucial step toward defining membership in the public occurred, more or less unintentionally, with the decision to hold elections for an Estates General, for the holding of elections demanded an answer to the question of who did and did not deserve political rights. With those elections, public opinion soon began to be associated with the opinion of the electorate, giving "the public" its clearest shape ever. Yet because there was no way to base the franchise on such an unverifiable quality as enlightenment, "public opinion" was now drifting further and further from the ideals of those who had formulated the concept. The events of the late 1780s were thus beginning to bring momentous changes in the concept of public opinion in France, as many illusions about the concept suddenly started to collapse.

Although the term "public opinion" has attracted the most attention from historians of this period, the French used several other terms to invoke new forms of collective authority before the Revolution. One such term was "the public spirit," which historians have often associated mostly with the period of Jacobin dominance in the Revolution, but which did appear before 1789. The term was not strictly synonymous with public opinion, as writers generally used it when they wished to describe the specific situation of people favoring the common interest over their own selfish interests. Condorcet called the public spirit "this zeal for the general good," and Necker, who contended that "the spirit of interest and attachment to one's fortune" were "the formidable enemies of the best public institutions," claimed that he used various methods "to promote [the] public spirit . . . and to link the people to the government through feelings of happiness and confidence."[39] As that passage suggests, the term could also denote a kind of harmony between the public and ruling authorities. According to Necker, public opinion had arisen in France well before he came to office, but a public spirit had only been "prepared and formed" toward the end of his time in office.[40]

Another important term was "the general will," a relatively old term in France, but one that gained currency at that time primarily through Rousseau's *The Social Contract*.[41] The precision of Rousseau's definition of the general will leaves much to be desired, but he used the term to describe the sense of a community when (and only when) its members were thinking of their common interests. Yet because individuals were often selfish, and because "sly orators" could mislead (though not corrupt) the people, Rousseau warned that "there is often a great difference between the will of all and the general will."[42] Among his various conceptions of the general will, then, Rousseau held that it consisted of what a community *would* want under the proper conditions — or at least what it *should* want regardless of what the individuals in it actually did want (or thought they wanted) at the moment; it was this dissociation between the general will and existing individuals' present perceptions and desires that allowed him to consider the general will "unchanging, incorruptible, and pure."[43]

This abstract, almost mystical quality made it hard for Rousseau to design a political system based on the general will. In *The Social Contract*, he saw the general will as the source of all legitimate political authority, calling for the people to express that will as they assembled periodically to make laws, elect magistrates to execute the laws, and oversee the work of those already elected. Yet if the expressed will of the gathered citizens could fail to coincide with the general will, how was the general will to be known? Offering a formula of apparent simplicity and precision, Rousseau wrote that "if we take away from [private wills] the pluses and minuses which cancel each other out, the sum of the difference is the general will."[44] Historians have often charged that the revolutionaries who later borrowed ideas from Rousseau misread *The Social Contract*, but as this example of Rousseau's advice for how to recognize the general will demonstrates, much of the blame for any misunderstanding belongs to the author of a political tract so full of ambiguities, contradictions, naïve assumptions, and crucial oversights. Indeed Rousseau himself may have come to realize how profoundly flawed the book was; according to historian Jacques Julliard, the writer Jean-Joseph Dusaulx claimed that Rousseau wrote him a letter in which he said of *The Social Contract*: "Those who claim to understand it as a whole are cleverer than me. It is a book that needs to be rewritten, but I have neither the strength nor the time to do so."[45]

Rousseau, of course, often staked out unusual positions, and his rejection of public opinion as a basis of political power is but one example of that tendency. That attitude toward public opinion reflected his definition of it, for as Baker writes, Rousseau treated the concept as "a social rather than a political category," a phenomenon consisting of "the collective expression of the moral and social values of a people, the shared sentiments and convictions embodied in a nation's customs and manners," which sounds closer to the pre-Enlightenment concept of *l'opinion* than to the notion of public opinion others held at that time.[46] Rousseau thus broke with the dominant ideas of his time in his definition of public opinion, in his use of the general will in place of public opinion in political matters, in his preference for will and virtue over reason and enlightenment, and in his desire to invest authority in a much broader group than others favored. In addition, whereas many considered deliberation essential to the formation of public opinion, Rousseau, fearing that demagogues would mislead the people, wrote that the general will could only emerge from a popular assembly "provided its members do not have any communication among themselves."[47]

And yet these two seemingly distinct concepts have several basic similarities, not the least of which is their shared goal of creating a new political legitimacy based on collective rather than personal authority. In both Rousseau's concept of the general will and the philosophes' notion of public opinion the addition of an adjective denoting universality transformed a noun denoting subjectivity and disagreement into a reliable, even infallible, foundation of authority. Both public opinion and the general will, that is, referred to abstract, disembodied forces virtually immune to human error, and that independence from individual judgments also made both forces necessarily indivisible and unanimous. These similarities help explain how the two terms could become largely synonymous once the Revolution began.

Another term often used in challenges to absolutism was "the nation." The term posed no inherent threat to absolutism, whose theorists had often used it to refer to the collection of groups and communities over whom kings ruled, but many now construed the term in ways threatening to absolutism. Proponents of the *thèse nobiliaire*, for example, offered elaborate historical arguments about the Franks and their noble descendants constituting a sovereign French nation long before kings sought to rule over them. Also, as Furet and Ozouf explain, many who used the term in the eighteenth century considered a kingdom "an ensemble of subjects," and a nation "a collectivity of citizens," insisting that the idea of a nation "includes the idea of *rights*."[48] And whereas absolutists portrayed the nation as a passive collection of dissimilar elements brought together only by the unifying authority of the king, others conceived of the nation as an already unified entity whose consent was essential to the ratification of laws and even to kings' right to rule.[49]

The idea of the nation thus appeared in various versions, as some emphasized its internal division into estates, corporations, and provinces, whereas others downplayed those divisions and saw it as more or less unified under the leadership of one group, such as the parlements or the nobility. The parlements themselves were never actually a unified entity, but their members often spoke in the name of the nation, rhetorically erasing the divisions that helped justify an absolute sovereign.[50] Though they envisioned the nation as composed of separate estates and corporations, the parlementary magistrates, writes David Bell, "contributed to the creation of a self-conscious national community" demanding the right to consent to laws and voice its will.[51] Also tending to portray the nation as having a single will or opinion were those who associated the term with public opinion. Necker, for example, did distinguish between public opinion, which he felt existed only in some countries, and "the national spirit," which could exist under despots, but in arguing that "it is only [public] opinion . . . that ensures the nation a kind of influence, in giving it the power to reward or punish through praise or contempt," he suggested both that public opinion was the opinion of the nation and that a nation could have a single will.[52] And as happened with the language of public opinion, the Crown unwittingly helped make the idea of a unified and sovereign nation with a will of its own more familiar by denouncing it publicly. These uses of the concept of the nation thus constituted another discourse that helped erode the legitimacy of absolutism much as the discourse of public opinion was doing.

The concept of the people, which became the central term in the new democratic politics of the Revolution, also appeared frequently in the Old Regime. Treatises on absolutism, such as Bossuet's *Politics Derived from the Words of Holy Scripture*, referred repeatedly to "the people," generally using the term as a synonym for the nation. In this outlook the term covered everyone under a king's authority. When Bossuet wrote, for example, that "the people must fear the prince" and that "fear is a necessary restraint upon men, because of their pride and their natural unruliness," he probably had in mind rebellious nobles as well as commoners, and his statement that "among the people, it is the weak whom the prince must protect most carefully" certainly suggests that the people included more than just the weak.[53] If "the people" and "the nation" often referred to the same royal subjects, the former term was more likely to be used in expressions of the king's paternalistic love for his subjects, although here the definite article often gave way to possessive pronouns, as in Bossuet's declaration that "the prince is the father of his people."[54] Outlining a reciprocal (if unequal) relationship between two parties, Bossuet wrote that "the prince must provide for the needs of the people," while the people must obey the prince and "must remain peaceful under the prince's authority."[55] Yet although Bossuet considered "the obligation to take care of the people . . . the foundation for all the rights that sovereigns have over their subjects," he did not mean that obedience to the king was conditional in any legal or contractual sense.[56]

For Bossuet, the people, like the nation, could have no independent will, and he insisted that "the will of all the people is contained within" the king's will.[57] In making this point, Bossuet was responding to nobles, Protestant political theorists, and others who were asserting such an independent will, but those groups conceived of the people in hierarchical and corporate terms, so neither party in these disputes imagined or defined the people in anything like the later revolutionary conceptions.[58] Although absolutism did allow individuals and corporations a customary right to petition the king for the redress of grievances, these petitioners were only supposed to speak for themselves or their corporation—and not publicly—so petitioners could not legitimately speak on behalf of "the people" or usurp the sovereign's role of unifying the multitude.

In the growing political discontent of the eighteenth century, some continued to portray the people as passive objects of the state's benevolent actions, as in Necker's plea to kings to pay "continual attention to the interest of the people," but others began to claim that the people (or nation) had a will of its own.[59] In an address to the King in 1775, for example, officials of the *Cour des aides* announced that "we . . . regard ourselves as representatives of the people," and they proceeded, as representatives often do, to put words in the mouth of the collective subject they invoked.[60] Warning that "the people groan under the weight of arbitrary taxes," these magistrates called for cutting royal expenditures, claiming that "this economy is demanded of you by the universal wishes of the entire nation."[61] Even more threatening was the declaration that "the unanimous wish of the nation is to obtain either the Estates General or at least the provincial estates," an assertion outlining a collective will not just to make specific demands but also to establish an institutional basis for ongoing demands.[62]

It may be significant that a text generally using "the people" and "the nation" interchangeably posed its boldest claims in the name of the nation, and if that choice did indeed have any meaning, the reasons probably involved the connotations of the term "the people." For although that term could be a pure synonym for "the nation," it could also refer to a population that did not include society's higher orders or classes. The jurist Charles Loyseau, for example, had equated "the common people" with the Third Estate, and Louis de Jaucourt's article on "the people" in the *Encyclopédie* noted a traditional definition of the term as an estate "opposed to that of the *grands* and the nobles."[63] Taking up an argument that the Abbé Coyer had made in 1755, however, Jaucourt contended that the term's meaning had been changing recently, so that whereas "the people" had once included "artisans, merchants, financiers, men of letters, and men of the law," the term was "limited these days to workers and agricultural laborers."[64] In this view, the growing wealth and social aspirations of the bourgeois led them to "secede" from "the people," and this change caused a traditional definition of the people as something like the Latin *populus* to give way to a narrower one corresponding to the Latin *plebs*. Also using this class-based definition, Voltaire described the people as "the populace which has only its hands to live by."[65]

Yet this idea of the people as the lower classes did not by any means completely displace other notions, and one can find at least three commonly used definitions in the language of the time: everyone other than the King and his ministers, the entire Third Estate, and the lower classes. Unfortunately, it is often impossible to tell exactly how a speaker was defining the term at any given moment, perhaps because the speakers themselves had not resolved these ambiguities in their own minds. In one typically ambiguous statement, for example, Necker emphasized the King's duty to provide "care for the people and protection for the poor," a statement that suggests the two groups were neither identical nor fully distinct.[66]

If the people, understood as the nation, were starting to become a political subject in the rhetoric of the upper classes, the people as plebs were hardly likely to do so given elites' generally negative perceptions of that group. One dictionary called the people "stupid, turbulent, [and] eager for novelties," and Holbach warned that "the people reads no more than it reasons," having "neither the leisure nor the ability to do so."[67] In arguing for the social utility of religion, Voltaire spoke of "a multitude of brutal, drunk, thieving little men," while Diderot wrote that "the little people are incredibly stupid," adding that they would never outgrow their superstitions and religious beliefs.[68] To Voltaire, it seemed hopeless, if not dangerous, to try to educate such creatures, and even Rousseau had doubts about the wisdom of trying to educate peasants.[69]

Yet the complexity of Enlightenment thought is quite apparent in the philosophes' discussions of the people. When denouncing tyranny, for example, the philosophes often referred to the people less disparagingly, and although they may have simply been thinking of the people as the nation in such cases, their comments were not always derogatory even when they specifically referred to the people as the lower classes. The idea that manual work was not entirely ignoble appears in various Enlightenment texts, including *Encyclopédie* articles on artisans and their work. And in his article on the people, Jaucourt said of the worker, "He drains our marshes, he cleans our streets, he builds our houses, constructs our furniture," while also calling agricultural laborers "sober, fair, faithful, [and] religious"; the people, he concluded, "always form the most numerous and most necessary part of the nation."[70] Similarly, Condorcet contrasted the people, defined as those who did honest work, with vagabonds and beggars, whom he called the "populace."[71]

An appreciation of the people's positive qualities even extended beyond their simple virtues or the useful labor they did, for as Ozouf notes, many had come to believe in "the presence of reason in every human individual."[72] Voltaire, who regularly dismissed the multitude as an ignorant tool of tyrants, and who often expressed skepticism about enlightening unskilled laborers, nonetheless wrote the following words in a 1767 letter to Simon-Nicolas-Henri Linguet:

> The highest sort of artisans, who are forced by their very professions to reflect at length, to improve their taste, to increase their enlightenment; these men are beginning to read all throughout Europe. . . . In several Swiss towns, and especially in Geneva, almost all who work in manufacturing spend their time reading when they are not working. No, *monsieur*, all is not lost when one leads the people to see that they have minds.[73]

Similarly, in his 1776 essay on the grain trade, Condorcet despaired of the people's current capacities, but he also argued that "the people are only imbeciles because one has for so long taken pleasure in brutalizing them"; the people, he added, "have long been the plaything of oppressors," and he cited changing popular notions about matters such as the movement of the earth and the circulation of blood to suggest that the people might someday become more enlightened.[74] Diderot also spoke of the possibility of educating "children of poor conditions," insisting that in the long run the multitude could at least learn to echo "the judgment of a small number of sensible men."[75] According to Roland Mortier, Diderot's pessimism about the people's ability to reason was "a passing temptation against which the whole weight of his work weighs in the balance."[76] Harvey Chisick has argued that although many philosophes derided the people's mental capacities in the first half of the eighteenth century, "a completely different spirit pervades a number of works on the lower classes published after mid-century," and Harry Payne has offered a similar view, noting the philosophes' many derogatory comments about the people's mental abilities but concluding that over time there was "a slight increase in the philosophes' estimation of popular capacities."[77]

Along with a more optimistic perception of the lower classes' intelligence went a growing concern for their well-being, for in Payne's words, "humanitarianism was in vogue in the eighteenth century."[78] The philosophes often denounced the toll that excessive work and taxation took on poverty-stricken peasants, and as the 1775 *Cour des aides* text's reference to "groaning" taxpayers shows, the rhetoric of magistrates sometimes expressed such concerns as well. Maza adds that by the middle of the eighteenth century lawyers often defended peasant communities against oppressive lords, and by the 1780s "progressively-minded barristers took up the cudgels for the truly wretched of their society."[79] Ozouf argues that some favored improving the lot of the lower classes out of humanitarian concerns, but also out of a belief that "inequality of wealth caused degeneration in individuals and before long decadence in states."[80] And as Darline Levy notes, Linguet warned of revolutionary consequences if the people's subsistence needs were not met, even speaking of the *salut du peuple*, which he called "the most sacred of laws."[81] If it generally remained, as Payne believes, "impolitic" to make legislative proposals in the name of equality, it had also become impolitic to speak of the people as Richelieu had when he compared them to mules needing a constant burden to remain obedient.[82] In short, traditional paternalistic concerns for the welfare of the people seem to have gained new vitality in late-eighteenth-century France, affecting overall perceptions of "the people."

In light of the rush toward egalitarianism and democratic politics that took place once the Revolution began, it bears noting that the vast majority of pre-revolutionary writers discussing public opinion, the political rights of the people, the universality of rational capacities, and the obligation to defend the poor were not trying to create democracy in France. Yet the articulation of these ideas tended to initiate processes that proved difficult to control. Here the kind of sociological changes Habermas identifies in eighteenth-century France probably did affect linguistic struggles, for as we have seen, the sociological referent of "public opinion" was gradually broadening with increasing literacy and participation in the developing institutions of France's public sphere. And whereas orators invoking public opinion had only sought to gain power for a rather limited portion of the population, achieving even that measure of equality required the articulation of what Ozouf calls "a devastating critique of privilege," which in time worked on behalf of the lower classes as well.[83] In addition, magistrates posing political claims in the name of "the nation" or "the people" helped redefine those terms, changing them from passive objects of paternalistic benevolence to active subjects with a common will independent of the Crown. Finally, because some members of the lower classes seem to have heard at least fragments of the ideas discussed in the public sphere, it is not surprising that the decades before the Revolution witnessed the kind of upsurge in popular protests and demands for political reform that historians such as Arlette Farge and Roger Chartier have discussed.[84]

These changes occurred in part because of linguistic ambiguities and other reasons internal to each discourse, but also because discourses invented independently and intended to remain separate eventually influenced each other, beginning to blend together even before 1789. For example, the critique of privilege intrinsic to the rhetoric of public opinion and the egalitarian sociability of the public sphere threatened the parlements' elitist assertions about the nation, while the ideas of publicness and universality inherent in the concept of public opinion also worked against the magistrates' hopes of confining authority to official institutions such as the parlements. Conversely, the parlements' posing of political claims in the name of a collectivity that included everyone—even those groaning under the weight of taxation—threatened efforts to keep membership in the public limited to the wealthy and enlightened. Similarly, assertions of the presence of reason in all individuals called into question the idea of vesting authority in a reasonable few and made the idea of consulting the common people on matters of state a bit less unthinkable, while Rousseau's idea of valuing virtue and will instead of birth or reason also helped prepare France for its future turn toward democracy. Finally, calls for measures to help the poor, a relatively innocuous project within the context of a stable absolutist system, had dangerous implications when voiced alongside these other ideas.

None of this is to argue that the events of the Revolution were preordained or that the Enlightenment caused the Revolution in some simple way, but the instability of these various discourses and their tendency to merge with each other support Furet's contention that "the *materials* of the revolutionary consciousness to come existed in France in the 1770s or 1780s."[85] If it would be excessive to attribute the egalitarian politics of the Revolution to the discourse of public opinion invented in the preceding decades, it would also be a mistake to ignore the ways in which these slowly converging ideas and discourses of public opinion, the general will, the people, and the nation helped make the events of the revolutionary decade possible.

II

❦

Sovereignty and Representation, 1789–1792

O f the many profound changes the French Revolution brought about, none had broader or more enduring consequences than the change from royal to national sovereignty. To a considerable extent, the other dramatic changes the Revolution caused, such as the abolition of nobility, the redrafting of legal codes, and the disestablishment of the Church, all flowed from the initial declaration of national sovereignty, which gave the revolutionaries a basis for those actions. The proclamation of national sovereignty also completely transformed ideas and practices of political representation, eventually helping to create a legitimacy crisis as intractable as the one it was introduced to resolve. And because the new doctrine of sovereignty led to a profound redefinition of public opinion and its political role—as public opinion came to be associated with the opinion of the new sovereign—any history of public opinion in the Revolution must include a careful look at ideas of sovereignty. Yet as this chapter will demonstrate, the revolutionaries failed to work out common definitions of the terms "national sovereignty," "popular sovereignty," or "the people," and they also could not agree on how the new sovereign's will should be represented. These failures not only helped undermine their efforts to create a stable and legitimate new order, but also led to persistent confusion about the meaning and political role of public opinion.

Despite the tremendous significance of the change, it is hard to pinpoint exactly when the shift to national sovereignty took place. The idea of national sovereignty had been around for years in France, and it began drawing increasing attention in the debates over calling a meeting of the Estates General in the late 1780s.[1] Yet despite considerable belief in the idea among the members of that assembly who gathered at Versailles in May 1789, support for a declaration of national sovereignty was not universal even among the deputies of the Third Estate, much less the deputies of the clergy and nobility, some of whom reluctantly began joining the commoners in a single assembly in June. As Michael Fitzsimmons observes, the commoners' decision to declare themselves a "National Assembly" on 17 June "presaged the assertion of national sovereignty," but they did not actually declare the doctrine at that time, and it remained possible to think of this National Assembly as an advisory body still operating within a system of either royal sovereignty or some kind of shared sovereignty.[2] As late as August 1789, when the deputies were drafting proposals for a Declaration of Rights to precede the new constitution they planned to write, many of their drafts made no mention of national sovereignty at all, and the phrase still did not appear in the text eventually chosen as a basis for debate.[3] Even the Abbé Sieyès, who had argued for national sovereignty in his recent pamphlet, *What Is the Third Estate?*, presented a draft that did not use the phrase, although some passages strongly suggested the idea.[4]

When deliberations failed to produce a majority for the draft they had chosen, the deputies decided to begin voting article by article. On 20 August, they spent much of a long day debating the preamble, and when a very long speech at the end of that day emptied out the spectators' galleries, one speaker moved to adjourn the session on the grounds that the Assembly's rules required its sessions to be public. An account in the *Archives Parlementaires* notes that "the hour was very late and yet the Assembly still had not adopted anything," so the frustrated deputies refused to adjourn. At that point Jean-Joseph Mounier proposed a vote on three articles, one of which declared that "the source of all sovereignty resides essentially in the nation."[5] Apparently without any debate, the deputies still present approved the articles and immediately adjourned the session. National sovereignty had become official doctrine in France.

When the deputies resumed their work, there was no further discussion of this article, and most newspapers did not even report this eleventh-hour decision. Part of the reason for the deputies' willingness to approve such a monumental idea so hastily may have been that the principle seemed so obvious that it needed no discussion. Of course its specific interpretation and ramifications did need extensive consideration, but the deputies expected to make further revisions to the Declaration once the constitution was done, which they expected to be very soon. By the time they finally finished the task two years later, however, few were inclined to tamper with the Declaration. That reluctance is understandable in light of one deputy's 8 August 1791 statement that the Declaration was "found on signs in all public places and even in the homes of those who live in the countryside," and in his words, that document had "acquired a sacred and religious character."[6] Nevertheless, there is no better proof for Marcel Gauchet's claim that the Declaration of Rights "was far from having been maturely weighed" than the way in which its article on national sovereignty was adopted.[7]

The deputies' haste in declaring national sovereignty also reflected a desire to act quickly given popular unrest—though they often spent hours debating far more trivial matters—as well as their view that the ideas in the Declaration were based in natural law, and thus needed no justification. Finally, the lack of debate on national sovereignty may have reflected the demoralized state of believers in royal sovereignty and divine right; although *L'Ami du Roi* insisted as late as September 1790 that "all power comes from God" and that "God did not give this power to the people, but rather to the King," few others spoke up for royal sovereignty or made positive arguments to justify it.[8] But if national sovereignty essentially had only to fill an intellectual and political void, the lack of discussion of it had serious consequences for the National Assembly's subsequent work. In stating that sovereignty resides "essentially" in the nation (or, even more vaguely, that *the source* of all sovereignty" resides there), the Assembly found a phrase that could gain wide approval, but one that produced endless misunderstandings over the next few years. Few at the time objected to the deputies' linguistic imprecision, though *Le Journal de Paris* did later complain about "this disastrous confusion of language and ideas" and the resulting "false ideas that the people have attached to certain words" such as sovereignty.[9] The failure to deliberate on the concept meant not only that the deputies would write a constitution while holding significantly different positions on the ultimate source of political authority, but also that they would repeatedly invoke this central term with little sense of what it meant to others.

One major source of uncertainty and misunderstanding about national sovereignty concerned the definition of the nation and its means of expression and action. Was it composed of separate estates, as many nobles and clergymen believed? Did it include all individuals, as others suggested? Or did it include only the members of the Third Estate, as Sieyès had written in his famous pamphlet? Was the King part of the nation, as some affirmed, or was the nation made up of everyone other than the King, as others contended?

And how could the nation express its will? Through the National Assembly alone? Through the King as well? Could the nation overrule the Assembly and the King? Could the nation express both minority and majority views, or did only the majority view count as the national will? Answers to these questions slowly took shape during debates on other issues, but the lingering ambiguities hampered the entire process of writing a new constitution.

If the concept of the nation raised difficult questions, so did the concept of sovereignty. For the sixteenth-century theorist Jean Bodin, sovereignty had meant a necessarily perpetual and unlimited power needed to create order by unifying an unwieldy collection of estates, orders, and corporations. Bodin and others did recognize custom as well as divine and natural law, so in a strict sense the sovereign's authority was not truly unlimited, but he rejected any formal separation of powers, insisting that sovereigns "not be subject in any way to the commands of others." In his view, "the Prince is above the law" and makes the law without needing "the consent of anyone above, equal to, or beneath him."[10] For Bodin and many later French theorists, the indivisibility of authority required that the sovereign be a king, and sovereignty became closely identified with both monarchy and absolutism.

Among the deputies elected in 1789, some clergymen and nobles continued to favor royal sovereignty, though many of them refused to participate at all once the three Estates were combined in a single National Assembly. Another group, the "Monarchiens," sought to reconcile the conflicting doctrines, as one leading deputy, Trophime-Gérard de Lally-Tollendal, did in calling the king and the nation "the two integral parties to sovereignty."[11] For another deputy, Pierre-Victor Malouet, the nation's sovereignty was largely theoretical, becoming practical and direct only in those rare moments when a nation had to overthrow tyrants; at all other times the nation had to transfer its sovereignty to those who could actually govern, namely, to a legislature and a king working together.[12]

Other deputies seemed leery of the whole concept of sovereignty, perhaps because of its absolutist connotations and the uncertainty over whether the king might retain a share of it. Although it proclaimed national sovereignty, the Declaration of Rights expressed an essentially liberal outlook that guaranteed individual rights and made a separation of powers a defining trait of any constitution. Well into the Revolution, many deputies adhered to this alternative to absolutist concepts of sovereignty, perhaps understanding the problems that transferring sovereignty from one man to an entire nation would raise. Summarizing those problems, Keith Baker asks, "How was the direct and immediate exercise of a unitary sovereign will to be guaranteed in a vast society where direct democracy was impossible? How was the indivisibility and inalienability of the nation's sovereignty to be sustained in the face of the necessity for representation?"[13]

One response to such questions was the theory that national sovereignty could only reside where the entire nation assembled, that is, in the National Assembly. This theory rested on two basic premises: that deliberation among all of the nation's parts was essential to the formation of a truly national will, and that the will of a majority of the nation's parts could stand for the will of the whole. Sieyès, a major architect of this theory, called France "a unified whole" and not "a confederation of municipalities or provinces"; consequently, "the deputy of one district is directly chosen by his district, but indirectly he is chosen by all districts," so "each deputy is a representative of the entire nation."[14] Only after representatives from every part of France had gathered and exchanged views, Sieyès believed, could one speak of a national will. Noting a particularly crucial implication of this doctrine, he concluded that "the people can only speak, can only act, through their representatives."[15] Lally-Tollendal asked "what the Assembly would be if each member arrived armed with a protest or a mandate that forced him to combat the general opinion," and he maintained that because "each part of society is subject" to the whole, "sovereignty resides only in the assembled whole."[16] Although many deputies rejected this theory, which could be interpreted as a denial of the nation's sovereignty, Mirabeau insisted that "no one can remain a member of the National Assembly if he does not recognize its sovereignty."[17]

Of course in politics theory usually follows practice, and in this case those formulating the idea of an indivisible sovereignty residing in a single chamber did so in the context of the Third Estate's campaign for a single National Assembly. Also, the idea that each district was subordinate to the whole developed in response to claims that many of the *cahiers de doléances* (the written grievances and instructions the electoral districts had issued their representatives) demanded the maintenance of separate estates. The theory that sovereignty resided in the National Assembly — which political theorist Raymond Carré de Malberg would later call parliamentary sovereignty — continued to prove useful to those deputies who increasingly sought to make the King their subordinate. Proponents of this theory had on their side the almost instinctive fears of national division noted earlier, and those fears now helped justify placing all authority in a single assembly, just as they had once justified placing all authority in one man's hands. Indeed, the possibility of dividing an assembly of representatives (unlike a king) made it all the more imperative to take a firm stand against any hint of dividing power. In this view, then, the indivisibility of sovereignty demanded the indivisibility of representation, an idea that would have profound consequences throughout the Revolution.

Once sovereignty (or at least its exercise) was safely located in the National Assembly, many of its members were also willing to call it an unlimited power. Defining sovereignty as "indefinite and absolute power," the Monarchien Mounier asserted during a debate on the royal veto in September 1789 that "no one doubts that a nation can do whatever it wants," and Jacques-Guillaume Thouret later asked "what authority could enchain the supreme power of the nation?"[18] By the time the deputies finished their text in 1791, the King's chances of exercising even a share of sovereignty had basically disappeared, and the final draft described the nation's sovereignty as "one, indivisible, inalienable, and imprescriptible."[19]

Any account of the deputies' ideas on sovereignty, however, risks overstating the degree of consensus and clarity of thought on a concept only discussed in brief digressions from other issues. Illustrating the confusion was a brief exchange in August 1791 over language regarding voting rights. Concerned about a reference to the nation transferring its sovereignty to representatives, Robespierre called sovereignty inalienable but also argued that even the "delegation" of "powers" amounted to "the alienation of sovereignty itself," and he cited Rousseau's point that "when a nation delegates its powers to representatives, that nation is no longer free." In his view, the constitution should state that powers, like sovereignty, can be neither alienated nor delegated, and he asked that the text speak only of the "delegation" of "functions."[20]

No one asked Robespierre to clarify his definitions of sovereignty, powers, functions, alienation, or delegation. Distinctions among those terms had mattered little before 1789, when one man was both sovereign and head of the government, but they now became vital with the transfer of sovereignty to an entity incapable of governing. Deputy Jérôme Pétion did argue that Robespierre's idea of inserting the term "inalienable" in the clause on sovereignty was unnecessary given that sovereignty was by definition inalienable, and he took issue with Robespierre's statement that "the nation could not delegate its powers."[21] Robespierre then denied he had said that, explaining: "I simply said that the nation cannot delegate its powers permanently, as the committee intends, which would be an alienation"; that claim was false, however, and it elicited mutterings of protest from the Assembly.[22] Now if one defines alienation as a permanent and irrevocable transfer of authority, Robespierre's reference to "delegation" was confusing at best. An ally of Robespierre tried to clarify this point by arguing that the nation does not del-

egate sovereignty, but "only commissions representatives to exercise the powers it wishes to confer on them," but he contradicted Robespierre's original
point by urging a delegation of powers rather than functions.[23] A proposal to
call sovereignty "imprescriptible" instead of inalienable merely added another undefined term to an already hopelessly muddled lexicon.[24] The Assembly voted at this point to call sovereignty both inalienable and imprescriptible and to state that the nation can delegate powers, but it appears that
a great deal of confusion still surrounded these terms.

As if the term "national sovereignty" did not generate enough confusion, the
term "popular sovereignty"—usually associated with the period from 1792
to 1794—also began to appear frequently by the early months of the Revolution.[25] In this period most of those who spoke of sovereignty belonging to
"the people" were simply using the term as a synonym for the nation. Sieyès,
for example, held that all public powers "come from the people, that is to say,
the nation," and Pétion declared that "the people are the nation, and the nation is the collection of all individuals."[26] Unfortunately, as Colin Lucas
notes, "the word 'peuple' was extraordinarily ambiguous because of its dou-
ble meaning," and few others joined Sieyès in stating definitions of this crucial term.[27] It was, after all, one thing to speak of sovereignty belonging to the
people (meaning the nation) but quite another to speak of it belonging to the
people (meaning the lower classes).

   Although Lucas is right to point out that basic ambiguity, the term actually had more than two commonly used meanings at that time. Among those
who defined the people as the nation, some imagined it as a unified entity
with a will of its own, while the King and some of his supporters continued
to use the absolutist definition of the people as passive objects of paternal
benevolence, often using the plural form to convey an image of a scattered
collection of dissimilar components. Noting approvingly that the King had
recently referred to the people as "his children," the Marquis de Sillery urged
his colleagues to think of themselves as "a gathered family" and to keep in
mind "the happiness of the peoples" under their care.[28] And as noted in the
previous chapter, whereas many defined the people as everyone other than
the King and his ministers, others applied the term only to the Third Estate.
Mirabeau, for example, referred to the nobility and clergy as "two orders that
are neither the people nor the prince," and during the Third Estate's debate
on naming the new assembly they were creating, some objected to Mirabeau's
proposed phrase "representatives of the people" out of fears of it implying
that their assembly only represented the Third Estate.[29] Yet another defini-

tion associated the people with the bourgeoisie, or perhaps the Third Estate under the bourgeoisie's leadership. Rejecting Abbé Coyer's 1755 argument that the bourgeoisie's rising wealth and social aspirations had led it to "secede" from the people, *L'Ami des Patriotes* wrote that the people were in fact "composed of the bourgeoisie," defining a bourgeois as "any man whose labor or whose fairly acquired property furnish means of existence." By including wage-earners in this category, the paper was using a remarkably wide definition of the bourgeoisie, but it made it clear that "the people" did not include vagrants, "brigands," and beggars — a rather sizable population in the France of that era.[30] Sébastien Le Chapelier also implicitly defined the people as the bourgeoisie when he held that the job of providing security in Paris should go to the *garde bourgeoise* (a force made up mostly of property owners), arguing that "it is the people who must guard the people."[31]

Most of those who associated the people with a specific class, however, had the lower classes in mind. If some rejected the phrase "representatives of the people" because it implied that the deputies would only represent the Third Estate, others resented its suggestion that they were representatives of the rabble.[32] Those who considered "the people" a derogatory term did so because of these class connotations, and they often associated the people with violence and disorder. On 14 July, for example, a deputy informed the National Assembly that although "the people" had killed the commander of the Bastille and placed his severed head on a pike, the "bourgeoisie of Paris" was now restoring order.[33] Similarly, during a debate over royal troops blocking the doors to the Estates General, a speaker argued that if "the nation" were barred from attending the sessions, "the people" would revolt.[34] For those invoking the people, of course, hints of dangerousness could be useful, as when Lally-Tollendal spoke of "the French people becoming indignant at their slavery [and] breaking their chains," or when an anonymous pamphleteer warned that "the People" were "getting excited [and] taking up arms," and that "one can no longer restrain them."[35] Many, however, preferred to use terms such as "the multitude" and "the crowd" when describing violent acts, thus protecting "the people" from denigration by those who would deny them a political role. The moderate revolutionary paper, *Le Patriote Français*, for example, denounced "these turbulent men who imagine that they *are the sovereign* when they have rioted and assembled a hundred men in public places," adding that "the people only have existence and political rights while in regular and non-tumultuous assemblies where one deliberates freely and calmly."[36]

In his study of the National Assembly, Timothy Tackett suggests that the violence of 1789 changed many deputies' images of the people, as "the

Rousseauist conception of the Common Man as repository of goodness and truth was frequently replaced, or at least strongly modified, by the image of the violent, unpredictable, and dangerous classes."[37] Tackett is right to emphasize the horror many felt over early revolutionary violence, but as we have seen, Rousseau's idea of the people was only one of many images widely held before July 1789. Moreover, while some were horrified at the violence, others defended it as a necessary and just response to tyranny. Indeed many portrayed the people in largely positive terms, carrying on the work of those philosophes who had recently begun to praise the lower classes and their mental capacities. The most important voice in this revaluation of the people in 1789 was that of Mirabeau, a disowned son of the old nobility elected to the Third Estate. To those who disliked his phrase, "representatives of the people," Mirabeau replied: "Will you go tell your constituents that you rejected this word, the people, and that if you did not blush at it, you have nonetheless sought to avoid a term that did not seem brilliant enough to you?"[38] Angered by "muttering" at another reference to the people, Mirabeau also said:

> Yes, it is because this term, people, is not respected enough in France, because it is darkened, covered with the rust of prejudice, because it presents an idea alarming to pride and against which vanity rebels; because it is pronounced with contempt in the Chambers of the aristocrats; it is for that very reason that we must not only force ourselves to rehabilitate it, but [also] to ennoble it, to make it respectable to ministers and dear to all hearts from now on.[39]

Others soon followed Mirabeau. In the session just noted, Sieyès, who had mostly spoken of "the nation" until then, reminded his colleagues that they were "envoys of the people" and that they had "sworn to reestablish the French people in their rights."[40] Replying to deputies who doubted the people's political abilities, a legislator recalled that people of all classes had elected them, and he asked if their electoral assemblies were really "so tumultuous and so disorderly" or if they produced "results unworthy of the nation?"[41] The people, another insisted, "have always had enough enlightenment to discern those who deserve their confidence."[42] Still another admitted that farmers, artisans, and others "have not had the time to perfect their intelligence, [and] are not well versed in the various branches of political economy and administration," but he called it "easier than one thinks to enlighten them, to interest them gradually in public affairs, and to inspire in them a taste for education." Noting that the classes now considered enlightened had barely known how to read several centuries ago, he concluded that "it is stunning how in the last few years enlightenment has spread even among the lower classes of society, and this progress can only continue to spread."[43] Some, echoing Sieyès, portrayed the people as numerically dominant, economically useful, and unfairly treated, while others, using the old definition of the people as those of humble birth and limited wealth, now associated those qualities with virtue rather than vice.[44] Nevertheless, many deputies retained negative views of the people, and while various orators were seeking to improve images of the poor, the Assembly was moving to disenfranchise them.

With so many definitions of the people in common use, one wonders how those both inside and outside the National Assembly could possibly have understood each other. A speaker uttering the phrase "the people" might have intended it to mean all individuals only to be interpreted as saying the lower classes, or intended it to mean the lower classes, only to be interpreted as saying the Third Estate, or the bourgeoisie. Consequently, though many who spoke of popular sovereignty early in the Revolution were not really seeking to revise the doctrine of national sovereignty or to suggest that sovereignty belonged to the poor, the ambiguity of the term "the people" helped concepts of sovereignty drift into new, often unintended meanings.

By the time of the October Days, when a crowd from Paris invaded the National Assembly and the royal palace at Versailles and forced the government to relocate to Paris, it appeared that some speakers referring to popular sovereignty were indeed trying to redefine the sovereign. When Robespierre, for example, stated that "the Constitution establishes that sovereignty resides in the people, in all the individuals of the people," he was in a way using the people as a synonym for the nation (since it was actually the nation that the deputies had called sovereign).[45] Yet in another way he was proposing a more egalitarian concept of sovereignty, for he made his statement in October 1789 in a speech against disenfranchising the poor. In short, while the words used to describe sovereignty changed little between 1789 and 1792, their meaning changed significantly, moving almost imperceptibly in a more radical and egalitarian direction. Thus long before the sans-culottes or their defenders began claiming that the principle of popular sovereignty justified rule by the lower classes, others with less radical ideas had already made phrases such as popular sovereignty and the will of the people familiar, removing much of their shock value and facilitating the transition to a new kind of politics.

Although the ambiguities in the deputies' declarations on sovereignty usually went unnoticed, a few observers did object. In August 1791 *L'Ami du Roi* wrote, "One wonders what is an inalienable, imprescriptible sovereignty that one can never make use of oneself." The paper also warned that "once you have placed this simple idea in the heads of the people, that they are sovereign, you will not be able to alter it by this other idea, that they cannot exercise its functions," and it called the new concept of sovereignty an "absurd, dangerous, [and] cruel principle that would upset the universe and would cause all crowned heads to fall on the scaffold."[46] Similarly concerned, *L'Ami des Patriotes* noted that it was "the entire collection of the nation that alone has the right to make an insurrection," and it insisted that while some "give the name 'people' to the class of citizens who agitate turbulently," those troublemakers "are *of the people* but they are not *the people*."[47] In August 1791 the conservative deputy Malouet (by then a pariah in the Assembly) warned of "simple and crude men dangerously misled by this declaration" of national sovereignty. That concept, he believed, was acceptable as an abstract notion, "but in saying that sovereignty belongs to the people and in only having them delegate powers, you give them the continual temptation" of possessing a right they cannot exercise. Calling the existing declaration "as false as it is dangerous," Malouet feared that governors would "take on, in the opinion of the people, a subaltern character."[48] Annoyed by the man and his ideas, the Assembly voted to prevent him from completing his speech.

Before long, however, such warnings about the implications of imprecise language regarding sovereignty would appear prescient. Political and social tensions were growing by 1791, as a period of relative calm that had begun after the October Days ended with the King's escape attempt in June and the National Guard's shooting of republican petitioners at the Champs de Mars in July. A radical republican movement based in the Paris sections (the districts originally created for the 1789 elections) then gained even greater momentum with the outbreak of war in April 1792 and the King's decision in June to veto two controversial measures and fire three popular ministers. On 20 June 1792 militants from the Cordeliers Club and some of the more radical Parisian sections engineered a demonstration, mobilizing thousands of Parisian sans-culottes and *fédérés* (National Guard members from the provinces who had recently come to Paris). Though the marchers were mainly angry at the King, they also disliked the many deputies who still favored a monarchy, and it is significant that the crowd went first to the National Assembly rather than the royal palace. While the Assembly was at work, a clerk informed the deputies that eight thousand armed citizens were outside the door, demanding to parade through the hall and read a petition.[49] Some deputies recalled that it was illegal for visitors to bring arms into the National Assembly, but deputies on the left dismissed the point, and a majority voted to admit the crowd.

A spokesman for the demonstrators then announced, "The French people have come today" to "annihilate" the executive power, convinced that "one man must not influence the will of a nation of 25 million souls."[50] Speaking "in the name of the nation," the spokesman declared that "the people are standing," awaiting "a response worthy of their sovereignty."[51] The rest of the marchers—thousands of men, women, and children armed with rifles, pikes, knives, and pitchforks—then entered the hall and spent nearly two hours marching, dancing, beating drums, chanting slogans, and singing "Ça ira" before their captive audience. The only hint of the deputies' control over the crowd came when a marcher with a bloody calf's heart on a pole—marked with the sign "Heart of an Aristocrat"—agreed to take his trophy outside.

How had this carnivalesque scene come to pass? The reasons behind the event, and behind the collapse of the first revolutionary regime, are of course many and complex. Both George Rudé's study of the crowd and Albert Soboul's work on the sans-culottes rightly emphasized the role of bread shortages in provoking the Parisians, but food crises, a familiar part of life in France, had often occurred without causing rebellions. Indeed both Rudé and Soboul acknowledge the role of new political ideas at this time; in Rudé's words, "the ideas and slogans of the revolutionary *bourgeoisie* . . . were beginning to take root among the *menu peuple* and to be turned by them to their own advantage," and "once these ideas began to permeate the common people . . . a new direction and purpose were given to popular unrest."[52] Among those ideas, none was more important than popular sovereignty, which by June 1792 had indeed led some citizens to view their political leaders as subaltern.

If a carnival involves a temporary inversion of ranks, a "world turned upside-down," then perhaps elements of carnival are inherent in popular sovereignty, which proclaims the governing few to be servants of the many. Democracies also follow the rituals of carnival by making that inversion of authority only a rare and temporary event, with the normal order of things being restored between elections. In revolutionary France, the deputies who proclaimed national sovereignty certainly expected authority to return to the country's political officials between elections, but it eventually became apparent that given prevailing definitions of sovereignty, nothing could justify forcing the sovereign people to accept a subordinate position at any time. Sovereignty, in other words, can be neither temporary nor restricted, or it would not be sovereignty. The sovereign people might choose to let representatives exercise political authority, but if they decided to make the inversion of authority permanent, no person or institution would have the right to stop them.

This whole theory, of course, assumed that "the people" were a real entity capable of thinking and acting, and the deputies' statements that any kind of direct democracy was impossible suggests that they knew better. Yet the awareness that the people could not actually repossess their powers may have led the deputies to feel safe in proclaiming their own subservience, as many did. In May 1789, for example, in a debate on keeping the Assembly's sessions open to the public, one deputy declared that "we deliberate here in the presence of our masters, and we owe them an account of our positions."[53] Unfortunately, if the deputies were right that the entire citizenry could not possibly govern, others held that a fraction of the citizenry could indeed legitimately claim the right to speak for the people and issue commands to the nation's representatives, which is exactly what happened on 20 June.

The ambiguities in the term "the people" undoubtedly contributed to the crisis that destroyed the first revolutionary regime, as it became clear that France's leaders had invested supreme political authority in a term whose meaning they could not control. Yet in some ways it mattered little whether a listener defined the people as the lower classes or the entire population, for the logic of democracy, which posits the equality of all individual wills, grants the majority the right to represent the whole. In France at that time the lower classes undoubtedly constituted a majority of the population, and given the common assumption that political opinions could be deduced from class status — an idea rarely challenged at the time — it was only a short step to the (unauthorized) conclusion that any member of the most numerous class could speak not only for his or her whole class, but for the nation as well. Thus for a sans-culotte addressing the wealthy deputies in the National Assembly, it must have been easy to feel justified in speaking for the people, or in proclaiming, as one marcher did on 20 June, "Legislators, we are not 2000 men but 20 million."[54] Deputies on the right often muttered and protested at such claims, but the sans-culottes, having heard that the people were sovereign and that sovereignty meant a supreme authority no one could limit, felt entitled to dictate to the deputies.

Although it was too late by 1792 to regain control over the meaning of political language articulated carelessly for three years, a few deputies did take issue with the militants' uses of the idea of popular sovereignty. One orator, for example, recommended sending a message to the sections, "explaining to them the sovereignty of the people, how it is exercised, and how it is usurped."[55] Yet the deputies on the left, seeing a chance to use the militants to oust their rivals from the Assembly, helped undermine any such efforts by endorsing the militants' claims. On 25 July the Jacobin deputy François

Chabot warned that "the nation will say to itself: [if] the National Assembly has not found in the Constitution enough force, enough means to save the commonwealth, the people must rise up and save themselves." When Chabot added that the people "always have the uncontestable right to change their Constitution," the president of the Assembly reprimanded him for violating his oath to protect the constitution. After a bitter exchange and a breakdown of order in the hall, the deputies voted to exonerate Chabot and to reprimand the President for having "misunderstood the sovereignty of the people." They then declared that popular sovereignty meant that the people have right to change the constitution "at all times."[56]

The question of the conditions under which a constitution can be replaced or revised has resurfaced frequently in France since the Revolution. In 1789 the idea that the sovereign can change a country's constitution at any time found many supporters among the deputies seeking to replace an unwanted political order, but before long concerns about the effects that doctrine might have on their own new regime led many to think again, and in their final draft they created a complex procedure in which three consecutive legislatures would have to agree to any revisions.[57] In the summer of 1792 deputies of the left, now seeking to rid themselves of both the King and the constitution that gave him his authority, once again began asserting the sovereign's right to change the constitution at any time, as one legislator charged that the authors of the procedures for constitutional revision had proclaimed the people's sovereignty but then "sought to enchain that sovereignty," and another held that the constitution's rules for revision "were merely advisory."[58] Voicing a common republican view, one Jacobin told the Club in 1792 that "the people cannot be despoiled of their sovereignty, and if the constitution does not lead them to happiness, they can rise up as a whole and seek a new constitution."[59]

Those who disagreed reiterated Sieyès's point that only the National Assembly could express the national will, or claimed that the nation, being sovereign, had the right to create binding rules governing revision—a claim weakened by the lack of any referendum on the new constitution. But although moderates protested the idea that the people could not be restrained by laws or constitutions, the radicals were merely repeating what even some moderate deputies had already argued. In *What Is the Third Estate?*, for example, Sieyès had insisted on the people's permanent right to change their constitution, asking how a nation could "impose on itself duties toward itself" and how it could have "a contract with itself." He concluded that "a nation not only is not subject to a constitution, but it *cannot* be."[60] The left, then, was not alone in articulating a vision of sovereignty that authorized the people to overturn their political system at any time.

Although the 20 June demonstration failed to destroy the monarchy and the constitution, a second uprising on 10 August 1792 finished the job. Once again, an armed crowd arrived in the National Assembly, addressing the deputies in the name of the sovereign people, and once again the deputies of the left embraced the movement, claiming, as one legislator put it, that "the nation is taking back all its sovereignty" from its representatives.[61] This time there were few deputies left to protest, for moderate deputies had recently fled after being chased by angry crowds and threatened with lynching. After a bloody but successful attack on the royal palace, the rebels jailed the King, and the deputies of the left, now dominating a rump parliament, announced elections for a National Convention to write a republican constitution.

Yet if these deputies no longer had to worry about the King or the moderates in the Assembly, they still had to deal with a highly mobilized, well-armed, and triumphant Parisian movement claiming the authority of popular sovereignty. That problem became apparent late in the day on 10 August, when a band of militants arrived to protest that the Assembly had only suspended and not deposed the King. In response, a leader of the remaining deputies unwittingly echoed the absent moderates, telling the petitioners that they "know perfectly well that Paris is only one section of the Empire," and that one section cannot dictate to the National Assembly in the name of the sovereign.[62] Unconvinced, the militants continued to speak for the nation, and the newly purged Paris Commune summarized the day's events by declaring, "The sovereign has spoken."[63]

As the previous section shows, the problematic nature of the new doctrine of sovereignty forced the French to confront the equally difficult issue of representation, and the ideas they articulated about representation, like those on sovereignty, established the basic framework within which orators made claims about public opinion. Unfortunately, the deputies gathering at Versailles had few theories or historical precedents to guide them as they fashioned a new system of representation. That practice was essentially unknown in the ancient world, as contemporaries often remarked. The theory and practice of absolutism was of little use, for under that system, as Baker explains, the Estates General assembled only "at the will of the monarch, and only . . . to give him aid and counsel on behalf of the multiplicity of corporate bodies comprising the particularistic social order of the Old Regime."[64] The deputies could also peruse the philosophes' texts, but unfortunately one of the more influential discussions of representation at the time was Rousseau's *Social Contract*, which denounced the evils of representation.[65] Ideas might also have been borrowed from England, but their association with a country viewed with as much horror as admiration usually sufficed to discredit them, and examples from America often struck French observers as irrelevant to France. Useful theories might be found in Montesquieu's work, as well as in texts by various Jansenists, disgruntled nobles, and *parlementaires*, but those designing a new system of representation in 1789 generally had to work without much theoretical guidance or historical precedent.

In creating the new system, the deputies of the Third Estate faced a troubling dilemma, for they needed to claim enough authority to allow them to challenge the king and the first two estates without claiming so much that they seemed to be merely new tyrants. Seeking to solve the former problem, the Third Estate claimed not just to be representatives of the nation but also to be the nation's *sole* representatives, following ideas in *What Is the Third Estate?*. Yet in asserting that they alone represented the nation, and in claiming a kind of perfect identity with the nation and an infallible ability to articulate its will, they risked matching Rousseau's portrait of usurping representatives. And by claiming an exclusive right to articulate the nation's will, they seemed to be denying the legitimacy of any rival voice emanating from the public, just as absolutists had rejected the legitimacy of "public opinion." The Third Estate's strategy for confronting its rivals thus called attention to its relationship with those it represented.

One of the first issues that forced the revolutionaries to discuss their relationship with their constituents was the binding mandate. Traditionally, voters electing representatives to the Estates General had had the right to give them strict instructions, a practice aimed at preventing representatives from being pressured into making excessive concessions to the king. In 1789, however, the deputies of the Third Estate found they could not carry out a revolution while adhering to instructions issued within the framework of the Old Regime.[66] Attacking the binding mandate in July 1789, Talleyrand insisted on the need for deliberation in the formation of the national will and noted the impossibility of citizens from all districts meeting for that purpose, calling it "impossible to deliberate when one has an opinion forced" upon one in advance. If deliberation were unnecessary, he added, a National Assembly would be as well, for "one would only have to count the wishes of each district one by one . . . and the least skillful clerk could carry out this operation." So instead of electing mere messengers, the voters chose representatives "to will as they themselves would will if they could transport themselves to the general meeting" and take part in deliberation.[67] In this view, each district was part of a whole, so when voters in one district let their representative overrule them, they were submitting not to the man they had elected, but only to the general will.

Critics of the binding mandate also contended that the voters themselves might not always want their instructions followed blindly. "Times have changed a great deal since we received our mandates," observed one deputy during a debate on the royal veto, suggesting that the voters' will had changed.[68] The voters, according to Talleyrand, "cannot know with certainty what [their] opinion would be after a question is freely discussed by all the other districts."[69] In this view, because the citizens could not meet, deliberate, and express their will after each new event, representatives needed the freedom to act quickly using their own judgment. Although a few deputies insisted that the cahiers remained binding, most soon ignored them.

In attacking the binding mandate, the deputies were trying to solve an immediate problem, but they were also indirectly formulating a rationale for representation. As they continued to do so, their principal argument involved noting the impossibility of assembling the entire citizenry in large modern nations, for as Sieyès explained, "it is obvious that five to six million active citizens, spread over more than twenty-five thousand square leagues, cannot assemble."[70] Even if there were some means of doing so, he added, the process would be so inconvenient that people would only wish to use it occasionally, making representation necessary at all other times. The impossibility of assembly thus justified a kind of parliamentary sovereignty.[71]

If those citing the impossibility of assembling the citizenry made a rather reluctant case for representation, some did make more positive arguments. Those opponents of the binding mandate who stressed the need for flexibility and discretion in the face of changing events certainly made such arguments, while others observed that because the direct democracies of ancient times had relied on slavery, representation permitted a broad expansion of liberty. Still others spoke of the need for enlightenment, expertise, and experience in matters of government, and they reinforced these arguments by invoking traditional images of the unruly, gullible, and ignorant multitude. Mirabeau, for example, considered it the deputies' duty to "to enlighten, to calm, to save the people from excesses that could produce the intoxication of a furious zeal," while Malouet doubted whether problems that even Locke, Montesquieu, and Rousseau "had found difficult to resolve" could be judged in "the cafés and public places."[72] According to Sieyès, the "uneducated multitude" chose "representatives who were much more capable than they were of knowing the general interest and thus of interpreting their own will."[73] Echoing Adam Smith on the efficiency of a division of labor, he also insisted that a political division of labor "is to the common advantage of all members of society" and that "the common interest [and] the improvement of the social state itself cry out to us to make government a specific profession."[74] Whereas some underlined the lawmakers' need for experience and technical knowledge in fields such as finance and the law, one legislator simply urged the people to entrust lawmaking to "an assembly of wise men."[75]

If the idea of enlightenment helped justify representatives' authority, so did the possession of property. As Furet notes, many associated enlightenment and property ownership, for the deputies had "learned from the century's books that aptitude for government and public life was born of independence and education, and therefore from property and affluence."[76] It therefore seemed rational to allow property owners to represent others and, in Antoine-Pierre-Marie Barnave's words, "to will for the nation."[77] Who better deserved this authority, asked one deputy, than "men who have some interest in legislation being good and wise, in government being stable" and "those who have something to lose?"[78] Others added that men of means were less susceptible to corruption and bribery.[79]

Nevertheless, many considered arguments about the impossibility of assembling the citizenry a safer basis of authority than such intangible qualities as enlightenment and concern for the general interest. Indeed, it was probably the deputies' sense that there was no way for the nation to assemble that best explains their dangerous habit of asserting their constituents' theoretical right to overrule them at any time, a tactic that they thought allowed them to prove their revolutionary credentials without taking any real risks. When Sieyès, for example, asked, "If [the nation] could gather before you and express its will, would you dare to dispute it?" he was undoubtedly outlining a scenario he considered impossible.[80] A few imaginative minds did seek ways to assemble the people; Jeremy Popkin describes a 1789 pamphlet entitled *Ways to Communicate Directly with the People*, which "offered drawings of a giant megaphone, a mobile sonic reflector, and other devices by which an orator could address a populace many times the size of the citizenry of the ancient city-states."[81] Yet such ideas must have seemed purely fanciful to most, serving only to prove that the French, unlike the ancient Athenians, could not assemble in one place.

Yet if every French citizen could not meet in one place, one could simply redefine what assembly meant, so that gathering voters in their local districts would solve the problem. As early as 1789 the newspaper *Révolutions de Paris*, citing the practices of the ancient Romans and modern Swiss, argued that the people could indeed assemble and that "the whole secret consists of divisions and subdivisions that facilitate the gathering of individual wills."[82] By 1792 Parisian militants and deputies on the left were making this case more and more frequently, proposing a new system of representation in which those who attended meetings in their sections represented those who did not, or in which the Paris sections represented the rest of the nation. And while volunteers from the departments were arriving in Paris in July 1792, *Révolutions de Paris* wrote that "since the eighty-three departments have sent numerous deputations to Paris, . . . the people of France have assembled."[83] Some might object that gathering the citizens in separate assemblies scattered throughout France did not permit truly national deliberation, or that political clubs sending deputations to Paris had no right to speak for their entire departments, but the deputies had helped prepare the ground for this challenge to their authority by repeatedly asserting the sovereign people's theoretical right to overrule them.

When the National Assembly turned to the design of specific representative institutions and procedures, one of its main tasks involved creating rules for elections. As the basic expression of national sovereignty and the source of representative authority, elections took a central place in the new system, and voters met repeatedly over the next four years to choose legislators, mayors, magistrates, town councilors, National Guard officers, and even clergymen. These constant elections helped to implant the idea of national sovereignty in people's minds, to teach principles of representation (replacing the corporatist logic of the Old Regime with a new individualism), and to reshape notions of public opinion as well.

When they came to the question of who could vote in future elections — a question that would soon have a profound impact on definitions of "the public" and "public opinion" — the deputies chose to retreat from the remarkably open franchise used in the Estates General elections, implementing property and residence requirements and also retaining the system of indirect elections.[84] Some feared that peasants and other poor voters would obey priests and landlords, while others worried, as the moderate deputy Barnave put it, about elections being "bought with pots of beer."[85] But while some were concerned about the poor being too obedient, others, shocked by the rash of revolutionary violence and attacks on property that swept through France in 1789, saw the opposite danger. Although many were reluctant to discuss the danger of enfranchising the poor, one deputy warned of the need to limit "the influence of numbers," adding that "it is impossible in the long run that the greatest number would not act in its own interest and that it would not radically and directly attack" private property.[86]

Reporting for the committee that drafted the electoral rules, Thouret offered a more positive argument, defending the restriction of voting rights to "a certain class of citizens" on the grounds of "the interest that they take in the success of the commonwealth."[87] In invoking the concept of interest, however, Thouret was using a highly ambiguous concept, for interest can have either a subjective sense (that one *cares* enough about politics to want to vote) or an objective sense (that one has some verifiable stake in a given order). If Thouret meant that only those who *cared* about politics should be allowed to vote (as his reference to the interest people "take" suggests), then any deliberate exclusion would be pointless, since the apathetic would not vote anyway. On the other hand, if he meant that only those who owned property could benefit or suffer from the course of political events, then he was making a very dubious argument. Challenging that argument, Robespierre insisted that even a lowly artisan has "his little savings," and he added that one's "interest in the conservation of one's things is proportionate to the modesty of one's fortune." Seizing both the patriotic and the egalitarian high ground, Robespierre denied that "one must be rich to love one's country."[88]

The deputies' decision to disenfranchise many of the poor is understandable given the ideas and events of the time, but the system they devised — in which deputies represented electors, who in turn represented "active citizens," who in turn represented disenfranchised "passive citizens" — created a kind of great chain of being more in keeping with the hierarchical Old Regime than with the newly declared principles. The often conservative behavior of national electorates throughout France's subsequent history suggests that the 1791 Constitution's multiple barriers against democratic excess may have been unnecessary, though the deputies had no past examples of electoral moderation to reassure them. Nevertheless, disenfranchising an entire class of citizens soon cost the new order a great deal of legitimacy, tainting the entire idea of representation and contributing to the downfall of the first revolutionary regime in 1792.

As for the design of new political institutions, it is important to note the deputies' initial uncertainty over the nature of their task and the extent of their authority. Most deputies seem to have come to Versailles seeking reform, not revolution (a word rarely used in the early months), so despite the common view of the summer of 1789 as a rare moment when a sharp break with the past allowed the creation of a completely new order, the political realities of the time in fact constrained the deputies in many ways. Perhaps most importantly, the existence of the monarchy remained beyond question in 1789, and no deputy even proposed to debate the issue at that time. So as the deputies began drafting a new constitution, it was simply given that it would feature both a monarchy and an assembly of representatives, a combination that soon proved very awkward.

It took little time for the National Assembly to become the prime locus of power in the new system. With the Assembly alone deriving its powers from election by the nation—and also holding the power to write the new constitution—the main question soon became what powers future legislatures would *not* have. Alarmed at the Assembly's increasing power, some cited the lessons of antiquity to warn of corruption and demagoguery in elected assemblies, while others cautioned that vesting all power in a unicameral assembly might produce what one deputy called "an alienation of national sovereignty."[89] One speaker said that because of the possibility of misrepresentation, "the liberty of any people who do not exercise all powers themselves only exists through a separation of powers," and Mounier cautioned that when all powers are in the same hands, "those who exercise them . . . consider themselves the supreme and infallible arbiters of the destiny of their peers."[90] Yet many deputies seemed to have held contradictory ideas, accepting the need for the separation of powers proclaimed in the Declaration of Rights (however interpreted) while also believing that the indivisibility of sovereignty required indivisible representation. So although the Constituent Assembly did create a system of plural representation, it rejected various proposals to limit the legislature's powers, and as conflicts with the King intensified, it became increasingly clear that many deputies had only a superficial commitment to a true separation of powers.

As the deputies' misgivings about sharing power with anyone became more and more obvious, the foundations of executive power came under increasing scrutiny. The wisdom of having a hereditary monarch in a system of national sovereignty had received virtually no discussion in 1789, if only because any talk of ending monarchy then might have jeopardized the whole enterprise, and the universal assumption that the King would head the executive kept the Assembly from giving much thought to the ideal nature or structure of the executive power. So aside from occasional statements that efficiency required one man to head the executive (an argument that justified an elected president as well as a king), few made positive arguments for why France should have a king. Nevertheless, though support for the monarchy declined with the King's escape attempt in 1791, it remained strong both in the National Assembly and throughout France, and Michael Kennedy reports that even the provincial Jacobins remained mostly monarchist well into 1792.[91]

One issue that did provoke useful discussions on the king's place in the overall system of representation was the royal veto. In creating a "suspensive" veto, the Assembly let the king delay enactment of any bill and make an "appeal to the people," giving citizens time to speak out before the Assembly reexamined it. Speaking for the veto, Malouet claimed that because the deputies' will and interests "can be found in contradiction with the general will and interest," there had to be some way to verify whether "a given resolution of [the] representatives is or is not the expression of the general will."[92] Other speakers later echoed Malouet, one insisting that the representatives' will "is not the real will of the nation, but rather its supposed will," and another contending that "representatives can be mistaken" about the people's will.[93] Taking issue with those who saw the national will only in the National Assembly, one deputy complained that "one has endlessly confused the National Assembly with the nation."[94] The veto's opponents, however, continued to see the National Assembly as the nation assembled, and Sieyès maintained that "the people or the nation can only have one voice"—that of the National Assembly.[95]

Yet justifying the royal veto on the grounds that the Assembly might misrepresent the nation failed to explain what gave the King the right to overrule the nation's elected representatives. Debate on the veto thus raised the crucial question of whether the king was a representative of the nation. If not, the source of his authority would be unclear, and he would certainly be subordinate to the Assembly. One monarchist claimed that the king necessarily represents the nation by virtue of exercising functions for it, a circular argument that said nothing about the source of his right to exercise those functions; Robespierre replied that carrying out functions merely made the king a "functionary" and an agent of the National Assembly.[96] Others claimed the king was a representative because the nation wanted it that way, having expressly delegated its authority to both branches and having "charged them jointly with expressing the general will."[97] Yet unless one based that claim on the cahiers, which the deputies had repudiated, it would seem to rest on an imaginary act of delegation. "Without election," declared Pierre-Louis Roederer, "there is no representation," so "the ideas of heredity and representation are mutually exclusive," and as Jacobin deputy Jean-Paul Rabaut Saint-Etienne said, if a representative "is not revocable he is not a representative."[98] Though the constitution ended up calling both legislators and kings representatives, the source of royal authority remained unclear, and the whole problem of the king's role in the new system of representation continued to plague this regime.

But if many came to believe that the National Assembly outranked the king in this new system, where did it stand in relation to its constituents? In other words, in the relationship between representatives and the represented, or between the government and "public opinion," which led and which followed? Many deputies accepted their theoretical subservience to the nation, but in practice they knew that no government could function if the governed refused to follow its rules.

Those who held that the national will existed only in the National Assembly offered a theory that effectively barred any citizen or district from overruling the Assembly, but few deputies accepted a theory that seemed to deny the legitimacy of public opinion. Instead, many deputies proclaimed the citizens' supremacy over them, often calling themselves "mandataries" to emphasize their subservience. Surprisingly, even some conservatives asserted the citizens' powers over their representatives, citing the cahiers as binding instructions in hopes of restraining an Assembly set on monopolizing the state's authority.[99] Others rejected the validity of the cahiers but affirmed other ideas such as the citizens' right to recall their representatives from office at any time, and when the King installed a new team of ministers to replace the popular Necker ministry in July 1789, some argued that governors must always have the public's support to hold office. Barnave, for example, stated that "when a minister does not have the confidence of the nation or its representatives, the National Assembly can and must declare that . . . the dismissal of that minister becomes necessary," and Lally-Tollendal insisted that "the pleas of a people are orders" for those in power.[100] Although these deputies were asserting the people's authority over the King and his ministers rather than over their elected representatives, they were nonetheless helping establish a significant principle.

Many deputies soon made clear their belief that they should also be subject to this permanent popular oversight, as they made countless arguments calling into question representatives' authority. In pleading for a royal veto in September 1789, Mirabeau charged that "the choosing of these representatives of the people will always result in a sort of de facto aristocracy," which "will always seek to keep [the people] in subjection."[101] During the same debate, some proposed that any veto should trigger new elections to clarify the people's will, and in reply to claims that it would be impractical to keep assembling the citizenry, the moderate deputy Alexandre de Lameth said that "once the districts are established, nothing will be quicker or easier than [to hold] elections."[102] The comte d'Antraigues considered representatives free to use their discretion when the people had expressed no view on an issue, but he told his colleagues that "when the people have spoken, it is your duty to give the first example of submission" and to "bend before this supreme authority."[103] The basic principle he cited was "this inalienable right that [the people] retain to elect those who represent them, to guide them, to instruct them, to judge them, finally, to enable them to be the organs of the public will and to prevent them from ever dominating that will." D'Antraigues also urged people to exercise "surveillance" over their representatives, a term that would soon take on increasingly ominous overtones.[104]

Initially, the deputies' assertions of their constituents' authority over them had little effect on their ability to govern, but activists in the Paris sections, hearing the principles the deputies were proclaiming, soon began posing their demands for a kind of direct democracy, at first only within Paris's municipal government but eventually in all of France as well.[105] By late 1789, *Révolutions de Paris*, which reflected the thinking of the more militant members of the Paris sections, rejected the idea of the national will existing only in the National Assembly, writing that "the will of the representatives can be in contradiction with the will of the nation."[106] That paper also insisted that unless "mandataries" were "revocable at will," the people would have no alternative to insurrection as a means of controlling them.[107] And also by late 1789 Jean-Paul Marat was proclaiming the people's unlimited powers over their representatives, writing in his newspaper, *Le Publiciste Parisien*, that the representatives' powers "are in the hands of their constituents, always masters who can revoke them at will."[108]

Egged on by such journalists as well as many deputies, militants in the sections asserted the people's rights over their representatives with increasing boldness. Indeed, just by meeting regularly the sections were demonstrating their rejection of the idea that the nation could not assemble (as well as disobeying a decree of the National Assembly) and by March 1790 a few sections were demanding the right to meet in permanent session. To ensure the deputies' obedience to their constituents' will, one district called for an "intermediary committee" to carry on "a continual correspondence" with the legislators, and Brissot (not yet a deputy) recommended a "frequent return of the delegates to their constituents" so that "the people will not be betrayed or sold out."[109] Illustrating the sections' outlook, one section asked, "Is it for the son to order, and the father to obey?"[110]

After the King's escape attempt and capture at Varennes, the sections grew even bolder, openly demanding a republic and questioning the Assembly's authority as well, and a group that gathered on the Champs de Mars in July 1791 signed a petition stating that as "members of the sovereign people," they were asserting their "right to express their will to enlighten and guide their mandataries."[111] The movement experienced a setback when the National Guard opened fire on the petitioners, but the outbreak of war in April 1792 and the deepening food crisis reinvigorated the movement, and by summer 1792 it was ready to challenge the representatives again. When a group from Marseilles came to Paris to demand a republic after the 20 June uprising, it informed the deputies that the nation "has the incontestable right to approve or reject the laws that its representatives impose on it, since it is the sole sovereign."[112]

Such claims certainly met opposition in the National Assembly. "The section," argued Le Chapelier on 10 May 1791, "is nothing; it is only a fraction of a whole and cannot have an isolated existence."[113] As another deputy told activists from one section who came to demand a republic in early August 1792, "it is not for one section of the empire to say, before the whole empire has pronounced" its will.[114] In this view, the sections at best spoke only for Paris, and Paris could not represent France, for only a simultaneous expression of all the electoral districts could bring the national will into view. But if many deputies refused to obey the Paris sections, we have seen that the Assembly as a whole was hardly united and consistent in opposing the citizens' right to dictate to their representatives. In spring 1792, for example, Robespierre, writing in his newspaper, *Le Défenseur de la Constitution*, attacked the whole idea of representation, arguing that if the people delegate their legislative authority to "a small number of individuals," then "it is only a fiction that the law is the expression of the general will."[115] During the August 1792 uprising, a sympathetic deputy argued that "it would be misunderstanding the sovereignty of the people to question whether they have the right to withdraw the powers they have delegated."[116] As in 1789, then, representatives facing insurrections often made arguments legitimating the crowds' actions and undermining their own authority, and by August 1792 that authority was collapsing.

As this political crisis deepened, calls for a "national convention" proliferated. Unfortunately, that term (borrowed from America) had no clear, broadly accepted meaning, as some seemed to be calling for the entire nation to gather once again in local assemblies and declare its will directly, while others merely envisioned the election of new representatives to write a new constitution.[117] The latter view, however, would not satisfy those who held that in times of crisis the nation had to "take back" the exercise of its sovereignty. In other words, because demands for a national convention reflected not only the lack of the present Assembly's legitimacy but also the legitimacy of representation itself, to end up with nothing more than a new set of representatives might seem a cruel betrayal to those dreaming of direct democracy. And yet as those merely calling for new representatives seemed to see, it was nonsense to demand that the nation voice its will directly, for there was no widely credible means by which "the nation" or "public opinion" could speak. So although calling a national convention did help resolve the crisis of August 1792, the problem of representation was far from settled.

The attempts of those outside the National Assembly to claim powers over the deputies are not surprising, but why did the deputies help undermine their own authority by asserting the people's supremacy over them? Many deputies who voiced these ideas were members of minority factions within the Assembly, and they were concentrating more on defeating their political rivals in conflicts at hand than on designing a viable future polity. More than once when a minority faction managed to take power, it abruptly abandoned its previous arguments and took up the case for representation, but because ideas and doctrines asserted in a given conflict could not be "unthought" once that conflict ended, the cumulative effect of minority deputies' repeated declarations of the people's right to instruct, overrule, and recall their representatives was to implant that idea firmly in revolutionary political culture. Yet those in power also frequently asserted the citizens' authority over their representatives, perhaps in hopes of seeming even more egalitarian and revolutionary than their challengers. (Here, Furet's concept of "egalitarian outbidding" seems particularly relevant.) Also, as we have seen, this ultimately self-destructive behavior rested on the assumption that there was no way to assemble the citizenry, which led the deputies to believe they could proclaim these rights with impunity.

Thus just as the revolutionary leaders' interpretations of national sovereignty laid the foundations for the upheavals of 1792, so did their ideas and rhetoric about representation. As historians have often noted, the attempt to fit a hereditary monarch into a representative system based on national sovereignty was bound to encounter serious problems, and the King indeed became the main object of the public outrage that eventually destroyed this regime. As for their own authority as representatives, the deputies did offer some justification, but their ideas on property ownership and political rights seemed to contradict core revolutionary principles, and by relying more on claims of the impossibility of assembling the nation than on positive arguments for a division of labor and a delegation of authority to those most qualified to judge complex legal, political, and economic problems, they left themselves vulnerable to refutation by those who saw national elections and ongoing section meetings as proof that the nation could indeed assemble. Moreover, the deputies consistently undermined their own case by repeatedly proclaiming the nation's theoretical powers over its representatives. By declaring both the nation's theoretical rights over its representatives and its practical inability to exercise those rights, the deputies helped create a sharp divergence of theory and practice that disappointed expectations and helped destroy confidence in the country's formal political institutions. And the more people's faith in those institutions eroded, the more essential it became for "public opinion" to provide an alternative source of legitimation.

III

🌿

Public Opinion and Legitimacy,
1789–1792

One of the first ways in which the concept of public opinion began changing in 1789 was in its relationship to governmental institutions and authorities. Those who invoked public opinion before 1789 in France necessarily alluded to a purely informal and extralegal authority, for absolutism made the king's opinion the only legitimate public opinion, and even those who called public opinion more powerful than kings generally conceded that at least in the short term, kings could simply refuse to bend before a force lacking any legal authority or institutional expression. With the election of the Estates General, however, that situation began to change, and within months public opinion no longer seemed to be merely an informal power. If public opinion was *la reine du monde*, many believed that this monarch had now begun to rule as well as reign.

These changes, however, drew attention to many hitherto ignored ambiguities in the concept of public opinion. As long as public opinion had lacked any official role, questions about how to define and represent it could remain unanswered, but now that "the public" was supposedly taking a direct political role, those questions became more urgent. One crucial event that helped, indirectly and unintentionally, to give public opinion more concrete form was the election of the Estates General, for it was not long before this perceived expression of the nation's will was also described as an expression of public opinion.[1] And with the declaration of national sovereignty, the concepts of the national will and public opinion became even more closely associated. Among those who identified public opinion with the electorate's opinion was the moderate weekly *L'Ami des Patriotes*, which wondered "how many votes a man must gather" to be "truly assured of public opinion" supporting him, and one deputy who called for annual elections on the grounds that "it is desirable that public opinion ceaselessly invest the legislative corps" with its authority.[2] Backing a plan to allow the reelection of representatives, Le Chapelier called it essential "that the censure of public opinion be clearly demonstrated, that the nation should have some means of expressing its confidence."[3] This growing tendency to associate public opinion with the opinions of the national electorate supports Timothy Tackett's claim that public opinion, previously "a somewhat disembodied abstraction, now took on a new and far more concrete meaning."[4]

There is an irony in this movement toward an electoral concept of public opinion in 1789, for it was around that concept that the French of the late twentieth century finally reached a broad consensus on the definition of public opinion and the means of its representation.[5] In this period, however, an electoral definition of public opinion was not universal, and support for it did not prove durable. One problem concerned the disenfranchisement of "passive citizens," which led some on the left to resist the idea of equating public opinion with the electorate's opinion. Yet while the left considered the electorate too small, others, who adhered to the prerevolutionary idea of public opinion as the product of enlightened minds, considered it too large. Part of the problem involved the sudden expansion of France's public sphere, which replaced a "republic of letters" in which many participants knew each other with an anonymous and disparate public sphere. France, in other words, lacked any national forum or arena of communications such as a newspaper that everyone read, and this led some to see only a chaotic babble of voices. Moreover, many of those voices belonged to members of classes that many upper-class observers did not want in the public sphere at all. Malouet, for example, distinguished between public opinion and the will of all individuals, insisting that public opinion "must only be that of the best minds, of the most decent and enlightened men," and not the product of "suffrage, and of the blind and seduced multitude."[6] Yet some simply resigned themselves to the idea that a much larger public now formed public opinion, even if, as *L'Ami du Roi* wrote, it was still "wise and virtuous men" and "property owners" who "alone *should* establish public opinion" (emphasis added).[7]

Despite these battles over public opinion's sociological referent, many believed that France's new government, unlike its predecessor, faithfully reflected public opinion. Yet at the same time many were claiming that France finally had a government that would obey public opinion. Though not clearly perceived at the time, these two ideas conflicted, for how could one claim both that the government was an infallible reflection of public opinion and that henceforth governments would obey public opinion? In other words, to insist that the government's opinion *was* public opinion would seem to deny the legitimacy of any nongovernmental expression of opinion in the same way that absolutist rulers had done. And yet if the government was *not* a true reflection of public opinion, what right did it have to rule or to resist public opinion? In short, equating public opinion with the sovereign nation's opinion helped give public opinion more concrete form, but it also raised troubling questions about the relationship between official powers and public opinion—questions that would persist throughout the Revolution.

Associating public opinion with the will of the new sovereign also helped fuel a general conflation of previously distinct political terms and discourses such as the physiocrats' rationalist concept of public opinion, Rousseau's voluntarist concept of the general will, and the nobility's theories of the sovereign nation. As the first chapter noted, distinctions among concepts such as public opinion, the nation, and the people had already begun eroding before the Revolution, but that process accelerated rapidly in 1789, producing an indistinct cluster of ideas and vaguely synonymous terms. Note, for example, the blending of formerly separate terms in this May 1791 statement by Robespierre:

> If, at a time when the public spirit was not yet born, when the nation was unaware of its rights . . . it managed to make a choice worthy of this Revolution, why would it not do even better when public opinion is enlightened and strengthened by the experience of two years? . . . I also think that the principles of this constitution are engraved in the hearts of all men and in the minds of a majority of the French and that it is not from the head of this or that orator that [the constitution] came, but from the very heart of the public opinion that preceded us and that has supported us. It is to it, to the will of the nation, that we must entrust its durability and perfection.[8]

In short, the philosophes' careful distinctions between public opinion and the opinion of the people were now fading. In March 1791 *L'Ami des Patriotes* wrote that "public opinion, clearly pronounced, is warning the National Assembly that it is time that it finished its work," for "the people are tired of waiting."[9] Also equating public opinion with the people's opinion was Mirabeau, who cautioned his colleagues that it was only in serving the interests "of the most useful and most unfortunate classes, that you will be able to count on their support, [and] that you will be invested with the irresistible power of public opinion, with the unlimited confidence and devotion of the people."[10] As for the general will, which Rousseau had contrasted with public opinion, deputy Marc-David Lasource told the Jacobins in June 1792 that the National Assembly "is waiting for public opinion to be expressed, because [the Assembly] must only recognize the general will, that is to say, that of the sovereign."[11] Similarly, another deputy called the general will "that of the greater part of the French citizens," and still another insisted that the general will "is composed of all the individual wills."[12]

One term that did often have a distinct meaning was *l'esprit public*, usually translated as "the public spirit." Although that translation is often appropriate, *esprit* can also mean "the mind," and in the Revolution *l'esprit public* sometimes meant "the public mind" in a sense not unlike Durkheim's later idea of a *conscience collective*. In such cases, the term was essentially a synonym for public opinion, albeit one even more likely to treat public opinion as unitary. Most often, however, the term served to describe a certain collective enthusiasm, a civic spirit, and a revolutionary zeal and consciousness. For many speakers, the public spirit referred only to people favoring "the general interest" over their own private interests, so that the term denoted the opposite of an *esprit de corps* or "party" spirit.[13]

Unlike public opinion, which speakers generally portrayed as having become a permanent part of life, the public spirit was something fragile, which could grow more or less intense and could even disappear altogether under adverse circumstances. Leaders therefore spoke of the need to promote the public spirit. Mirabeau, for example, said that the public spirit had been incapable of forming at all until the three orders had merged, and in recommending the use of frequent elections, he asked: "By what better means will you form this public spirit?"[14] Also suggesting this fragility, the staunchly revolutionary weekly *Révolutions de Paris* wrote that "a public spirit cannot exist" as long as "each person prefers himself to the fatherland," and Robespierre warned of counterrevolutionaries who wanted "to kill the public spirit by reviving prejudices, frivolity, and idolatry."[15] For some, the public spirit also differed from public opinion in that it strongly implied unanimity, whereas references to public opinion more often allowed for a range of views. In Mona Ozouf's words, whereas public opinion was "suggestive of subjectivity and liberty," public spirit was "a more homogeneous and coercive term."[16] Although Ozouf associates the term "public spirit" with the period of Jacobin rule, it did appear frequently before 1793, and the Jacobins were not alone in using it.

At the same time that revolutionary orators were turning formerly separate terms into synonyms, they also frequently took apart existing terms and rearranged their parts into seemingly endless permutations and combinations. The familiar terms "public opinion" and "the general will" now spawned hybrids such as "the public will" and "general opinion," and the National Assembly's minutes also contain a staggering array of terms such as "the will of the people," "the national will," "national opinion," "the national wish," "popular opinion," "the public voice," "the voice of the public," "general confidence," and "national confidence." A few observers complained about this linguistic chaos—*L'Ami des Patriotes* wrote that "there are no words that have been abused more than 'nation' and 'people'"—but no one seemed able to impose order on the political lexicon.[17] Given this situation, historians seeking to define each term risk imposing too much sense on the past, for it is hardly clear that the speakers themselves had in mind distinct definitions for each term, much less that others all agreed on their definitions. So whereas a broad movement toward identifying public opinion with the will of the sovereign or the electorate supports Tackett's point about "public opinion" becoming more concrete in 1789, that term's tendency to blend with countless other terms offset that trend, making terms such as "public opinion" and "the general will" even less clear than they had been before the Revolution.

As for the characteristics of this variously named force, a few older ideas about public opinion survived the recent changes. A sense of its irresistible power, for example, appears in Mirabeau's 1789 claim that the king's finance minister "can no longer go against the current of public opinion . . . [and] must go with it or be submerged by it."[18] Similarly, Parisian militants about to overthrow the monarchy in August 1792 called public opinion a force that "makes and unmakes kings," while others saw it as an all-seeing "sentinel," "overseer," or "solid anchor" for the nation.[19] The idea of a powerful and enlightened public opinion thus persisted for some time after May 1789.

Yet with the opening of political life to millions of citizens whose political capacities seemed dubious to many educated observers, the belief in public opinion's rationality soon began to collapse. Illustrating this apprehension about a suddenly expanded public, the conservative daily *Le Journal de Paris* complained that whereas it had once been "enlightened men, good writers, . . . [and] that portion of the Public that read and discussed that alone formed opinion," now "there is not a single butcher, a single stonecutter, a single market woman who does not believe they are specially qualified to decide if the King should have an absolute or suspensive veto, if the legislature should have one or two chambers, etc." The paper summarized its view of the new public, calling it "a sheeplike flock of ignorants and fools, always ready to follow out of weakness and to obey out of fear."[20] And if the intrusion of the poor into public life fueled some observers' anxieties about public opinion's rationality, so did the growing presence of women, as *Le Journal de Paris*'s reference to the "market woman" suggests. In a fairly typical comment, *Le Patriote Français* warned against allowing women in the National Assembly's galleries, writing that women would only add "a spirit of frivolity" to the sessions and would "cause distractions and bring disorder to the discussions."[21] Of course women had figured prominently in the prerevolutionary Republic of Letters, but the *salonnières* had belonged to the upper classes, whereas the women who now played such vital roles — marching to Versailles in the October Days, shouting at the deputies from the galleries of the National Assembly, and so on — were mostly from humbler classes, and they behaved, dressed, and spoke very differently from the *salonnières*. Given that the men in power at this time were all from the middle and upper classes, it is not surprising that their views of public opinion were affected by such women's participation in public life, or that they began to describe public opinion as irrational, fickle, gullible, and volatile.

As the rapid expansion of the French public sharpened tensions between the legitimacy of enlightened reason and the legitimacy of numbers, some sought ways for the two principles to coexist, while others abandoned all hope of saving reason from what *Le Journal de Paris* called "the irresistible ascendancy of the mass and of numbers."[22] Still others simply ignored the problem. But an erosion of belief in the public's rationality was only part of a more general growth of pessimism about the concept. One common complaint concerned the time it took for public opinion to act, a problem already noted before 1789, but one that seemed even more serious given the rapid pace of revolutionary events. Public opinion might eventually overpower tyrants, observed Mirabeau, "but exactly when can one count on this power of public opinion?"[23] *Le Patriote Français*, noting that kings had long ignored their subjects' wishes, urged people not to rely "on public opinion alone, which has defended them so poorly for ten centuries," and in the National Assembly the Abbé Henri Grégoire opposed the royal veto by asking, "Doesn't experience show that the tyrants of all centuries ignored the cries of reason and defied public opinion?"[24] In this view, unless public opinion could act more quickly, its vaunted power might amount to little.

Among those who now despaired of public opinion's reliability and rationality, some held out hope of it growing more enlightened, and many called for new efforts to educate the citizenry. Some also sought to create order in

France's suddenly expanded public sphere. In his prospectus for *Le Patriote Français*, for example, Brissot warned that "the mass of pamphlets that have appeared since the birth of the Revolution" and the sudden growth in their readership had harmed the transformation of individual opinions into a unified and reliable public opinion. Because "few people have the means" to read everything now published, he added, France lacked a common arena of discussion. In his view, the "unity of opinion" France needed could "only be the fruit of gradual instruction" carried out by a single national newspaper, one "written in the heart of the capital, at the center of the movement toward enlightenment, and circulating rapidly" into the provinces. "It is the only means," he concluded, "of educating a large nation that is limited in its powers, unaccustomed to reading, and yet anxious to escape from the servitude of ignorance."[25] Unfortunately, because no one could say when a single, universally read newspaper might succeed in unifying and enlightening the citizenry, France would have to build its new order while public opinion remained a chaotic and unreliable force.

Some observers even worried that public opinion might grow less enlightened as time passed. Opposing the postponement of a decision on the King's fate after Varennes, Lameth, who wished to preserve the monarchy, charged that the delay "would only help to promote confusion" and "create more room for the techniques some use to form a public opinion" designed to bully the National Assembly.[26] In the same debate, Lameth's close associate Adrien Duport worried "that an artificial public opinion, that exaggerated feelings, that a public opinion lacking any base in reason or the interest of the people might sway you," while Pétion warned that "factions, cabals, [and] intrigues have sought to distort public opinion."[27] Many blamed public opinion's errors on the Jacobin Club, which one speaker called "a machine" led by men "versed in the art of seducing the impulsive multitude."[28] "Public opinion," complained a disillusioned deputy, "wanders aimlessly and changes every day," and given "the skill with which one complicates the questions" facing the public, "everything converges to create a dangerous fermentation of minds."[29]

By the end of 1791, then, little seemed to be left of Enlightenment concepts of public opinion, although a broad belief in its power remained — and that power now provoked more anxiety than confidence. Taking issue with the sacred idea that the law was the expression of the general will, Malouet urged the lawmakers not to follow the general will, for "the general will can be unjust and passionate but the law can never be."[30] Few were willing to speak as bluntly as Malouet, but amid a growing crisis of faith in public opinion, many seemed sympathetic to his basic point. Speaking more diplomatically,

Duport charged after Varennes that "the lasting good of [the] country seems opposed to a passing expression of public opinion," or at least to "an artificial opinion . . . that has no basis in either reason or the interest of the people." Duport thus urged his colleagues to "resist, once again, the influence with which one seeks to surround you."[31] Such calls to resist the dangerous force of public opinion, which resembled the attitudes of prerevolutionary rulers, offered another example of the ironic continuities between the political culture of the Old Regime and the Revolution.

One important way to describe images of public opinion is to note the way in which speakers portray its internal composition, or texture, and in the case of the French Revolution orators generally portrayed that composition in either corporatist, individualist, or unitary terms. The unitary approach was the first to appear in France, as prerevolutionary theorists had seen public opinion arising only when the chaos of contrary individual opinions coalesced into a single, indivisible force; from this point of view it would have been nonsensical to speak of public opinion being divided. The events of 1789, however, undermined this broad prerevolutionary sense of public opinion's unitary composition, opening debate on the issue.

Given France's old tradition of organization into royally sanctioned "corps," such as guilds and other socio-professional bodies, it is not surprising to find corporatist images of public opinion during the Revolution. In 1790 Mirabeau, advising the King on the monitoring of public opinion, recommended that observers file reports indicating the opinions of "the nobility, the clergy, the old magistracy, the courtiers, the military corps, the bourgeois, the merchants, the artisans and peasants, [and] the inhabitants of the cities and countryside."[32] Lucien Jaume rightly notes, however, that Mirabeau's was "a very rare attitude," and although Old Regime political culture undoubtedly left an imprint on the Revolution, one could often discredit an idea or practice simply by associating it with the Old Regime.[33] Nevertheless, corporatist images of opinion continued to appear in the first years of the Revolution. During the National Assembly's 1791 debate on petitions, the Jacobin François Buzot argued for people's right "to express their wish under the name of an entire corporation," and contending that "the general wish is expressed by the corporations, by the cities, by the administrative corps — who know the desires of the people — and by associations of citizens," he urged governing authorities to heed corporate petitions.[34]

Many references to public opinion's texture took the form of rejections of rival approaches, particularly the corporatist one. Opposition to corporatist notions of opinion appeared in debates over the election of an Estates General, and they continued with the Third Estate's struggle against voting by order, when, as Tackett observes, many deputies denounced "the 'cabal' of nobles and clergy that was opposing them and voting as a bloc."[35] From then on, writes Lynn Hunt, "factional politics was synonymous with conspiracy," and a search for "'transparency' between citizen and citizen, between the citizens and their government, between the individual and the general will" brought suspicion on anyone purporting to speak for a whole category of individuals.[36] In opposing the Jacobins' use of collective petitions in 1791, Le Chapelier warned that members of a group who declined to sign their names would become "unwilling petitioners," and that any group presenting a collective petition "would soon become a corporation tainted with all of the spirit, all of the passions, all of the despotism that accompanied the corporations" of the Old Regime. Contending that "the people can only delegate powers they cannot exercise themselves," and that the power to express an opinion was one that the people could certainly exercise, he concluded that no individual had the right to speak for others without their written authorization.[37]

As for the individualist outlook on public opinion, one of its first and most prominent affirmations appeared in *What Is the Third Estate?*, where Sieyès argued that "the will of a nation . . . is the result of individual wills, as the nation is the assemblage of the individuals" in it.[38] Attacking the vote by order, he asked, "How can one argue on the one hand, that the law is the expression of the general will, i.e., the majority, and on the other hand that ten individual wills can cancel out a thousand individual wills?"[39] When the Declaration of Rights proclaimed a long list of individual rights and liberties, individualism gained official status, inevitably affecting ideas of public opinion. For its adherents, individualism offered an equality long absent in France, and it was partly on the grounds of serving individual equality that they banned corporations in 1791. As a foe of the Jacobins argued, political clubs threatened liberty and equality because those "joined together will always have a much greater influence than those who are isolated," and even the Jacobins consistently denounced the formation of "parties."[40] The constitution, Le Chapelier concluded in 1791, "no longer recognizes anything but the social body and the individuals" who compose it.[41]

Yet to speak of a public opinion composed of individual opinions was to admit the possibility of division, and the French horror of division led many to shun both corporatism and individualism in favor of unitary images of opinion. From this perspective, even the idea of individuals seemed suspect. "Individuals," proclaimed one Jacobin, "are those who isolate themselves, or rather who know less how to work for the public good than to calculate their private interest."[42] As Gunn has noted, it seemed that the deeper and more obvious France's political divisions became, the more emphatically orators announced the unity of national opinion.[43] After the King's capture at Varennes, when civil war seemed a dire possibility, a deputy reporting on the events declared that "all of France had only one wish, . . . that of living under a free constitution," and he rejoiced in knowing that the nation's will "is manifested with so much unanimity."[44] And in August 1792 a group of militants from the Thermes-de-Julien section, speaking for "all the citizens of the capital," told the deputies that "the uniformity of all our wishes" and "the union of wills" would lead the Parisians to succeed.[45]

The Thermes-de-Julien deputation, however, also complained that "citizens from this section have recently brought you a disavowal of the petition presented in the name of the entire [Paris] Commune," and they declared themselves "gravely insulted by this strange alteration of the truth."[46] As this comment shows, some could speak in unitary terms even when discussing dissent, whose very existence disproved their claim. How was this possible? More broadly, how did orators turn obvious division into images of unity? The answer involves definitions and interpretations of key terms, for some felt that by definition the public spirit or public opinion only existed when divergent views coalesced into one homogeneous view. Hence, any divergent opinions simply did not qualify as public opinion. Here it may be significant that the French term *le peuple*, unlike the English term "the people," is a singular noun whose conjugation invites a unitary language, but the existence of English terms such as "the nation" suggests limits to such explanations.

One of the more common techniques orators used to turn diversity into unity involved describing the opinions not of individuals but of political districts such as the nation's departments or Paris's sections, in effect blending elements of corporatist and unitary notions of opinion. In 1791, for example, the Champs de Mars petitioners claimed that "all sections of the realm simultaneously demand that Louis be tried," and in 1792 a deputy argued that the 20 June insurgents had behind them "the votes of all the departments of the kingdom" and support "from all the parts of the Empire."[47] Such rhetoric, of course, simply ignored any contrary opinions that existed in each district. A second means of manufacturing unity can be seen in Sieyès's claim that because the general will was only formed in deliberation, "the people, or the nation, can only have one voice, that of the national legislature."[48] That concept, which recalls Hobbes's notion of the sovereign creating unity by the very act of representation, allowed Sieyès to speak of a nation composed of individuals, and even to admit disagreements among them, while still portraying national opinion as unanimous. The key to this system was parliament, a site for the production of national unity, and an enclosure that kept discord contained within its walls as long as its members followed common rules and agreed to let majorities within it represent the whole.

Yet another rhetorical technique for manufacturing unity involved defining dissenters out of the nation altogether. Once again Sieyès had marked the way, calling the Third Estate "a complete nation" and the nobility "a foreigner in our midst."[49] The Jacobins proved particularly fond of this technique; one speaker at the Paris Club claimed in July 1792 that a desire to depose the King was "the wish of all the departments and of all who are neither nobles, nor priests, nor scoundrels," and *Le Patriote Français* wrote that "all the good citizens of the empire are raising a unanimous and spontaneous cry against the crimes of the Court."[50] Moderates also used the technique, such as when Lafayette asserted that the 20 June demonstration outraged "all the good citizens" of France.[51] As Furet and others have noted, this kind of linguistic exclusion helped pave the way for the physical exclusion of unwanted elements later in the Revolution.[52]

One source of this unitary notion of public opinion was the concept of indivisible sovereignty. Unitary accounts of national opinion had also become familiar before 1789 both through invocations of public opinion and through claims about the will of the nation. Of course the Old Regime had also promoted corporatist outlooks, but even corporatism promoted unitary thinking, for the spokesmen of Old Regime corporations, being limited to describing the view of their own groups, were accustomed to speaking in unanimist terms. With the fall of the monarch who had structured French corporatism, and with the rise of popular sovereignty, the transition from unitary descriptions of one's own corporation to similar descriptions of one's nation was probably not hard to make. Yet another source of the penchant for unanimism in the Revolution was the incommensurability of competing principles of legitimacy, which made it hard for rivals to tolerate or even acknowledge each other's views. Commenting on revolutionary electoral practices, historian Patrice Gueniffey writes that "a search for unanimity seems to have been the rule from as early as 1790," and because many saw "no room for minority opinions" in electoral assemblies, "those whose 'candidate' appeared not to be in a position to win often preferred to withdraw, possibly to form a parallel assembly."[53]

As for the consequences of such rhetoric, one question to consider is whether anyone believed it. Our sources allow no definitive answer, but such rhetoric probably did little more than galvanize one's own supporters, and the howls of protest that often greeted assertions of unanimity in the National Assembly suggest that listeners often found such claims absurd.[54] As a result, rivals often talked past each other, preventing deliberation from uniting competing groups in a coherent political community. The unanimist penchant also harmed prospects for broad national cohesion by promoting hostility toward dissent. In 1791 Pétion complained of "public tranquillity" being disturbed by "the constant revolt of the minority against the majority"—a phrase that touched off "tumult" on the right side of the hall—and he added that anyone who still opposed a law after its passage "places himself in a state of insurrection."[55] Throughout the Revolution, a common term used to describe rivals was *factieux*, which means factious or subversive, but which one speaker defined as "those who are constantly in the minority."[56] Even worse was one petition's description of rival petitioners as "venimous insects," or a deputy's claim that only "criminals" could disagree with his view.[57]

Given these deeply illiberal statements, which match familiar images of revolutionary political culture, it is important to note that not everyone thought this way. *Le Patriote Français*, for example, contended that "one speaks foolishly if one claims that the opinion of the majority must determine the opinion of the minority," and *L'Ami des Patriotes* wrote that while a victorious majority can expect obedience to the law, "it can never impose silence" on dissenters.[58] *L'Ami des Patriotes* also rejected the suppression of political clubs with unwanted viewpoints on grounds reminiscent of James Madison. "The more political clubs there are," it claimed, "the less concern they should cause," and it offered the following explanation: "If you have only one, it will be oppressive; if you have two of them, they will fight each other; if you have a thousand of them, they will live in peace."[59] So although unanimist images of public opinion filled these debates, some voices did favor pluralism and individualist notions of public opinion.

Insofar as rivals favored incompatible principles of legitimacy, the choice to describe opinion in unitary terms probably did not account for France's failure to end the Revolution through deliberation, for it matters little how one describes the opinions of a sovereign others do not recognize. Deliberation, in short, cannot resolve all conflicts, and even the best rhetoric may be ineffective on certain audiences. Some of the French were indeed stubbornly committed to the principles of the Old Regime, and were thus impervious to any invocation of public opinion. But after the initial defections from the Estates General and National Assembly, few of those remaining on the right side of the hall were truly implacable foes of the principles of 1789. Why, then, were the groups in the National Assembly unable to coexist in a system with an elected majority and a loyal opposition? Here, unitary descriptions of opinion probably did matter, for they weakened the credibility of the rhetoric of public opinion, helping prevent a force widely embraced in theory from serving as an arbiter of political disputes. A unanimist outlook also helps explain the inability of many, especially on the left, to distinguish among varying degrees of political opposition. This lack of political depth perception and this bitter intolerance of any kind of dissent fueled a tendency to demonize opponents, to exclude them entirely from the nation, and to shift political struggle from the field of linguistic and electoral contestation to that of physical violence.

Even among those who accepted the legitimacy of national sovereignty and some measure of pluralism, invocations of public opinion could not really resolve disputes until the parties involved found some broadly acceptable means of ascertaining opinions. Those using the concept of public opinion before 1789 had paid relatively little attention to that problem, in part because they imagined public opinion as unitary and self-evident, and in part because there was no urgent need to resolve disagreements about a force lacking any legal authority. Some continued to speak of public opinion as self-evident after 1789—Malouet wrote that "public reason announces itself, as the sun does, with bursts of light"—but the persistence of sharp disagreements showed that what one group found self-evident another did not see at all.[60] Thus whereas rivals had once brought their disputes before a sovereign capable of speech, they now brought them before an abstraction that issued different messages to different observers.

Although some orators simply ignored epistemological questions about public opinion, others acknowledged them, and as Jaume notes, "the *anonymous*, because collective or semi-collective, character [of public opinion] bothered the revolutionary personnel."[61] A sense of public opinion as elusive and subject to manipulation and misinterpretation led many to warn of *opinions factices*, or false images of public opinion designed to deceive. *L'Ami des Patriotes*, for example, called for distinguishing between "two kinds of public opinions: one imaginary, solicited, feigned, [and] exaggerated," and one that is "calmer, wiser, but more solid."[62] Expressing his mistrust of Parisian claims about public opinion, one deputy urged his colleagues to look to the provinces to find "true public opinion."[63] Voicing a similar mistrust of the loudest voices in the public arena, Barnave refused to "call public opinion that momentary buzz that a few writers produce around themselves."[64] Yet if the most audible and openly expressed opinions constituted unreliable evidence, then ascertaining public opinion was going to be difficult indeed.

As the Enlightenment belief in the self-evident nature of public opinion eroded in the first years of the Revolution, a few leaders began seeking means of investigating people's views. Perceiving public opinion as a complex national phenomenon, Mirabeau advised the King to use a network of surveyers to file periodic reports, while the journalist and politican Roederer considered studying newspaper circulation to learn the distribution of opinions.[65] Royal officials and revolutionary administrators sought to monitor public opinion by using the police (as in the Old Regime) to listen in on conversations in cafés and other public places and by having agents read newspapers and attend debates in political clubs. As Ozouf writes, authorities were "constantly preoccupied with evaluating the state of public opinion or 'the public mind,'" but their findings remained secret, so when participants in public debates sought to support claims about public opinion, they had to look elsewhere.[66]

As orators and writers sought ways to prove their claims, they looked for specific forms of expression that could serve as manifestations of public opinion, as well as certain individuals or groups who could legitimately speak for the public. In other words, because the entire nation could not express itself to the country's elected representatives, these individuals and groups would be granted the right, in effect, to represent the represented. One of the first forms of expression suggested as evidence of public opinion were the cahiers, which speakers often cited in 1789, and which a committee undertook to study systematically in July of that year. Speaking for that committee, Clermont-Tonnerre made several quantitative judgments about the cahiers, noting, for example, that monarchy, royal inviolability, and male inheritance of the Crown were "recognized and authorized by the greatest number of the cahiers, and called into question by none."[67] Yet others questioned the cahiers' value by pointing out that the well-to-do had dominated their drafting, and, as noted earlier, many deputies ignored the cahiers because they knew that obeying them would constrain the Revolution. Of course the deputies could have solicited new cahiers, but doing so would have required the risky step of reconvening the same assemblies that had elected them.

Outside the National Assembly, some argued that newspapers could articulate public opinion. As Popkin writes, "The political press was an indispensable symbol of the public opinion of a people that lacked the means to speak for itself," and unlike the cahiers, the press "could react quickly to changing events."[68] But as Popkin adds, "newspapers provided a babble of voices" rather than a coherent message—a problem that inspired *Le Patriote Français*'s plea for a single national newspaper everyone read.[69] *Le Journal de*

Paris also addressed this problem, asking whether a rival paper's opinion was "really the general and public opinion or merely one of the opinions that are in the public."[70] So although one might gauge the range of opinions by surveying the press — an idea supported by the common assumption that people adopted the views they read in the press — that method could not really establish the size of each current of opinion. One major problem involved the lack of reliable circulation figures, but even had such figures been available, they would have provided only a rough portrait of the distribution of opinions in a country where many could not read or afford newspapers. Moreover, the idea that people adopted the ideas they read was hardly reassuring, and many equated published opinion with artificial and illegitimate opinion. Much of the skepticism about published opinion owed to suspicions of the bribery of journalists; *Révolutions de Paris*, for example, in complaining about newspapers supporting the King, denounced what it saw as "solicited, extorted, and dearly bought articles."[71] In the National Assembly few deputies cited newspapers as evidence of public opinion, and when they mentioned them at all it was usually to protest their latest outrage.

Those skeptical of newspapers' ability to articulate the public voice often looked for ways in which the people might speak for themselves. One such idea consisted of the *bouche de fer*, a precursor of the modern "suggestion box" in which anyone could place written messages. Gary Kates reports that one political club, the Cercle Social, used a *bouche de fer*, though he notes that the club did not simply publish the messages collected, but rather condensed and interpreted them before printing the results in its newspaper. The final product, then, was merely another newspaper, albeit one with its own approach to ascertaining public opinion.[72] This idea, however, did not catch on.

Another proposed manifestation of public opinion consisted of the views of the sections. These organizations could make a particularly compelling claim to represent public opinion given their origins in the electoral districts that had chosen representatives to the Estates General. In other words, if public opinion was a force that both invested governing officials with their authority and continued to supervise their actions, then what better voices of public opinion could there be than the entities that had elected representatives in the first place? The lawmakers, however, were not eager to face any real oversight, as one can see both from their attitude toward the cahiers and from their refusal to let the sections meet between elections. And they were hardly alone in mistrusting the sections, which became the target of countless complaints about hidden oligarchies dominating them. *Le Journal des Clubs*, for one, complained of the sections being run by men "who ceaselessly give their own view, who interrupt each speaker so that they themselves can orate," in short, by "domineering men who cannot stand others having an opinion that differs from their own."[73] In the same year, a disgruntled citizen complained that in his section five or six men always managed to secure the floor before the session began and then monopolize it all night. "When these men are finally tired," he explained, "and when many citizens have gone home for the night, it is decided that the discussion is closed and a decree is produced matching the views of the speakers and the wild men who alone have been allowed to speak."[74] Early in the Revolution the exclusion of passive citizens (the poor, domestic servants, women, et al.) from the sections created resentment among the Parisian lower classes, but when members of these classes forced their way into the sections in 1792, it was the middle and upper classes' turn to allege foul play.[75] Such accusations, along with frequent charges that the sections abetted Parisian domination, explain why many observers rejected the sections' claims to speak for public opinion.

Also making a case to be the voice of the public were the political clubs, or *sociétés populaires*. The clubs, which rested on the right of association stated in the Declaration of Rights, may seem to fit Habermas's concept of public opinion being formed by private citizens gathering freely to discuss public affairs in sites independent of the state, and Raymonde Monnier indeed accepts the clubs' claims to be the voice of the people meeting freely in an open and democratic public sphere.[76] Early in the Revolution few objected to their existence, but before long many grew alarmed that one club overshadowed all others, as the Jacobin Club was the only club with chapters throughout all of France. And because the leaders of the Paris Jacobin Club were also deputies in the National Assembly, and because these men used the Club meetings to coordinate their tactics in the Assembly, the idea that these were ordinary citizens exercising a right to oversee the government gave way to perceptions that the Club was a parallel — and unelected — power interfering with the work of the people's legitimate representatives.

As the Jacobins went through a series of schisms and purges that saw the exit of their more moderate members, the Club's detractors grew louder and more numerous. *L'Ami du Roi* denounced France's "clubocracy," calling the clubs "conspiracies against public tranquillity" where "all the passions heat up and ferment," while *La Gazette Universelle* called them "the renewal of powerful corporations" as well as "a means for a few ambitious men to direct opinion at their whim" and "smother the real public opinion."[77] In the words of *Le Journal de Paris*, the clubs "do not represent one hundredth of the nation."[78] Anxiety over the Jacobin Club's growing power and its tendency to speak for the nation led to Le Chapelier's September 1791 successful proposal to ban popular societies; these "corporations," he argued, were no longer necessary now that the Revolution was ending, and if allowed to exist, they would replace true public opinion with "a cry of agitation destined to disturb the work of legitimate authorities."[79] By 1791, then, the debate over the clubs was essentially a debate over the Jacobins, with their members seeing them as an authentic voice of the people and their adversaries denouncing them as the tools of fanatic minorities bent on dominating public opinion.

In the Revolution's first months, one mouthpiece of public opinion that many deputies seemed to find credible were the crowds that attended their sessions and filled the streets outside the National Assembly. Although few offered any serious arguments for why the crowds should be taken to represent the nation, their visible, physical presence made them hard to ignore, and for deputies lacking a clear legal or popular mandate for the bold course they were taking, the crowds' encouragement probably meant a great deal. Tackett notes that in their diaries and letters, several deputies "remarked on the exhilarating effects of the spectators' enthusiasm," and he adds that in the streets of Versailles, "the crowds were constantly in evidence, following the deputies wherever they went, cheering, chanting, encouraging the Third at every step."[80] Affirming the crowds' representativeness, Mirabeau proclaimed: "The movement in Versailles is soon the movement in Paris; the agitation in the capital is communicated to nearby provinces, and each commotion extends to a broader circle . . . [and] finally produces a universal agitation."[81] After the National Assembly moved to Paris in October 1789, crowds congregating in the Palais Royal area offered deputies a chance to mingle with constituents right outside their hall. One Jacobin told his colleagues in July 1792 that he had just visited the Palais Royal "to sound out the public spirit," and he found it "excellent."[82] The terms speakers used to describe crowds in the galleries and streets also show a belief in their representativeness, as deputies, having declared their sessions "open to the public," soon referred to the crowd as "the public" or "the people."

The crowds' influence, of course, was not limited to those who appreciated their presence. Etienne Dumont, a friend of Mirabeau who attended many sessions, wrote that Mirabeau's colleagues disliked him and wished to silence him, "but the galleries took too much pleasure in hearing him for the Assembly to dare refuse him the floor."[83] Also noting this influence, *L'Ami du Roi* complained that "the majority of the assembly rejects that which might sadden the tribunes and embraces that which can provoke applause."[84] Moderate and conservative deputies, however, apparently believed in the crowds' representativeness at first, perhaps because they assumed that a crowd made up mostly of their social inferiors represented the thinking of a nation made up mostly of the same kind of people. But if deputies on the right limited themselves at first to complaints about applause and jeers interrupting their debates, some began to question the crowds' representativeness. Fueling this change were growing doubts about the spontaneity of the crowds' outbursts. Dumont, for example, noticed one day that "a fishwife . . . was directing the reactions of about a hundred women and young people who were awaiting her orders to cry out or be silent," and he also saw that she was on familiar terms with some of the deputies.[85] Others eventually charged that their rivals were paying "claques" to fill the galleries, and the presence in those galleries of many women—usually viewed as more "unruly"—also led some to view these crowds with suspicion.[86]

Resentment of crowds reached a new level with the October Days, when marchers demanding bread took the symbolically profound step of invading the deputies' portion of the hall before forcing the Assembly and the King to move to Paris. Describing the scene, Tackett writes that women "began entering the hall in large numbers, muddy and bedraggled, wedging themselves onto the benches between the deputies, shouting for bread when the Assembly tried to conduct business as usual on matters concerning the constitution."[87] Subsequent investigations focused both on the role of certain deputies in engineering the episode and on participants' tales of armed militants forcing them to join the march to Versailles, suggesting the value that some placed on spontaneity and individual liberty in any manifestation of public opinion.[88] From that moment on, many moderate deputies waged a running battle with crowds in the galleries (and the radical deputies backing them), trying, mostly unsuccessfully, to keep them from interrupting the Assembly's work with their cheers, jeers, and heckling. Yet in asking the spectators to watch in silence, the deputies were essentially assigning them a role like that of the passive crowds that had watched displays of royal authority under absolutism. Unwilling to accept that role, the crowds found it outrageous that the deputies would dare try to silence the voice of the people, while many deputies found it equally outrageous that a band of troublemakers would dare interfere with the work of the people's representatives.

Crowds, of course, played a central role in the Revolution from its very beginnings, but as that role expanded in 1791 and 1792, claims that crowds spoke for the people, or indeed *were* the people, encountered increasing skepticism. Crowds' use of violence and intimidation provoked especially sharp reactions. *L'Ami du Roi*, for example, denied "that the wish of the citizens can only legally be spelled out using the tips of murderous bayonets and the blood of victims," and that "it is only by these signs that one can recognize the national will."[89] Even those sympathetic to the Revolution began to express alarm, with *Le Patriote Français* writing that "under a free constitution the path of posing demands to the legislative power is the only one permitted" and that "insurrection is the resource of slaves."[90] Among those protesting the 20 June demonstration was Strasbourg's city council, which called the marchers "an armed multitude" and "men who call themselves the French people," and the council insisted that "a handful of perverse men . . . and a few fanatics, blind instruments of a criminal element, are not the nation."[91] In that crowd, the moderate, constitutionalist *Gazette Universelle* wrote, "some were profoundly guilty, while the greatest number were fooled, seduced, [and] misled."[92] A group of citizens from Abbeville was among many who wrote to the Assembly denouncing the marchers. "They should know that the people of all the departments disavow them," the letter explained. "Paris is not the French people; more precisely, a fraction of Paris, several of its sections, a part of the *faubourgs*, cannot take for itself such a grand, respectable, and holy name."[93]

A somewhat less controversial image of public opinion could be found in letters and petitions, which were usually read aloud at the start of each session of the National Assembly. Referring to petitions, Danton told the Jacobins in 1792 that "there is in the constitution one means to express, to obtain the national wish," and he believed that a petition could resolve the stalemate over the royal veto, since no one could remain unconvinced "once the sovereign will is mathematically demonstrated."[94] When a deputy declared that "the Constitution gives the nation two . . . means of making its voice heard: that of petitions and that of naming its representatives," he was in effect saying that petitions were the only legitimate expression of public opinion between elections.[95] For those who favored unitary portraits of opinion, petitions had the advantage of presenting only one current of opinion; one Jacobin, for example, told his colleagues on 5 August 1792 that if they sent a petition to all their affiliates, it would come back "covered with signatures, and within a month you will have the unanimous wish of the French."[96]

Yet as long as others could present petitions for rival viewpoints, this form of expression was not likely to settle questions about national opinion. In June 1792 one speaker announced that "the true wish of the people . . . cannot be doubted" given "this infinite number of petitions that you hear read at the podium each day, and which announce to you unequivocally the wish of the nation," but a skeptic, reminding him of petitions expressing the opposite view, asked "how the wish of the majority of the people could thus be clearly known, even if these petitions were multiplied?"[97] The numbers of petitions received and the number of individuals signing them might seem significant, one deputy noted, but in a large country, "It is difficult to add up a number of individual wishes" and to know "in what relation [it stands] to the majority of the nation."[98] *Révolutions de Paris* dismissed a petition signed by 300 citizens by noting that there were 25 million people in France — implying that 24,999,700 citizens had refused to sign the petition.[99] In this view, petitions were a legitimate form of expression, but they were, as *La Gazette Universelle* put it, "insufficient to indicate the national wish."[100]

Some observers even denied that a given petition or letter was legitimate. In June 1792, when the Assembly's president began reading a violent republican diatribe that "6620 citizens of Lyons" had sent in, deputies on the right began shouting, "That comes from the Jacobins!"[101] Soon after that, the Assembly heard from a witness who saw false signatures being added to petitions at the Jacobin Club.[102] Although the moderates seemed most likely to question the authenticity of petitions, *Révolutions de Paris* charged that one moderate petition was filled with "some signatures purchased at a notary's office," and a deputy on the left charged that petitions against the 20 June demonstration "were fabricated in Paris and sent out to be signed."[103] That paper also dismissed letters protesting the demonstration on the grounds that they had been solicited by the Crown and written by government officials, echoing a prior complaint from *L'Ami du Roi* that letters to the Assembly proved nothing because they were "solicited and extorted" rather than spontaneous and authentic.[104] Petitions and letters, in short, could not settle disputes about public opinion, which left the sovereign largely unable to express itself between elections.

As if to admit the inability of all of these representations of public opinion to secure general acceptance, some turned to the idea of the referendum as a means of ascertaining public opinion between elections. One referendum proposal came from the Champs de Mars petitioners, who asked the National Assembly in July 1791 to "ascertain the will of the eighty-three other departments," and those petitioners refused to obey the King "unless the majority of the nation expresses a desire contrary to that of the present petition."[105] At the time, however, the procedure was unfamiliar, and many greeted the proposal skeptically. "But how will the eighty-three departments be consulted?" asked *La Gazette Universelle*, insisting that "the directories, the municipalities, and the clubs are not the departments."[106] The petitioners had ignored such practical matters, leaving vital questions unanswered.

Would voting take place in primary assemblies, in the electoral colleges, or in both? How would the questions be worded, and would the petitioners or the Assembly have that power? Who could then call future referenda? And once the French began holding referenda to sanction the Assembly's acts, how would they ever stop?

Not long after that referendum proposal, *L'Ami du Roi* made its own plea for the procedure as part of its campaign for the royal veto. Any act vetoed, it argued, should be brought up for "examination by the nation, convoked in primary assemblies, . . . so that the nation's wish may be perfectly established."[107] Though it may have seemed odd for a royalist paper to endorse such an idea, the paper disliked the National Assembly and believed that most of the French remained loyal to the King. The deputies, however, refused to open a legally binding parallel channel for the expression of the national will, and even those on the left ended up opposing the idea.

Even some members of the Paris sections opposed the use of the referendum. During an April 1791 debate over the King's intended trip to Saint-Cloud — during which some feared he would try to flee France — many sections protested proposals for a referendum on whether to allow the trip. Some resented having to answer a "yes-or-no" question, and the Théâtre-Français section complained that asking a section, "whose opinion is essentially unlimited," to choose between two preformulated answers subverted democracy.[108] As this section realized (and as twentieth-century critics of opinion polls and referenda often charged), enormous power would accrue to those who chose when to hold a referendum, what issues to raise, how to word the questions, and how to interpret the responses. Of course no section could think of any way to allow millions of citizens, or even thousands of sections, to carry out those tasks, which are simply beyond the competence of large numbers of people. The Marché-des-Innocents section admitted this in discussing a proposal to submit all laws to popular ratification, accepting the use of a yes-or-no vote given "the impossibility of reaching a precise result if several thousand assemblies were to make additions and modifications."[109] So with both the deputies and many sections opposing the idea, it is not surprising that no referendum was held in this period.

The rejection of all of these methods left elections as the best remaining method of learning the national will, but unfortunately even elections elicited great skepticism. As noted earlier, the composition of the electorate remained bitterly contested, for conservatives were alarmed at so many of their social inferiors being able to vote, while many on the left were outraged at the exclusion of the "passive citizens." Moreover, even those who protested the exclusion of passive citizens often harbored deep concerns about how they might vote, fearing the influence of priests and nobles in rural areas. In addition, the same perceptions of foul play, coercion, and intimidation in the primary assemblies that discouraged some of the French from voting also led many observers to mistrust election results; R. B. Rose writes that when Parisians were chided for not voting, they "tended to protest that the elections were all fixed by a cabal anyway."[110] Finally, even for those satisfied with the fairness of election results, the rapid pace of revolutionary events made them seem outdated before long.

In short, the French in this period could not agree on any way of knowing public opinion, and as a result the rhetoric of public opinion suffered from a pervasive crisis of credibility. In the National Assembly those who invoked public opinion without citing any evidence were frequently met with heckling, derisive laughter, and counterassertions, but even those citing evidence such as election results, the actions of crowds, or letters and petitions still faced strong skepticism. Though the nature of the evidence itself had much to do with the problem, the question of who was citing it often mattered even more, suggesting that the lack of any independent, impartial observer of opinion was also keeping public opinion from settling political disputes.

Although skeptics often dismissed any evidence presented, at other times they accepted the truth of the claims about a given group's opinion but denied that that group's opinion represented public opinion as a whole. Such was the case when the speaker noted earlier suggested that the cahiers merely contained the opinions of the rich, when another orator mentioned above asked how petitions could establish what a majority thought, or when speakers denied that the sections or the Jacobins could speak for the nation. In dismissing the opinions of small but vocal groups, these skeptics alluded to a kind of silent majority. In a letter to the National Assembly in June 1792, for example, a group of citizens complained of the Jacobins' and other militants' ability to give an exaggerated image of their numbers, writing: "The silence of the good emboldens the malicious and perhaps gives them all their dominance." Urging others to raise their voices, these citizens concluded that their foes "must no longer fool people . . . about their apparent majority."[111] A month later, Strasbourg's city council wrote a letter claiming that "there is a mass of good citizens who [have] remained in the silence of disdain up until now," and after Varennes, *L'Ami du Roi* wrote that the number of monarchists "is still bigger than one thinks," adding that in revolutions "it is almost impossible to know the real public opinion, for the ignorant and the subversive cry out, while the decent and educated citizens fall silent, out of fear or prudence."[112] Unfortunately, in pointing to a "real" public opinion made up of silent, private opinions, these observers were offering a concept that would be too elusive to resolve disputes.

While some accepted evidence but questioned its representativeness, others questioned the fairness of the process by which the opinions were produced, charging that signatures on a petition were forged, that members of a crowd were bribed or threatened into participating, and so on. One of the most frequent and troublesome charges concerned demagoguery, a concept not always distinguishable from skillful persuasion or from the kind of egalitarianism that flourished in the Revolution. Conservatives were perhaps most likely to complain about demagogues and those who knew, as one monarchist put it, how "to operate all the levers of opinion," but they were hardly alone in voicing such concerns.[113] One radical journalist, for example, defined "proletarians" as "all the citizens easily susceptible to being corrupted."[114] These accusations of manipulation, though aimed at political rivals, also revealed deep misgivings about the newly proclaimed sovereign and the wisdom of basing power on public opinion.

By 1792, then, ideas about public opinion bore little resemblance to pre-revolutionary notions. Although the French still theoretically believed in the irresistible power of public opinion (at least in the long run) and still valued unanimity, nearly all its other characteristics had been transformed. No longer associated with the judgment of an enlightened few, it now referred to a much wider group, though one without any broadly accepted definition. No longer presumed rational, it was now thought to blend will, reason, and blind impulse. No longer necessarily formed in deliberation, it now carried connotations of unreflective instinct and hasty, visceral reaction. No longer necessarily public, it now might include the opinions of the silent. And no longer presumed infallible and incorruptible, it now raised suspicions of artificiality and manipulation.

Even to summarize notions of public opinion, however, is to risk overstating their clarity at that time. Before 1789, of course, there were key disagreements on public opinion's meaning, as well as many ambiguities in terms such as "the general will" and "the people." But in 1789 those terms all began merging, creating a jumble of vaguely synonymous but ill-defined terms that both reflected and compounded the futility of revolutionary deliberation. Yet if rivals had reached an impasse on the means of invoking the people's authority, they continued to believe in a force no one seemed able to grasp. The Revolution, in short, faced a basic dilemma: that public opinion both had to and could not serve as the arbiter of France's political disputes.

• • •

Given the democratic principles introduced in 1789, assessing political legitimacy in revolutionary France requires some examination of the opinions of
millions of people, a project historians have traditionally equated with the
study of public opinion. Lacking better sources, historians have generally
avoided that entire project—as the lack of monographs on public opinion in
the Revolution indicates—but the literature on other aspects of the Revolution
is full of comments about national opinion based on evidence such as a crowd's
actions or words. Unfortunately, judging national opinion from such evidence
is risky for many reasons, not the least of which is the infinitesimal percentage
of the adult population that took part in any given uprising or demonstration.
Even elections, which might seem to offer the best record of patterns of opinion, have limited value given the same set of problems that led so many contemporaries to look upon the returns with such skepticism. Perhaps most importantly, because declared candidacies were prohibited for most of the
Revolution, voters were not really choosing between clearly articulated policy
options, making it all but impossible to deduce people's opinions from elections. We have, in short, very poor evidence of people's opinions on most issues.

An even more serious problem than the scarcity of evidence or the illusions
inherent in collective manifestations of opinion is the choice of standards the
historian should use. Should one only take into account opinions expressed
publicly or should one try to infer the opinions of those afraid or unable to
speak publicly? Should one view opinion in individualist, corporate, or unitary
terms? Should one consider only the opinions of "active citizens," or should
one also take into account the opinions of women and the poor? Should one ignore the opinions of emigrés and opponents of the Revolution? What forms of
expression should one consider legitimate? To attempt a study of public opinion in the Revolution using the term's traditional historiographical definition,
or to try to answer these questions and then proceed on that basis, would be to
treat as settled some of the very questions that were most at issue at that time.

Yet it seems necessary to offer some comments on national patterns of opinion in light of statements such as Furet's that in the Revolution "power was in
the hands of those who spoke for the people," or Gueniffey's reference to legitimacy being "granted and withdrawn by 'opinion,'" without which "one could
not remain in power."[115] It is true that the weakness of formal powers made legitimation by public opinion more crucial, and also that competitors for power
claimed to have the support of public opinion, but it would be quite another
matter to suggest that "public opinion" or "the people" actually determined

who had power in the Revolution. In sum, to speak of public opinion as a true power rather than a potential or supposed source of authority is to take the ideas and perceptions of revolutionary actors at face value.

One reason not to call public opinion the true power early in the Revolution is simply that orators invoking it were pointing to an imaginary force. Yet the problem was not just that orators vastly overstated the number of people who supported their ideas, or that many citizens were too uninformed or confused about events in Paris even to have opinions at all, for fictions can certainly be sources of real power. Instead, the problem was that public opinion was only a set of *proposed* fictions, with no single one yet enjoying broad credence. This is not to say that the rhetoric of public opinion had no effects, for linguistic struggles undoubtedly played a major role in the formation and mobilization of each faction, but reactions to claims about public opinion in the National Assembly and elsewhere suggest that speakers were often preaching to the converted. In short, because ideas about public opinion remained too fragmented and contested for that fiction to play much of a role in resolving conflicts and allocating power, it makes little sense to argue that power in the first years of the Revolution belonged to "public opinion" or to those who enjoyed its support.

If public opinion was a chaotic field of sharply contested principles and terms rather than an actual social force, then what did give competing groups and individuals their power between 1789 and 1792? Elections did play some role, but as Gueniffey rightly notes, "at most they confirmed . . . changes and purges that had *already* taken place."[116] Instead, at crucial moments such as the taking of the Bastille, the October Days, the King's arrest at Varennes, the Champs de Mars massacre, and the August 1792 uprising, what gave victorious groups their power was sheer force, specifically an ability to marshal regular or irregular armed forces at key times and places. So although many implied that the National Assembly's decisions expressed the view of a majority of the deputies, which in turn reflected the view of a majority of the citizens, such claims were false. Intimidation and harassment of deputies began as early as July 1789 in Versailles, where, as Dumont noted, people "routinely insulted those one called 'aristocrats' in the streets and at the doors of the Assembly."[117] In the October Days, Tackett reports that "a crowd of men came by Mounier's house at night threatening to cut off his head," and that "Malouet was surrounded on the Place des Armes by a dozen men with pikes until Mirabeau rushed over to extricate him."[118] Many deputies left the Assembly for good at such times, "no longer hoping for anything," as Dumont writes, "from a Revolution that worked by these methods," and the co-

erced departure of so many deputies — eventually a majority of those elected
in 1789 — calls into question the idea that the Assembly's decisions reflected
the opinions of the French citizenry.[119]

When this regime finally fell in August 1792, it was not, as Robespierre
and others suggested, an insurrection of "the entire people," but rather, as
Mathiez and others have shown, the work of militants from the Paris sections and some of the *fédérés* still gathered in Paris.[120] Moreover, the uprising
was not the spontaneous act that some claimed it was, but was engineered by
the leaders of the Paris Commune and the Paris Jacobins. Of course these
leaders needed a substantial following to act as they did, and there is no
doubt that effective rhetoric was essential to their building a successful movement, but the roughly twenty thousand men who overcame the royal guards
on 10 August still represented a tiny portion of even the "active citizens" in
France at that time. So given that it was the use of force by a small number of
relatively organized militias that toppled this regime, it might be best to
speak of the 10 August *journée* as a coup d'état rather than a revolution or an
insurrection of "the people." In short, the pivotal events of this period primarily reflected configurations of force, not public opinion in anything like
the sense in which contemporaries and historians have generally used it.

As if to acknowledge that point, revolutionaries began in this period to
argue for the legitimacy of revolutionary violence. But how was it that the
French had moved so quickly from valuing the authority of a public opinion
based on reason to embracing the use of physical force? One concept that
served as a bridge between the legitimacy of reason and that of revolutionary
violence was the legitimacy of numbers, whose place in French thought before 1789 reflects an important continuity. Despite the many allusions to reason in the discourse of public opinion before 1789, the latter concept had
quantitative dimensions as well, with public opinion being regarded to some
extent as the product of a kind of poll of the members of the Republic of Letters. In other words, though the members of that Republic did not generally
acknowledge the point, and though they certainly denied that the opinions of
the many could prove a proposition, they essentially believed that a large
number of enlightened minds subscribing to a given idea indeed suggested its
validity.[121] What primarily began to change in 1789, then, was simply the size
of the public whose "votes" suggested a proposition's validity, and the ground
for this expansion of the relevant public had already been prepared before
1789 by the philosophes' tentative reappraisal of the mental capacities of artisans and others. Moreover, the concept of force had also figured in ideas about
public opinion before 1789, as phrases such as *la reine du monde* suggest. The

roots of revolutionary France's adoption of the principles of legitimation by both numbers and force can thus be found in prerevolutionary thought.

There was of course opposition to the idea of legitimation by numbers before the Revolution, but some still questioned the idea after 1789 as well. *L'Ami du Roi*, for one, considered most of the people "incapable of having an opinion of their own," suggesting that "votes must be weighed and not counted," and as noted earlier, speakers such as Malouet still adhered to elitist notions of public opinion after 1789.[122] Such views, however, soon became unpopular, and even Condorcet wrote that given France's adoption of democratic ways, "everyone should adopt as a guiding rule not that which seems most probable, but that which seems most probable to the greatest number."[123]

Yet as belief in the legitimacy of reason gave way to belief in the legitimacy of numbers, the continuing presence of people refusing to accept a given view forced the revolutionaries to see what the philosophes would have seen had they actually tried to govern France—that "error" did not simply melt away when faced with the blinding light of truth, and that consensus would be elusive in a self-governing polity. As a result, the transition from a legitimacy of reason to a legitimacy of numbers soon led to a further shift toward belief in a majority's right to impose its will by force. One can see this movement in the way in which Parisian militants presented petitions to the National Assembly; not content with sending delegates holding pieces of paper full of signatures, the militants eventually took to descending on the National Assembly in person, hoping to overawe the deputies and to give their numbers an imposing physical presence. When the militants then showed up bearing arms on 20 June 1792, they took the process one step further, and they took it further still when they chose to use those arms on 10 August. Whether or not these militants really had the support of a majority of the French, they probably believed they did, and they felt that their superior numbers entitled them to dictate their will.

If it was thus force rather than "public opinion" that mainly determined the course of events in this period, it is still hard to avoid the suspicion that this regime's legitimacy could have been much stronger. Why, in other words, did so many turn to violence? Why was France unable to create a constitution that would end the Revolution and begin a new era of legitimate and stable government? Part of the answer concerns familiar issues beyond this study's scope, including controversies over religion, property, and the state's obligation to the poor, and there can be little doubt that recurring bread shortages, which were often most severe at times of political violence, made political legitimacy and stability more elusive. These religious and socioeconomic struggles would have strained the legitimacy of any government, but the ability of previous and subsequent French regimes to survive conflicts over those issues suggests the need to consider certain problems in the country's political institutions and culture.

Among the conservatives who opposed the new political order, some still considered the King sovereign and rejected the National Assembly's authority altogether, while others accepted national sovereignty and backed the National Assembly until they began to see it as a captive of the Jacobins and the Parisian militants. These conservative and moderate revolutionaries' disillusionment turned especially bitter when the Assembly suspended the King's functions after Varennes, at which time nearly three hundred deputies, angry over what they saw as the end of any separation of powers, refused further cooperation with the Assembly in matters unrelated to the King. Many on the left, however, opposed the regime because of its use of property requirements for voting and election to office. Attacking the idea that one needed wealth to have sensible opinions, the Jacobin bishop of Blois, Abbé Grégoire, said he knew passive citizens in Paris "who live on the sixth floor, penniless, but who are nevertheless able to offer very sound opinions," and Robespierre asked if it was true "that probity, that talents are really measured by fortune?"[124] The exclusion of passive citizens was particularly unpopular in Paris, where a rather high property threshold disenfranchised a large number of citizens.[125]

The left also questioned the National Assembly's legitimacy because it contained many former members of the first two estates, who, in the words of *Révolutions de Paris*, "do not represent the nation since they were not elected by it."[126] The left, in other words, questioned the National Assembly's legitimacy both because of its origins and its actions. But the main issue that led militants to move against the Assembly in 1792 was its support for monarchy. In short, while the Assembly's decision to suspend the King's functions undermined its legitimacy on the right, its decision to retain the King in any capacity weakened its legitimacy on the left.

Before Varennes critics had mostly followed the old pattern of distinguishing between the King and his entourage, but after that episode many began attacking both Louis himself and the very idea of monarchy. As the conflict escalated, it became increasingly clear that an unelected hereditary power fit poorly in a system of national sovereignty. In 1791 the Marseilles city council, noting that the Declaration of Rights had ended hereditary distinctions, denounced "this monstrous pretension of a private family to whom royalty would be delegated hereditarily," and it also denied that it had ever been the nation's will to give executive power to kings.[127] Replacing the King with an elected president might have made sense, but republicans mistrusted any kind of "personal power" (a remarkably durable aspect of French republican political culture), and the Assembly never gave the idea serious thought.

Republican deputies did propose an executive committee, but others felt that would defeat the purpose of having a power that could act swiftly and efficiently, and a speaker denouncing that idea in July 1791 received "the repeated applause of a nearly unanimous Assembly."[128] As late as summer 1792 most deputies remained committed to monarchy; when an antimonarchical letter was read to the Assembly in July 1792 it was reported that "the very great majority of the Assembly stood up almost simultaneously to call for either the censure of that address or the punishment of its authors."[129] Particularly in Paris, however, the republican camp continued to grow, and France soon reached a stalemate over the monarchy, with one group demanding that a king check the power of a potentially dictatorial popular assembly while another rejected the very idea of hereditary monarchy. Under such conditions, it would have been hard for any kind of deliberation or rhetoric to produce consensus.

The entire question of the monarchy thus revealed profound flaws in this regime and its constitution, which Dumont called "a veritable monster" with "too much of a republic for a monarchy and too much of a monarchy for a republic."[130] It is true that regimes often survive despite having illogical and incoherent principles — especially when they enjoy the inertia of tradition or a better security force than this Assembly had — but the French concept of sovereignty as a limitless authority made it harder for rival camps to coexist. For that view of sovereignty made those in power intolerant of dissent, helped undermine basic liberties, and weakened the ability of laws and the constitution (often seen as illegitimate constraints on the sovereign) to structure and contain political conflict. In addition, by insisting that the indivisibility of sovereignty demanded undivided representation, French leaders essentially sacrificed the benefits of a separation of powers, creating a government so strong that it alarmed rivals of the faction that controlled it and practically forced them to pursue power outside the system.

A less widely held idea of sovereignty that also harmed legitimacy at this time was the concept of parliamentary sovereignty that Sieyès and others outlined. With public debate and political associations flourishing in a country finally freed from the restrictions of absolutism, the idea that the National Assembly had a monopoly on expressing the national will was a fiction few would accept—and none viewed it more skeptically than the militants who eventually overthrew the regime. Brissot probably captured many people's feelings when he wrote in *Le Patriote Français*, "I no more believe in the infallibility of this Assembly than in that of the Pope."[131] Even Sieyès himself had once insisted (unlike Hobbes) that a nation exists prior to its representation and "never relinquishes its right to will" even after choosing representatives.[132] Those who claimed a parliamentary monopoly on expressing the general will, in short, seem not to have convinced many listeners, and their claims may even have fueled suspicions about the deputies' intentions.

Finally, as explained in chapter 2, it did not help that the National Assembly declared national sovereignty without discussing it long enough to forge some common definition of it. From the moment the Assembly declared national sovereignty, French leaders continued to act as if they had already reached agreement on its meaning and political ramifications, and the confusion that continued to surround the concept cannot have helped the National Assembly build consensus on a new political order.

Confusion and rancor also surrounded the theory and practice of representation. As we have seen, much of the controversy focused on rules and structures of representation such as suffrage and the nature of the executive power, but at least as troubling as questions about how representation should work was the question of whether it should exist at all. Part of the problem was that while many deputies were striving to build public confidence in representation, angry voices outside the Assembly were working to undermine it. Already in 1789 *Révolutions de Paris* warned of "a new aristocracy, . . . the aristocracy of our mandataries," and charged that France was "less free than under royal despotism," while another paper, urging citizens to watch their representatives closely and control their every action, wrote that "there is no middle ground between [the people] uniting and reigning and being oppressed."[133] Before long this rhetoric turned even more virulent, as Marat called a majority of the deputies "traitors to the fatherland," a "gangrenous horde of valets of the Court, dissolute prelates, royal satellites, corrupt jurists and nobles of the robe," and "a bunch of imbeciles."[134] Attacking the deputies from the other side of the spectrum, *L'Ami du Roi* reminded the people that "their representatives are not their sovereigns" and told the deputies that "far from giving [the people] orders, it was their place to receive orders from them."[135] Such attacks on representation, which often denied there was any middle ground between pure direct democracy and the most abject slavery, undoubtedly harmed the regime's legitimacy.

Given these ongoing attacks, creating a legitimate representative regime would have required French leaders to make a consistent and concerted case for vesting authority in elected representatives. In a poorly educated and politically inexperienced nation with only rudimentary and fragmented means of communication, however, it would have been hard for even a well-designed and well-executed campaign of public education to disseminate an understanding of the rationale for representation. Unfortunately, attempts to make that case were neither well-designed nor energetically and consistently executed.

When leaders did give reasons for representation, they relied too much on the argument about the impossibility of assembling the nation, which the citizens' ability to gather in their sections and primary assemblies seemed to contradict. Moreover, not only did many deputies fail to articulate a clear case for representation, many even attacked the idea, fueling suspicions toward representatives by warning of their temptation to become "oppressors," "aristocrats," "masters," and "tyrants."[136] Much of the problem involved the Jacobins and other minority factions attacking representation in hopes of toppling the moderates who controlled the Assembly, but Article 6 of the Declaration of Rights itself stated that "all citizens have the right to participate personally, or through their representatives, in [the law's] formation," a phrase that made direct democracy sound possible and failed to explain why citizens might prefer that representatives make the laws. Even Sieyès, who offered some of the most carefully crafted justifications for vesting authority in representatives, also said that no one should become a representative "if he does not have the confidence of his constituents, [and] no one can keep that status in losing that confidence."[137] Such statements, by suggesting that representatives must remain popular at all times in order to remain in office, raised unrealistic expectations incompatible with political stability.

The problem with calls for direct democracy was the lack of any practical means of implementing them — a problem that the idea's supporters rarely addressed. For the most part, that is, orators asserting the people's powers over their representatives could offer little more than the idea that "public opinion" or some other equally nebulous concept should dictate to the National Assembly. Yet even if the French had found some means of letting the citizens approve or reject everything their representatives did, it was unclear that most voters even wanted such powers. Voter turnout, after all, was already so low that many placed little stock in election results, and the problem would have grown worse if people had to vote on every new piece of legislation. In short, it was simply not practical to dispense with representatives, even if attacking representation continued to make for effective rhetoric. Direct democracy thus became a theory without a practice, and if the Parisian sections happily filled the vacuum by designating themselves the sovereign people, theirs was a solution of highly dubious legitimacy.

Compounding these problems concerning the theory and practice of sovereignty and representation was a pervasive spirit of mistrust and hostility that hampered efforts to produce consensus through deliberation. In the National Assembly, deputies routinely used violent epithets to describe men sitting across the room from them, ignoring repeated pleas for restraint and civility by the Assembly's presidents. Rivals in the Assembly, Dumont observed, "were too irritated with each other to work in concert, and they sought only to hinder and defeat each other." Indeed his comment that "one cannot begin to imagine the passions that devoured that assembly" probably applied equally well to conditions outside the Assembly.[138]

Given this atmosphere and the distance between rival positions and principles, it was all the more imperative for the French to find broadly legitimate institutions and procedures they could use to resolve their conflicts, but as we have seen, France's formal political institutions and procedures had little legitimacy. The law, which under proper conditions restrains a society's centrifugal tendencies, often elicited little respect in revolutionary France, as lawmakers themselves disregarded it when it suited them and often defended the illegal actions of crowds. As we have seen, for example, the National Assembly dismissed the complaint that the 20 June demonstrators would break the law by bringing weapons into the hall, and on the eve of the 10 August attack a moderate deputy's account of being threatened with lynching produced "bursts of laughter" and applause from the Jacobins, who refused to investigate or prosecute those responsible.[139]

The problem of disrespect for the law naturally plagues all revolutions, for they cannot begin without destroying obedience to the law but cannot end without restoring that obedience. Unfortunately, the principles used to destroy one regime can prove just as corrosive to its replacement; in the French Revolution the idea that the *salut du peuple* superseded any written law was one such principle, and that idea, generally associated with the Jacobin regime, was already heard in this period.[140] This idea of "the people's safety" at times meant that the people could always overrule any law or act of their representatives, but at other times it meant the opposite — that in emergencies leaders should ignore the people's will in order to ensure their safety. This concept became increasingly familiar by 1792, and references to it may be taken as signs of a collapse of consensus and a crisis of existing institutions' and leaders' legitimacy.

Perhaps the contradictions in the 1791 Constitution made that collapse likely, but the *salut du peuple* idea helped inspire and justify the regime's destruction, setting a dangerous precedent that fueled further instability. Early in the Revolution the constitution had seemed almost sacred, but as the previous chapter showed, even at that time orators had often asserted the sovereign's perpetual right to change its constitution, and by 1792 a growing number were insisting that the people's safety required ridding France of its current constitution. So although a referendum on the 1791 Constitution might have given it greater legitimacy, even such a manifestation of the people's will might have done little to stop its future revision. In short, respect for the sanctity of laws and constitutions — a crucial source of political stability in any society — was very weak in France at this time.

The legitimacy crisis affecting France's formal political institutions increased the pressure on informal representations of the sovereign's will, but the French could no more agree on informal methods of invoking that will than they could on formal procedures and institutions. Suggesting the disorder in thinking about public opinion was the proliferation of poorly defined neologisms and hybrids of previously distinct terms such as "public opinion" and "the general will," and although the ambiguities in the language of public opinion at first allowed the French to operate under an illusion of consensus, it soon became clear that observers disagreed sharply about issues such as just who made up "the public" or "the people." Most did seem to agree that "public opinion" now referred to a much larger group than before 1789 — the electorate being its most common sociological referent — but with the contours of the electorate themselves remaining contentious, the question of whose opinions constituted public opinion remained deeply divisive.

The sudden broadening of the public whose opinions now counted also helped destroy a broad prerevolutionary faith in public opinion's rationality and reliability, as countless orators soon revealed their misgivings about the wisdom and maturity of the entity they had just proclaimed sovereign. Moreover, nearly everyone began to suspect their rivals of seeking to manipulate or bribe this gullible public and to manufacture a false public opinion. Amid this atmosphere of suspicion, rivals viewed each other's unsubstantiated assertions about public opinion with profound skepticism, and though orators sought to persuade their listeners by citing various forms of evidence, none satisfied skeptics, who either called the evidence unreliable or considered the group in question unrepresentative. Finally, the French also disagreed over the texture, or composition, of public opinion, and if unitary images of public opinion gradually began to prevail, that victory seemed little more than a vain attempt to deny the very obvious lack of unanimity in France. France, in short, was far from reaching consensus on either the formal or informal means of representing the sovereign's will, posing a severe problem for the establishment of political legitimacy.

IV

✣

The Beginnings of the Republic,
1792–1793

B y the end of the day on 10 August 1792, the King and his family were prisoners of the Paris Commune, while much of the Tuileries palace lay in ruins. Figuratively, the Legislative Assembly also lay in ruins, with many of its members having fled and with the rest now essentially taking orders from the Paris Commune. Indeed, the entire constitution was in ruins, as the uprising had brought down a regime as well as a government. While the militants celebrated their victory, some feared how "public opinion" might react, but given the time it took news to travel, their leaders were able to consolidate their power before most of the French even heard about the events.

Immediately after the uprising, its defenders portrayed it as the work of the entire sovereign people. Some also invoked the precedent of 14 July, but this "second revolution" had overthrown an elected government based on national sovereignty. Stepping into the background, the Paris Commune and the Jacobins allowed the rump parliament to address the nation, and in a 16 August communiqué, the Assembly downplayed the militants' role, casting itself as the motive force and explaining why it had suspended the King. The document gave various arguments, from the need to avoid a "civil and religious war" to an assertion that the King had abdicated by various actions, but its main strategy was to claim the support of public opinion. Focusing on the King's veto of measures for which "public opinion had strongly manifested itself," it asserted that "from one end of the empire to the other, the people expressed their somber concerns" and their demand for a republic. As evidence, it cited "numerous petitions sent from a great number of departments [and] the wish of several Paris sections, followed by a general wish expressed in the name of the entire [Paris] Commune," and it concluded that on 10 August "the people" had "appeared in their entirety, gathered with a single goal and a single will," to depose the King.[1] Yet the Assembly, fearing that many would doubt these claims, decided "to turn to the supreme will of the people, and to invite them to exercise the inalienable right of sovereignty" by electing a national convention to write a new constitution.[2]

Within weeks an electorate now open to many former "passive" citizens elected a National Convention, which met in Paris on 21 September. On its first day the Convention unanimously abolished royalty, but that unanimity did not last, as two groups, known as the Gironde and the Mountain, began seeking the support of the Plain, a much larger group of uncommitted deputies.[3] The Girondins, part of the left in the last regime, now formed the Convention's right wing, and though most of them were still members of the Jacobin Club, Brissot and other Girondins soon stopped attending its meetings. In Paris the main forces outside the Convention were the Jacobins, the Paris Commune, and the Paris sections (the latter two being strongly partial to the Mountain without being under its control), while in the provinces power lay primarily with local officials, sections in the larger cities, and the Jacobin Clubs, most of which were still committed to neither the Mountain nor the Gironde. Not represented at all in the Convention were royalists and conservatives, who had been barred from participating in many of the electoral assemblies, and whose newspapers had been shut down in the August uprising. In that uprising many prominent royalists had also been executed.

Despite having been elected to write a new constitution, the National Convention quickly became distracted from that mission by the tasks of governing the country, fighting the war, determining the King's fate, and, as of spring 1793, crushing the counterrevolutionary rebellions that broke out in the Vendée and elsewhere. Having scrapped the 1791 Constitution, the French now had to wage their political battles without any charter to guide them, placing more weight than ever on the rhetoric of public opinion. Unfortunately, the delay in drafting a new constitution also meant that the confusion over basic terms and concepts that had plagued the previous two assemblies would persist.

One idea on which all seemed to agree was the doctrine of popular sovereignty. Although historians have often considered national sovereignty a less radical doctrine than popular sovereignty and have associated it with the first phase of the Revolution while identifying popular sovereignty with this phase, that distinction can be misleading. Conceptions of sovereignty did change at this time, but the terms "popular sovereignty" and "sovereignty of the people" had already been used extensively in the previous period, and many spoke of "national sovereignty" after August 1792, with even Montagnards using it as a synonym for popular sovereignty.[4] Thus the main disputes focused not on whether to call the nation or the people sovereign, but on how to envision this sovereign and its powers.

One very common definition of the people remained the totality of France's citizens. When orators referred, for example, to "the working portion of the people" or "the needy portion of the people," they implied that the people included some who were neither workers nor needy.[5] One Girondin made this explicit, saying, "I do not distinguish this or that class; the people are not one portion, they are the totality of the French."[6] Equally common, however, was the old concept of the people as the lower classes, which Robespierre used when he said the people were "still persecuted by the rich," and which another deputy illustrated by declaring, "The people do not go to the theater [because] they do not have the means."[7] Complicating the lexicon was the term "sans-culottes," which was often, but not always, a synonym for "the people." When one Jacobin, for example, claimed on 19 December 1792 that the Club was on the side of "the people and the sans-culottes," he implied that the two terms might not be pure synonyms, though this speaker, like many others, may not have been quite sure what he meant by each term.[8] So although the left generally favored a class-based definition, "the people" remained a term that left ample room for confusion.

In much the same way that some prerevolutionary writers had distinguished between "the multitude" (used for denigration) and "the people" (reserved for praise), some orators in this period made positive qualities defining traits of the people, in effect defining the people morally and politically rather than sociologically. The Jacobin deputy Collot d'Herbois declared that whereas some thought the people included "the totality of the French, I mean by the people the totality of the good citizens, without including those who conspire against the people," and Robespierre wrote in his newspaper that there were only two groups in France, "the good and the bad citizens, that is to say . . . the French people and . . . the ambitious and greedy men."[9] In the National Convention, he called the people "the majority of the nation, not excluding the most numerous, the most unfortunate, and the purest part of society," an ambiguous statement that follows Rousseau in linking wealth and vice but also implies that some members of the people were not from the

purest or poorest part of society.[10] At times Robespierre made his moral definition even clearer, as when he noted that the people included "men of all
conditions who have a pure and lofty soul," from "philosophes who love hu-
manity to the sans-culottes."[11] Once again, though, there is some danger in
looking for precision and consistency in these definitions; in the speech
quoted above, for example, Robespierre called the people "the majority of the
nation," but he also used the terms "the people" and "the nation" interchangeably and said he "considered these words synonymous."[12]

The left was not alone in defining undesirable elements out of the nation
or the people. The Girondins often claimed it was "brigands" or "anarchists,"
not the people, who were committing acts of violence in France. And when a
Jacobin deputy referred to "the people" having smashed a moderate newspaper's presses on 10 March 1793, the Convention reacted with "murmurs,"
leading the president of the Convention to inform the speaker that "it is not
the people who broke the presses."[13] That statement may have simply meant
that a mob was not the people, but the Girondins often proclaimed their faith
in the people's wisdom, defining them in moral terms not unlike those the
left used.

In addition to defining the sovereign, the French also had to consider sovereignty's precise location. Activists in the sections saw sovereignty in the sections, but others argued that it lay in the communes or the larger districts
known as cantons.[14] The Girondins, aware of the threat from the sections,
specified, as Condorcet put it, that "each assembly is not sovereign" and that
"sovereignty can only belong to the whole of the people."[15] A committee of
the Convention later adopted Condorcet's view, charging that "anarchists
abuse this word by applying it endlessly to little sections that they treat as
sovereign," and the committee announced that sovereignty rested only in
"the complete gathering of all the French citizens voting in the primary assemblies."[16] Yet another view appeared in the debate over the Girondins'
proposal for a referendum on executing the King, when the Rennes Jacobin
Club protested that this "appeal to the people" was unnecessary because the
people had vested their sovereignty in the National Convention, and deputies
occasionally reiterated this parliamentary sovereignty idea.[17]

As the latter argument suggests, resolving sovereignty's location required
saying something about the terms on which representatives might exercise it,
but unfortunately this period saw continuing confusion over whether and
how sovereignty was "conferred," "transferred," "delegated," and so on.[18]
Some also claimed that popular sovereignty meant that the citizens had certain rights over their representatives—such as the right to approve all legisla-

tion by referendum or to recall representatives from office — and these claims often led to heated debates on the nature of representation (examined below). Once again, however, orators discussing sovereignty usually moved on to other business before working out some common understanding of that term.

As for sovereignty's characteristics, most continued to believe in a limitless authority, even if disagreements persisted on whether such authority should be transferred to representatives. After the 10 August uprising, *Révolutions de Paris* reacted angrily to those who wondered just what the marchers had intended in coming to the palace that day, writing that "when the people rise up as a whole, they owe no one any explanation."[19] Also illustrating this belief in sovereignty's limitless authority were the September massacres, in which a Parisian mob slaughtered over a thousand prisoners considered counterrevolutionaries. In historian Pierre Caron's view, the people were exercising a right of summary judgment that royal sovereigns had traditionally claimed, in effect saying that the people, being the source of the law, were above it.[20] One can assume that few in the crowd knew of that legal doctrine, but most had by then absorbed the basic idea that the people were sovereign and could thus do anything they wanted. Robespierre did propose one limit on the sovereign's powers, arguing that a nation could not subject itself to a monarch, and he called this "the only proper restriction on the too-unlimited and often poorly advanced principle of the sovereignty of peoples," but even that limit seemed excessive to one of his fellow Jacobins.[21]

The Girondins, despite their reluctance to deny that sovereignty meant unlimited authority, continued to take issue with those Paris clubs and sections that tried to act in the sovereign's name. Reporting to the National Convention in October on the Paris Commune's powers, the Girondin Interior Minister Jean-Marie Roland complained that some were misinterpreting popular sovereignty, trying "to persuade the people that they can do anything in order to make them do what they want," and Girondin deputy Pierre Vergniaud later told the people, "The anarchists have fooled you by their abuse of the word sovereignty."[22] Others maintained that a National Convention (a "constituent power") differed from an ordinary legislature (a "constituted power") in having been granted unlimited powers until it finished its task. According to one orator, "the assembled Convention is the sovereign will."[23]

As the preceding section shows, the idea of representation came under increasing fire after 10 August. Hébert's newspaper, *Le Père Duchesne*, called the country's elected representatives "a pile of blowhards, lawyers, prosecutors, notaries, bailiffs, and other sorts of vermin who devour the food of the poor," and the paper proclaimed that "the legislators of a free people must get it through their damned heads that they are only the people's clerks and not their masters, and that they must obey their sovereign's will while trembling with fear."[24] Echoing Rousseau, a spokesman from the Quinze-Vingts section denounced the "imbecile politicans and professors of public law" who had written the last constitution and "all these great minds, armed with the title of *constitutionnaires*," who knew less than those "who have only studied the art of government in the book of nature."[25] Not surprisingly, such groups continued to demand either strict controls over the country's representatives or forms of action that circumvented representatives altogether.

In response to such attacks, some representatives continued to note the impossibility of assembling the citizens, and one Girondin cited Rousseau in support of his claim that "purely democratic government is a chimera."[26] Offering a more positive argument for representation, the independent deputy Bertrand Barère asserted that the nation wanted to delegate its powers, an argument that enlisted a powerful source of legitimacy, but one with no defense against the nation then changing its mind and choosing to do away with representatives.[27] Placing representation on somewhat firmer ground, Robespierre maintained that the people lacked "the time to assemble . . . to judge questions of State," while another deputy referred to the Convention's members as "745 deputies whom the people considered the elite of France in courage and virtue."[28] Some deputies also took up the argument that the people had to entrust their powers to the country's most enlightened men. Paraphrasing Rousseau, one deputy said that "the people always want what serves the national interest, but they do not always see it, and that is why they delegate" some of their powers.[29]

The Paris militants, however, were generally in no mood for such arguments. Moreover, many deputies once again helped undermine faith in representation, either in hopes of establishing their credentials as true friends of the people or in attempting to weaken their rivals in the Convention. Despite having defended representation at times, Robespierre often called representatives "masters" and representation a form of "aristocracy"; he also declared, following Rousseau, that though "the people are good . . . their delegates are corruptible," explaining that "the corruption of governments has its source in their excess power and in their independence from the sovereign."[30] Some deputies spoke of ending representation altogether, as Danton suggested there were "a thousand ways to maintain liberty without having recourse to representative government," and Augustin Robespierre (Maximilien's brother) favored "democratic government" over representative government.[31] Some even insisted that the citizens could indeed assemble in person. In proposing a referendum on the King's fate, Salle, a Girondin, told the Convention it could use special couriers to summon the people to their primary assemblies, and "in less than two weeks," he told his colleagues, "the wish of the Republic will be clear to you."[32] Also dismissing logistical concerns, another Girondin concluded that "nothing is simpler" than gathering the citizens to vote in a referendum.[33] The Montagnards opposed the Girondins' proposal for a referendum on the King, but they generally did so not by making positive arguments for representation, but rather by attacking the Girondins' motives or by emphasizing the dangers of a vote at that moment on that topic.

In proposing specific means by which citizens might control their representatives, a few voices still favored a binding mandate. A speaker at the Jacobin Club insisted that the sovereign declares "its imperative wish" when voting, and he likened representatives to royal ambassadors, who were "carriers or communicators of orders from their masters."[34] When the remnants of the National Assembly had summoned the primary assemblies to elect a National Convention, they had advised against any kind of binding mandate, but some departments ignored the advice and issued their representatives specific instructions and limits.[35] The members of the Convention generally ignored these binding mandates, but they offered little reason for doing so other than occasional claims that binding mandates had no place in a system in which each deputy represented the entire nation.

More common than support for the binding mandate were assertions of the citizens' right to give their representatives instructions between elections and to recall them from office at any time — the latter right being asserted with increasing frequency as the Parisian militants became furious at the Girondins for their moderation toward the King. Aware that petitions had long been a kind of supplication before the sovereign, a *fédéré* told the Jacobin Club that when the people spoke to the Convention, they came "not as petitioners, for the people do not make petitions, but to declare their will," and another speaker said the citizens "always have the right to force their agents to follow their orders."[36] According to one Parisian petition, the ability to recall representatives from office was "the eternal right of all constituents" and "the safeguard of the people."[37] And in March 1793 a group of Jacobins from Marseilles announced they were using their "rightful share of sovereignty" to order the Girondins to resign, telling them, "Flee, cowardly and perjured mandataries, or fear being the first to feel the avenging sword of the republican people who are rising up for the third time."[38]

Few of those asserting this right of recall, however, stated any clear and consistent principles or guidelines for when or how a recall might take place.

Le Père Duchesne simply affirmed the people's "right to recall and replace those who do not march in the proper path," and the paper was equally vague about how a recall might work, stating only that if representatives did not do a good job, "we must not be afraid to show them our teeth."[39] Robespierre was just as vague about methods, writing that the people can revoke their representatives "following the forms that the general will must establish."[40]

Despite temptations to embrace a right of recall as a way to rid themselves of their rivals in the Convention, the deputies knew that doctrine threatened their own power, and they sought ways to limit its use without contesting the principle. One means involved the idea that each deputy represented the whole country; when one section demanded the Girondins' ouster, the Convention's president noted that those deputies represented "not the people of Paris, but all of France," and insisted that "the National Convention only recognizes the entire people as sovereign."[41] Replying to the Jacobin petitioners from Marseilles, Barère called it "a shame that we do not all have the citizens' unanimous confidence" but said that because "our constituents are the entire nation," deputies should resign only "when the entire people, or a majority of them, have expressed their wish."[42] Some still insisted on a department's right to recall its own representatives, but most seemed to reject any formal link between a deputy and the department that elected him, and proponents of a department's right of recall were often branded as "federalists."[43]

Yet ironically, the idea that deputies represented no specific district, which had been intended to give them greater independence, ended up weakening rather than bolstering representation. Once the deputies were dissociated from a specific district, that is, removing them from office would not cause the region that elected them to go unrepresented (though some voters from the departments that had elected the twenty-nine Girondins ousted on 2 June 1793 disagreed). After all, if each deputy represented all of France, what difference did it make if there were 745 or 716 deputies? Also, dissociating the deputies from the departments that had elected them promoted the idea that the Parisians had as much right to revoke deputies from the Gironde as voters from Bordeaux did. In the Girondins' view, of course, no single district had that right, but that was not how Parisian activists saw things, and because the Convention was in Paris, only the Parisians were really in a position to force anyone from office. Turning a logistical question into a political doctrine, Robespierre argued "that a great nation cannot rise up in a spontaneous movement," so "tyranny can only be struck down by the portion of the citizens who are closest to it."[44] In short, in the absence of clear procedural rules, the idea of a right of recall, when combined with the idea that deputies represented no one district, was taken to mean that Parisians had a special right to recall deputies from any part of France. The Cordeliers Club expressed this view in a March 1793 decree, declaring that "the Paris Department, an integral part of the sovereign, is invited to take hold of the exercise of sovereignty" and that "the electorate of Paris is authorized to replace the deputies who have betrayed the people's cause."[45] Just over two months later, that call was answered.

The idea of using referenda to let the people approve or reject their representatives' work received a great deal of attention in this period. Some proposed holding a referendum to prove the nation's support of the 10 August uprising, but most deputies preferred the safer approach of simply asserting that the nation had carried out or supported the insurrection. Nearly all, however, agreed that the new constitution would need approval in a referendum, even if disagreement remained on whether citizens should vote on each article or on the text as a whole. Some even insisted that the citizens vote on all new legislation, or at least, as one deputy argued, on "all the important resolutions."[46] Rejecting Condorcet's idea that any law not challenged by a petition would be considered binding, *Révolutions de Paris* denied that one could presume the people's acceptance of a law "through the silence of the departments," but the paper said nothing about the practical difficulties of holding so many referenda.[47] One who did address that problem was Chabot, who told the Jacobins in September 1792 that citizens should meet every Sunday in their towns and villages to review the legislature's work, to deliberate on it, and then to vote on all laws.[48] Another deputy opposed the idea, arguing that it "would paralyze the legislature," but even one of the Girondins claimed that "every act of the people's representatives is an assault on their sovereignty if it is not submitted to their formal or tacit ratification."[49]

Many of the same arguments reappeared in debates over the Girondins' demand for an "appeal to the people" on the King's fate. That proposal involved a role reversal given that the Girondins usually resisted the left's demands for direct democracy, and though it outraged those who wanted Louis's immediate execution, it did put them on the defensive. In proposing that referendum in December 1792, Salle called it "a real homage to national sovereignty," and he argued that those who opposed it "abuse the word sovereignty very strangely."[50] If the people voted for the King's execution, he noted, then those who wanted him to die would get their wish anyway, but if the people voted to spare him, he asked, "By what right would you send him to the scaffold against the national will?"[51] What was at issue in this debate was not only the King's life, but also the Convention's legitimacy, for although the referendum sought to compensate for the dubious legal basis of the King's conviction, it also addressed the fear that many citizens would resent the King's execution and question the Convention's right to order it. Several Girondins called for the referendum on the grounds that people outside Paris were irate over Parisians pressuring the Convention; one told the deputies that the Convention was "absolutely detested" outside Paris, and another warned that if the Convention passed a death sentence on its own, many would say "that we were forced to pass it," having been "influenced and intimidated by the Parisians."[52] As Salle explained, by allowing the departments to have their say, "the Convention will be exempt from any reproach."[53]

Though caught off guard by the Girondins' populist outbidding, the left attacked the referendum proposal as nothing but a ruse to save and perhaps restore the King. For Robespierre, a referendum on the King was unnecessary, for "the people truly expressed their own will" through "the spontaneous and universal movement" of 10 August.[54] Another Jacobin added that the people had already spoken by electing the National Convention, and he told the deputies, "The people have given you full powers [and] have charged you with doing all that is useful for their safety and liberty."[55] Raising a question relevant to all referendum proposals, many asked how, once the deputies began submitting their decisions to popular sanction, they would draw a line between actions that did and did not require popular sanction, and some noted that they had made many vital decisions on war, taxation, and public liberties without seeking the voters' confirmation.[56] One normally pro-Girondin deputy called the plan "a trap, because it risks . . . placing the people and their representatives in formal contradiction," and Robespierre warned that "this project can only lead to destroying the Convention itself."[57] In short, the plan's opponents called it a threat not only to the Convention's legitimacy but also to representative government. One Montagnard even contended that whenever the sovereign people reassemble, all representative authority automatically ends. "The government is no more," he insisted, "and everywhere the departments, the districts, the municipalities, the tribunals cease to exist, at least legally. . . . What horrifying chaos, what deplorable and dangerous anarchy!"[58]

The Girondins considered these arguments disingenuous, and several of them pointed out that many who now called referenda dangerous had supported the Champs de Mars petitioners' call for a referendum on monarchy as well as the more recent plea for a referendum on the new constitution. In what would become a French tradition over the next two centuries, those who proposed the referendum accused the party resisting it of fearing the people's judgment; as the Girondin deputy Armand Gensonné put it, that party "does not want the people to make use of their sovereignty . . . because it wants to exercise it in their name."[59] The Girondins thus took the popular high ground, dismissing suggestions that the issues and evidence were too complex for voters to judge. Brissot called that "an accusation against the good sense of the people" and charged that the Mountain's strategy amounted to portraying "the ignorance, the stupidity, and the vices of the people they pretend to adore."[60]

The Girondins' stratagem failed when the Convention voted to reject the idea and execute the King. Explaining the Convention's decision, David Jordan writes that many deputies considered the idea "dangerous or impractical or unnecessary," and he rightly adds that many also saw royalist motives behind the appeal.[61] Yet the failed tactic did have significant consequences, as it helped to discredit the entire idea of the referendum, a procedure that might have served to restore some of the legitimacy the state kept losing through the constant denigration of representation. Direct democracy, in other words, remained a theory without a practice, as orators raised people's expectations for political equality without offering any way to fulfill them.

If prevailing ideas on the representative relationship left the deputies in a precarious position, so did current ideas about constitutions. Some saw constitutions as social contracts in which individuals agreed to limit their future freedom by granting powers to representatives; in this view, the powers given to representatives and the authority vested in a constitution would be considered compatible with popular sovereignty on the grounds that the people had deliberately created them. Provided there was some reasonable way for the constitution to be revised, citizens might then be persuaded to accept these limits on their will, giving constitutions some hope of stability and representatives some leeway to use their discretion. Unfortunately, strict obstacles to revision in the 1791 Constitution had marked many people's thinking by this time, and the rhetoric of direct democracy also weakened respect for constitutions. Many, in short, came to see a constitution as a set of rules that bound governing authorities but not the sovereign people (a view Sieyès had expressed in *What Is the Third Estate?*). In November the spokesman for a key committee of the Convention expressed such a view, stating that "the nation was not restrained by the constitution" and that "it has the imprescriptible right to change its constitution" at any time.[62]

Yet despite declaring that right, the deputies could not agree on how revision might begin. Offering one possible answer, they decreed that the people always retained a right of insurrection against rulers or constitutions they considered oppressive, though proponents offered few specifics about who could use that right or how the process would work. One who did address the point was Robespierre, who, as noted earlier, contended that the Parisians had a special right and obligation to overthrow a tyrannical government for the good of the nation.[63] In effect, Robespierre was amending the principle that the nation had a permanent right to change its constitution or government by force, asserting that the people of Paris had that right, and though the argument persuaded few deputies outside the Mountain, its reception in the Paris Commune and sections was another matter.

Another crucial matter affecting the country's search for a legitimate and stable order was the separation of powers. The King's removal threatened the existence of a separation of powers, which worried those who felt that the war and other problems increased the need for an independent, efficient executive. Such concerns led some to recommend direct popular election of an executive council, and *Révolutions de Paris* called for "a chief of the executive power" who "would no longer be hereditary or chosen for life."[64] Yet for much of the left, the belief that the indivisibility of sovereignty demanded indivisible representation, when combined with fears of monarchy and resentment of the Girondins' current control of the executive ministries, led to demands for a full concentration of authority in the Convention. So despite complaining in March 1793 that "we do not have a sufficiently active government," Robespierre advised the Convention to take full powers on the grounds that it is "unity of action that gives a government force," and his colleague Collot d'Herbois called an independent executive "useless in a free constitution."[65]

Reinforcing this concentration of power in the Convention was what one might call republican antipersonalism, a deep resentment of any individual holding power. So even deputies who still favored having an executive seemed to agree with the Jacobin leader Georges Couthon that "it is not only royalty that must be removed from our constitution, it is any sort of individual power."[66] *Le Père Duchesne*, as usual, put things more bluntly, writing that "any head that seeks to raise itself above the others must be cut down."[67] Among the deputies, this hostility toward individual authority arose in part from a desire to prevent anyone outside the Convention from challenging their monopoly on popular representation, but it also arose from their own mistrust of each other. Eventually, the Convention ended up vesting nearly unlimited powers in the Committees of Public Safety and General Security, but it did so gradually, working under the illusion that it could continue to control those committees.

Yet as the early-twentieth-century historian Cochin observed, a country obsessed with the unity of authority nonetheless had a bewildering array of authorities and institutions, including sections, municipal and departmental governments, revolutionary committees, tribunals, primary and electoral assemblies, popular societies, and various other formal, semiformal, and informal bodies.[68] Some proliferation of institutions is to be expected in any revolution, but given the pervasive spirit of mistrust and fear — a cause as well as a consequence of economic crisis, war, and counterrevolutionary revolt — this degree of fragmentation probably confused many citizens, and it certainly alarmed the Montagnards, who saw counterrevolution in all organizations they did not control. Moreover, a recurring pattern of schisms had often resulted in duplicate versions of many of the bodies noted above, reflecting the refusal of many leaders and citizens to accept the legitimacy of any body that rivals controlled. In May 1793 the Montagnards and their Parisian allies decided to solve the problem by mounting yet another armed uprising, which ended with the arrest of the Girondin leaders on 2 June 1793.[69] Unfortunately, the Mountain's takeover of the National Convention and its subsequent attempt to centralize all power violated many of the Revolution's basic principles of sovereignty and representation. In so doing, it also deepened the mistrust already affecting France's formal institutions, thus spiraling the legitimacy crisis into greater depths.

As the French searched desperately for sources of authority in this perplexing time, they looked for ways to invoke the will of the sovereign people even more effectively, and according to several recent studies, their methods now began changing. The most notable change, these works suggest, involved a movement away from the term "public opinion" toward the term "the public spirit." J. A. W. Gunn, for example, writes that public opinion "changed its name" at this time, as there was "a gradual and halting process whereby references to public opinion, the language of the pre-revolution and of the friends of authority, gave way to talk of 'public spirit.'" Gunn adds that as the Revolution proceeded, "the Left continued to favour talk of public spirit" over public opinion, which "remained the preferred vocabulary of the Right."[70] Gunn's comments echo Mona Ozouf's statement that "Jacobin texts shunned the use of 'public opinion,' a term too suggestive of subjectivity and liberty."[71] Both of these authors see "public spirit" becoming the dominant term as the Revolution turned more unanimist and coercive.

Although Gunn and Ozouf are right to note a decline of pluralistic notions of public opinion, the suggestion that one term replaced another, or that one term belonged to the left and one to the right, needs rethinking for several reasons. For one, we have seen that orators often referred to the public spirit before 1792. Second, the term "public opinion" remained very widely used in this period, appearing at least as often in the texts examined here, and it is simply not true that the Jacobins shunned the term. Third, the Girondins and other moderates also spoke frequently of the public spirit. More broadly, even to limit one's scope to the terms "public opinion" and "public spirit" would be misleading, for those were but two of many largely synonymous terms used to draw authority from the same basic source.

If it remains impossible to identify distinct meanings for most of these terms in this period, it is possible to note changes in the meaning of the basic cluster of terms. The opening of the electorate and the sections to passive citizens undoubtedly affected these terms' sociological referent, and with the sansculottes now playing a greater role than ever, terms such as "the people" acquired even stronger class connotations. Yet "the people" could still refer to the entire citizenry as well as to various other groups such as the lower classes, the Parisian sans-culottes, or the "good citizens," so once again the opportunities for misunderstanding were extensive.

One phrase that did have a distinct referent was "the opinion of the departments," an important category at a time when the representativeness of Parisian opinion stood very much in question. Another term that often had a distinct meaning was "popular opinion," which had pejorative connotations. Barère, for example, lamented that "reciprocal hatreds have created excessively erratic and dangerous movements in popular opinion," and Pétion complained that because of slanderous rumors launched at the Jacobin Club, "a certain popular opinion, false and depraved, forms."[72] As for "the general will," most speakers simply used it as a synonym for terms such as "public opinion," but Robespierre, who often complained of public opinion being manipulated and corrupted, told the Convention, "I trust the general will."[73]

At times, the term "public spirit" indeed differed from "public opinion" and other phrases, denoting harmony between citizens and authorities and devotion to the community.[74] In an essay on the public spirit, Roland called it "this profound and religious sentiment that places above our dearest interests that of the common motherland and makes us feel fraternal affection toward our fellow citizens, prescribing to us as the first of our duties that of loving, respecting and observing the laws"; he also saw it as "the most complete deference toward constituted authorities."[75] For many, the term also meant a revolutionary spirit or "patriotic" zeal whose intensity fluctuated. Condorcet told the deputies they must calm current agitations "without weakening the activity of the public spirit" or destroying "this temporarily useful heat," and *Révolutions de Paris* warned of a "sudden decline of the public spirit" and of increasing "apathy" and "discouragement."[76]

Yet if it is sometimes possible to identify distinct meanings of terms such as "the public spirit," at other times the distinctions simply disappear. Gunn writes that for the left, the public spirit (unlike public opinion) was "good by definition," but this period saw endless complaints about both public opinion and the public spirit having become "corrupted" or "depraved," and in his text on the public spirit, Roland complained that people constantly confused it with *l'opinion*, a more unstable and less universal phenomenon.[77] And whereas some followed Rousseau in distinguishing between the general will and public opinion, or between the general will and the will of the majority, others did not. In calling for a referendum on the King's fate, Buzot argued that only "this general will, pronounced out loud," could resolve the problem, and in announcing that the Convention had voted against holding a roll-call vote on one issue, the assembly's president stated, "It is the will of the majority, and consequently it is the general will."[78] Very rarely did anyone object when speakers blended such formerly separate terms.

In describing this many-named force, many still spoke of its omnipotence, and even Robespierre used the old royal metaphor, declaring that "patriots, armed with the scepter of opinion, will easily smash the scepter of despotism and conspiracy."[79] Royal metaphors might seem inappropriate at this point, but this monarch resembled Solomon more than Louis XVI. *Révolutions de Paris*, for example, called the public conscience "infallible," and Robespierre predicted that his evidence against the Girondins would "suffice for public opinion, for the nation, which, like history, will judge impartially."[80] As for references to the people's opinion, the traditional denigration of the people, which now risked sounding counterrevolutionary, gave way to a torrent of emphatic praise, as *Le Père Duchesne* called the people "wiser than scholars," and *Le Patriote Français* wrote that "the class of citizens that one calls the people . . . has more good will, more good sense, fewer prejudices, and fewer calculated interests than the other classes."[81]

Yet many speakers were not so sure of public opinion's omnipotence. A spokesman for a committee studying the press's abuses explained that "your committee believed at one time that the force of public opinion would suffice to render these criminal writings harmless," but it now held that "the public spirit was being perverted," necessitating regulation.[82] Similarly, the Cordeliers demanded a purge of the administration and the army "to get rid of all those whom the whip of public opinion has not chased away," and Danton

predicted that France would need to find more effective means "once we
have exhausted all the means of public opinion."[83] Aware of such concerns,
various orators called for patience. Buzot noted that although slanderers
might do harm at first, "those who have served their country and who love
virtue will regain the degree of public opinion's esteem that they should
never have lost," and the Jacobin Philippe Fabre d'Eglantine reassured the
National Convention that the people "never err in the confidence they accord, or at least they never err for long."[84]

Unfortunately, the pace of events made such delays seem intolerable, and
anguished descriptions of public opinion and the people now proliferated.
Late in 1792 Buzot regretted that the people were "so easy to mislead by
speaking to them of their happiness" and he also worried about "the people's
extreme volatility."[85] Even former radicals now voiced doubts. In *Révolutions
de Paris*, Pétion wrote that whereas before 1789 "a few educated men" and "a
few philosophes" had studied political problems and formed public opinion,
"the masses of the nation" were now "seeking enlightenment," but "they
mistake their first ideas for knowledge." In his view, "the man who has done
the least to develop his reason launches into a harangue, speaking boldly on
the most difficult questions," and "those who hear him generally being no
better educated than him, applaud him, quickly absorb his errors, and then
propagate them." Soon, he concluded, "public opinion is corrupted and takes
a wrong direction," and "this wayward opinion then proceeds to put all its
weight on the authorities, dragging them along with it."[86]

Pétion and other moderates were not alone in voicing such views. *Le Père
Duchesne* complained that "more than three-quarters of the French do not see
what they are and what they can do," and Robespierre observed that the people
may have courage but "they have neither finesse nor eloquence . . . [and] are
often duped by scoundrels."[87] The Girondins' referendum proposal brought
out many of the Montagnards' misgivings about the people, leading Joseph-
Marie Lequinio to fear "the remains of ancient idolatry for kings" and monarchists' efforts to sway "a multitude lacking enlightenment."[88] Some did express
a kind of Rousseauian faith in rural virtue, but perceptions of what speakers
called "the simple people of the countryside" and "country people still lacking
in foresight" colored the mostly urban political class's overall perceptions of the
people, with many fearing the nefarious influence of rural priests and nobles.[89]

For many, then, public opinion was neither omnipotent nor wise. In his
Lettre à ses commettans Robespierre wrote that public opinion might be the
queen of the world, but "like all queens, it is courted and often fooled," and
similar allusions to the public's gullibility filled the debates of the time.[90]

Many also feared that public opinion was too unstable and fickle to be a foundation of the state. Whereas one orator in 1791 had called public opinion a "solid anchor" of the state, one Montagnard now warned that "opinion is floating uncertainly," and *Le Patriote Français* wrote that "public opinion is a stormy sea on which the ship of state ... must navigate."[91] Nor was the public spirit immune to such problems, as Roland announced that "public spirit, which should have made such rapid and firm progress after four years of revolution, only manifests itself in convulsions" and remained prone to "languor" and "the subversion of principles."[92] Reflecting perceptions of the public spirit's volatility were metaphors of temperature, electricity, and flame, as orators spoke of "a fire that is ready to ignite," an "explosion whose consequences cannot be known," and a "spontaneous implosion [that] electrifies people's souls."[93] A certain zeal was of course welcome, but it often seemed that the public spirit was either about to erupt in uncontrollable flames or to freeze over completely; one deputy warned that "the public spirit that some have already sought to cool down could be extinguished" altogether, and another leaving for the departments promised to "heat up the patriotism that has gone cold."[94]

Ironically, in calling the public spirit and public opinion volatile, fickle, and prone to error, these orators were using the same terms that had once been applied to individual opinion, suggesting that something had gone wrong in the transformation of unreliable and dangerous individual opinions into a steady and reliable public opinion. The problem most often cited was counterrevolutionaries' efforts to manipulate the people, or to wield what one speaker called "the magic power of opinion."[95] Fueling fears of manipulation was the discovery of a cache of documents in the King's secret *armoire de fer* in November 1792. One document described the sums the King had paid to everyone from journalists and spies in the Jacobin Clubs to hecklers and claques in public places, as well as plans for helping the King gain popular favor through bizarre schemes such as riding on horseback through Paris and throwing coins to the people.[96] The discovery of the King's correspondence with foreign courts also raised concerns, and it soon became almost automatic to see William Pitt behind every expression of opposition to the Revolution. Deepening the Montagnards' anxieties was the creation of Roland's "Bureau of the Public Spirit," through which the interior minister subsidized various Girondin newspapers until his resignation in January 1793.

Alarmed at manipulation of a gullible public, leaders repeatedly called for efforts to "direct" and "fix" public opinion. One Jacobin proposed that "a committee composed of enlightened persons" summarize the opinions expressed at the Paris Club and then "propagate these opinions from one end of the empire to the other so as to shape, so to speak, the public spirit into a uniform mold."[97] Unfortunately, when the Girondins and Jacobins warned of nefarious forces corrupting public opinion, it was mainly each other they had in mind, so the more the Jacobins strove to mold their affiliates' opinions, and the more the Girondins developed their state-subsidized publishing empire, the more they exacerbated each other's anxieties. For many, the only real remedy for the problem lay in education, which *Le Patriote Français* called "a salutary oil that calms the waves provoked by ignorance and passions."[98] Expressing a pervasive yearning for a unanimous, enlightened, and docile public opinion, the Jacobin deputy François-Xavier Lanthenas outlined plans for a Ministry of Public Instruction that would oversee a thoroughgoing national education system and spoke of "the public opinion that it alone will rule over."[99] Regrettably, that solution offered little hope in the short run.

At the root of many anxieties over public opinion and others' efforts to mold it lay a visceral fear of pluralism, which had pervaded eighteenth-century French political culture and which only worsened now. Once again, the more severely opinion became divided, the more loudly orators proclaimed its unity, and speakers often veered manically from proclamations of public opinion's unanimity to warnings of its division—even within a single speech. More and more, speakers declared unanimity by defining unwanted elements out of the nation, as one deputy called it "the wish of all the republicans in France" that the Convention judge the King, and another, using an even more unfalsifiable rhetorical construct, argued that there was not a single "true republican" who wanted the King to live.[100] Orators also continued to argue that a given opinion was unanimous because it had been heard in "all the departments" or "all the parts" of France.[101] Jaume has rightly spoken of the "mystic unanimism" that marked the Jacobins' conception of the general will, but that outlook was limited neither to the Jacobins nor to the concept of the general will.[102]

If unanimist rhetoric now dominated the language of public opinion, a more corporatist language did occasionally surface as well. Much of this language came from the sans-culottes, whose rejection of individualism historian Albert Soboul pointed out. In spring 1793, for example, one Paris section responding to a call to arms against the Vendée rebels promised to come "en corps."[103] Of course the Old Regime's *corps* had spoken with a single voice, so it is not surprising that the sans-culottes who now ruled most of the sections occasionally blurred lines between unanimist and corporatist rhetoric. The corporatist tradition also lived on in allusions to the opinions of the Revolution's new political units such as the departments or the primary assemblies.

Ozouf and others are right to stress a movement toward unanimist conceptions of opinion in this period, yet some measure of pluralism and individualism did persist, especially among the Girondins. Buzot, reminding the Convention that "the right of petition is a purely individual right," declared that if petitions were not signed individually, "twenty or twenty-five individuals would have the right to represent all the citizens of a section without their consent," and another deputy, commenting on a petition from the faubourg Saint-Antoine, said he did "not believe that this faubourg . . . shares the sentiments expressed in the petition."[104] During the King's trial, many Girondins contested the left's assertions of a unanimous demand for the King's death, and indeed the entire idea of holding a referendum on the issue reflected an individualist outlook. At times, even the Jacobins used an individualist outlook, such as when Danton proclaimed that "the general will as a whole can only be made up of individual wills."[105] Thus despite a trend toward even greater unanimism, individualist and pluralist descriptions of opinion still figured in the language of this period.

As orators outlined public opinion's role at this time, many continued to use the familiar concept of an informal "court of public opinion," in effect portraying public opinion as an alternative to state power. That outlook can be seen, for example, in one Jacobin's recommendation that France "extend [its] conquests by the path of opinion" rather than by the formal annexation of conquered territories.[106] In a slightly different formulation, however, public opinion appeared as a loyal auxiliary to official powers. Replying to calls for a new security force to defend the National Convention, *Le Patriote Français* maintained that "public opinion is the only dike that defends the legislators," and *Le Père Duchesne* wrote that the deputies would be "better guarded by opinion."[107] Others, however, preferred to portray public opinion as the leading partner, and Barère's claim that "opinion made the revolution of liberty, opinion alone can maintain it, [and] opinion alone can give activity and nerve to the Committee of Public Safety" supports Cochin's view that as the Revolution progressed, "opinion, a controlling power in its normal state, became a force of initiative and action."[108] Seeking the arrest of the Girondins, members of the Bonconseil section told the deputies that "the public voice indicates to you" who the guilty are, and these speakers ordered the Convention to "turn over to the tribunals these monsters that public opinion has already proscribed."[109] So whereas some viewed public opinion as a jury before which the accused might plead their case, others portrayed it as a prosecutor, dragging the guilty before formal authorities for punishment.

While some orators and writers depicted public opinion and the government cooperating, others saw a more adversarial relationship. This perspective arose in part from the Convention's rejection of a true separation of powers, which led some to assign public opinion the role that rival branches would otherwise have played (a concept that recalls the physiocrats' ideas).[110] Hence the repeated insistence of deputies and others that ministers explain their actions to the public, and the many petitioners who invoked public opinion in demanding the censure or recall of unpopular deputies. Of course public opinion lacked any legal means of coercing governments, forcing frustrated citizens who invoked public opinion against the state to seek other ways of implementing their will. A group of petitioners from the faubourg Saint-Antoine came up with one idea in May 1793, ending its list of demands by warning of an insurrection and by informing the deputies "that nine thousand men are at the doors of this hall."[111] So whereas some had envisioned public opinion surrounding the Convention to defend it, others had in mind a force surrounding the Convention with its weapons pointing inward. Unfortunately, given the anxieties about public opinion described above, the idea of public opinion dictating to the state seemed just as troubling to many as a government unchecked by its power.

The task of reaching consensus about the public's wishes should have become somewhat easier with the expulsion of monarchists and conservatives from public life after 10 August, but despite that narrowing of the political spectrum the ascertaining of public opinion remained problematic. Much of the difficulty in reaching consensus had to do with the mistrust and bitterness separating the Girondins and Montagnards, but it also arose from many people's growing sense that things were rarely what they seemed on the surface. The Revolution, in short, had become obsessed with conspiracies and the unmasking of traitors—a consequence, in large part, of the Revolution's own strictures on public expression, which forced the disgruntled to hide and to use clandestine means of communication. Also complicating attempts to discover public opinion were fears of an "artificial" public opinion based on the manipulation and deception of the people.

This pervasive air of suspicion naturally made the reading of public opinion seem even more difficult. "Citizens, do not be fooled," the Girondin Marguérite-Elie Guadet warned the Convention in April. "One only seeks to surround you with artificial opinions in order to hide from you the real public opinion."[112] Also, as modern students of public opinion often note, people tend to assume that the opinions they hear among their own circle of friends and associates accurately represent national opinion, and though there are countless examples of that illusion in revolutionary France, at least some of the French questioned such samples' representativeness. Buzot, for one, pointed out the difficulty in a large republic of knowing the opinions of "those whom one does not see and whom one knows poorly," and indeed for anyone in Paris, the patterns of opinion in the rest of the country often remained a great mystery, a kind of latent force that might alter the Revolution's course at any moment.[113]

Among those who tried to investigate what people were thinking outside Paris was the National Convention, whose decision to send "representatives-on-mission" to the provinces reflected a desire both to ascertain and to shape opinions. Illustrating the Paris Jacobins' similar interest, one speaker at the Club explained that "the Society is convinced that one of the subjects most worthy of its concern is to know what the public spirit of the departments is," and Chabot told the Jacobins that "the only way to know [the] general will is to consult it."[114] The idea that public opinion needed careful verification certainly figured in the Girondins' pleas for a referendum on the King, as one orator averred that "a presumption cannot dispense with the duty of recourse to the sovereign."[115] Yet when Louis-Pierre Manuel said "we will only work amid uncertainty" without a referendum to prove the public's support for the end of monarchy, Brissot replied that holding a referendum would itself create uncertainty.[116] As that exchange showed, it was one thing to agree on the need to verify people's opinions and another to agree on a suitable method.

One possible method, more often implied than formally proposed, involved deducing people's opinions from their socioeconomic status, reducing the study of opinion to a kind of census operation. For those who saw France divided into two groups, the "sans-culottes" and the "aristocrats," there might still be the problem of deciding who belonged in each category, but one Jacobin seemed quite sure that the sans-culottes outnumbered aristocrats by ninety-nine to one.[117] Dismissing proposals for a referendum on the Girondins' fate, Chabot claimed that "the sans-culottes are the majority of the republic, so it is unnecessary to appeal to the departments."[118] Answering the question of how the sans-culottes might articulate their will, some suggested that because they had, in effect, voted with their pikes on 10 August there was no need for a referendum, an argument that supports Soboul's idea that "armed insurrection constituted the extreme manifestation of popular sovereignty."[119] Yet others suggested that because the foot soldiers who stormed the palace had been mere pawns, that insurrection was not an authentic expression of the popular will. Robespierre answered such charges by writing that "this immense people, this innumerable multitude of citizens of all conditions [had been] acting in concert, without leaders and without any rallying point," but insurrection remained a sharply contested form of expression of public opinion.[120]

For those on the left, taking Parisian opinion as proof of public opinion seemed appropriate. If nothing else, this method was easier than sounding out opinion in distant provinces, and speakers often described public opinion based on quick tours of the local cafés and public places near the National Convention. Aware of doubts about Paris's representativeness, various speakers offered theories to justify this method. For Danton, Paris was "the advance sentinel of the Republic"—so that Paris expressed the opinions that the provincials *ought* to hold whether they actually did or not—and for Chabot Paris was "the center of enlightenment, where that of all of the departments ends up."[121] Others made a virtue of necessity, saying that Parisians had to speak for France because the National Convention met in Paris. For the Jacobin leader André Jeanbon Saint-André, Parisians were "obliged by their position" to play a special role, and a group of Parisian petitioners claimed that "their position alone" entitled them to speak for France.[122] Addressing the "sans-culottes of the departments," *Le Père Duchesne* argued that "if . . . you had witnessed all the betrayals" the Parisians had seen, "you would not have waited as long" as they had to demand the Girondins' ouster.[123] Finally, many simply denied there was any difference between the Parisians and the rest of the French; a deputation from the Paris Commune claimed on 31 May that Paris was an "extract of all the departments" and "the mirror of opinion," and Robespierre called Paris "a kind of general gathering point . . . that is constantly renewed by citizens of this vast state" arriving there. "It is not a city of 600,000 citizens that you accuse," he told the Girondins, "it is the French people, it is the human species, it is public opinion."[124]

As these comments' defensive tone suggests, however, many rejected such claims. Invoking the principle of equality and warning of "the despotism of Paris," Lasource insisted that "Paris must be reduced to a one eighty-third share of influence, like each of the other departments."[125] Although not everyone in the departments resented Paris's power, the Convention did receive countless complaints, including a letter that asked how Paris could "give a fair idea of the wishes of the departments" and called on the Convention to "study public opinion . . . [but] not in the combined wishes of the Paris sections."[126] In addition to denying that Paris could represent France, many questioned whether the militants who spoke for Paris even deserved that right. When Danton, for example, referred to a group of anti-Girondin petitioners as "the people of Paris," a heckler called out, "They were not the people of Paris."[127] Sounding several common themes, Jean-Bonaventure Birotteau claimed that "only eight to ten thousand citizens vote in the sections, the others being kept away by terror," and that "twelve to twenty individuals" often met in the section's hall after the meetings adjourned and passed decrees "often disavowed the next day" by the rest of the section's members.[128] Buzot undoubtedly spoke for many in saying, "I am far from regarding the clamors of a portion of the inhabitants of a city as the expression of the national wish."[129]

A closely related issue was the ongoing controversy over the role of spectators in the Convention's galleries. As we have seen, that role had been debated since 1789, but these debates now grew even more bitter as the spectators, now made up almost entirely of sans-culottes, became even bolder. Buzot attacked the "habitués" of the galleries, "bribed, no doubt, by the aristocracy," and reminded his colleagues, "We are not the Paris Convention, nor that of the galleries, but of the entire Republic."[130] Emphasizing the small number of individuals in question, one deputy said it was only "some fifty citizens [who] sow confusion and disorder in the Convention," and *Le Patriote Français* wrote that "the galleries are almost always filled with the same individuals, . . . two or three hundred lazy people who besiege all the entry ways early in the morning and keep out the patriots, especially those from the departments."[131] Even *Révolutions de Paris*, which shared the crowds' political views, admitted that "the entire people are not in the galleries."[132]

Seeking some way to keep Parisians from monopolizing seats in the galleries, the Convention adopted a system in which each deputy could distribute a certain number of admission tickets, but that system quickly broke down. The spokesman for a committee investigating complaints from citizens denied entry reported that "some women have seized the right to police the doors of the Convention's galleries and . . . they have been tearing up the tickets of those who appeared, insulting and threatening them."[133] The Montagnards, of course, opposed any measures to keep the militants out of the galleries; Robespierre even wished the Convention could build "a vast and majestic edifice open to 12,000 persons" where "the general will alone would be consulted."[134] But when a Jacobin deputy, opposing the use of admission tickets, asked rhetorically whether the galleries would be open to the public or not, one of the Girondins shot back that "the real question is not that, but the following: will the galleries be salaried by the Jacobins or not?"[135]

As these debates showed, many considered the sans-culottes in the galleries and streets mere puppets of the Jacobins. But for their supporters, the clubs were the very voice of public opinion, or, as one petition put it, "centers of the public spirit."[136] In November, Robespierre told the Convention that "experience has proved . . . that the opinion of the Jacobins and the popular societies was that of the nation," and a month later a speaker at the Club asserted that "the public spirit is only pure at the Jacobin club."[137] For the Jacobins, gauging the popular mood outside Paris often involved little more than sending a member to visit the Club's many provincial affiliates and then report back on "the public spirit" or "public opinion," but their findings were often unpleasant, and as Michael Kennedy reports, the reading of letters from the affiliates "often reduced the Paris Jacobins to 'sober silence.'"[138]

Facing skepticism about their claims to speak for public opinion, Jacobin leaders often sought to orchestrate a popular cry, sending their followers petitions to sign and messages to repeat. Hoping to get rid of the Girondins, Augustin Robespierre asked the Club in April to "direct public opinion" and urge the people to "come to the bar of the Convention and force us to place the unfaithful deputies under arrest."[139] He thus outlined a kind of circular process, as Jacobin leaders (nearly all of whom were deputies) created a message and sent it out to their followers, who then came to the Convention repeating it in the name of the people. The deputies could then invoke these statements of the popular will, even if doing so amounted to quoting an echo of their own voices. These messages needed to seem spontaneous in order to have much credibility, but the endless accusations that the Jacobins were behind the petitions suggest they were unconvincing. At the Convention on 26 May, while Marat was helping a barely literate sans-culotte read a petition protesting Hébert's arrest, Chambon interjected: "The speaker does not know how to read very well. Since the address's author is next to him . . . and is spelling it out for him, why doesn't he just read it himself?"[140]

Even if virtually no one was contesting the right of petition, just what a petition proved remained in dispute. When Rabaut Saint-Etienne called the "multitude of addresses" the Convention had received on the King's fate "the only means we have of knowing public opinion," he was referring to that correspondence as a whole, but individual petitions routinely claimed to speak for all of France.[141] Much of the problem with petitions, then, involved the difficulty of using them to learn the overall distribution of opinions in France, and many complained that the number of petitions arriving at the Convention said less about patterns of opinion than about the ability of a well-oiled political machine like the Jacobin Club to mobilize its members.

Moreover, petitioners' claims to speak for entire categories of the population often elicited protests from those supposedly represented. Replying to an inflammatory petition that had purported to speak for "the entire city of Marseilles," Barère suggested that the citizens of Marseilles "will no doubt be surprised to read in the papers the opinion that a handful of men" had attributed to them, and a rival deputation from Marseilles later told the Convention, "You have not always heard the free wish of the people of Marseilles, [as] one has sometimes presented you with nothing more than a phantom of it . . . put forth by a small number of anarchists."[142] Amid bitter power struggles in the sections, such disavowals became common, as many complained of signatures gathered by force, the drafting of after-hours declarations, and the signing of petitions by women and children. These complaints severely weakened a primary channel of public expression.[143]

The suspicions surrounding all of these informal images of public opinion led many to look to election results. Those citing the Convention's election as a manifestation of public opinion saw messages such as approval of the 10 August events and a desire to punish the King, and many argued that the voters had granted the deputies what Jeanbon called their "unlimited confidence."[144] Given that many departments sent in no written texts containing any such grant, Jeanbon's conclusion amounted to a claim that simply by voting people had approved the request for unlimited powers, but if the mere act of voting meant a positive response to the Assembly's request, then what was one to make of the roughly 85 percent of the eligible electorate that had chosen not to vote?[145] Questioning claims about positive mandates from the voters, Pétion told the Montagnards, "You say that the people sent you to decide Louis's fate. . . . So where are these mandates that have thus extended your sovereignty?" Barère replied by asking, "Where are the limits on our mandates?" but if that reply managed to nullify Pétion's challenge, it also produced a rhetorical stalemate that illustrated the limits of trying to glean information about public opinion from election results.[146] Finally, deepening concerns about strong-arm tactics in the voting halls and other irregularities now generated even more skepticism about election results' ability to represent public opinion.[147]

Even had elections provided a clear view of the citizens' opinions, they would still have offered only a snapshot of their views. For some, referenda offered a way to know a changing or undeclared popular will, but as we have seen, the Girondins and Montagnards, despite taking turns supporting the principle of the referendum, clashed whenever either party actually proposed one. In contesting their rivals' proposals, speakers also raised certain theoretical objections. Asking, "How could one gather 6 million citizens?" and "How could one manage to make them deliberate?" Barère held that referenda could not work "in a numerous nation, which cannot gather in a single place," and he also embraced the idea that all representative authority dissolves once the sovereign assembles.[148] The following Montagnard proposal for a referendum question on the Girondins perhaps best illustrates the difficulty of finding broadly acceptable questions to ask the voters in such a polarized environment: "Will the French people keep these cowardly men who have betrayed equality, these men who trembled before the idol of the dethroned tyrant, among the mandataries who are writing a constitution for them?"[149]

With so many methods of ascertaining public opinion subject to bitter disagreements, some deputies looked to the Convention to act as the public's voice. Calling it "impossible to believe that a nation spread across more than 25,000 square leagues of territory could speak in any way other than through its representatives," Barère declared that "the National Convention is the voice of the people," and that "it alone strikes down all abuses, by the force of public opinion, to which it gives birth."[150] In the view of another deputy, "The National Convention represents the French republic entirely and perfectly," and still another held that "it is here, in this hall, that the nation's spirit must reside."[151] Although one might expect the deputies to favor such a convenient doctrine, not all of them did. Chabot maintained that the deputies' reading of the general will needed constant verification by referendum, without which "you will never have anything but the opinion of the deputies, which is not always in accord with the general will."[152] And though Robespierre insisted that each "patriot deputy" indeed articulated the popular will — arguing that "to stifle his voice is to stifle the voice of the people" — he refused to equate the Convention's opinions with public opinion as long as the Girondins remained part of it.[153] So with all these formal and informal representations of opinion provoking bitter controversy, public opinion remained a source of authority that all recognized in theory but that no one could really use to settle disputes or legitimize authority.

As for the difficulties historians face in analyzing France's legitimacy crisis, the problems already noted in chapter III certainly still apply in this period, but one problem that became even more serious after August 1792 was the pervasiveness of violence and intimidation. Deputies and citizens alike were already subject to extensive coercion by August 1792, and all of the Legislative Assembly's decisions on or after 10 August were tainted by the absence of deputies who had fled for their lives. Some of the French did protest the 10

August events, but the administrators of the Somme Department learned the consequences of doing so when the Convention voted to arrest them for saying that the 10 August uprising had been illegal.[154] The September massacres and the government's failure to punish the perpetrators (or even to condemn the events in clear terms) certainly heightened the atmosphere of terror in late 1792, and rumors of violence again circulated during the King's trial.[155] This atmosphere of intimidation naturally raises serious questions for historians seeking to assess patterns of French opinion in that period.

A related problem concerns the lack of reliable measures of opinion. In this period there are reports on local opinion filed by the representatives-on-mission, and though they contain some useful information, they are marred by the reporters' failure to adjust for their own biases. Indeed some of these reporters, whose mission included shaping opinion as well as observing it, seem to have done little more than visit the local Jacobin Clubs and radical sections and then proceed to describe opinion in the entire department. But if the reporters did not mention those biases, others certainly did. A group from Marseilles, for example, complained to the Convention that "your representatives, upon their arrival in Marseilles, surrounded themselves with nothing but subversives and anarchists."[156]

As for using elections for the National Convention as evidence of national opinion, the many problems noted earlier raise serious questions. Also, as Alison Patrick points out, most people voted with little sense of what had happened in Paris on 10 August, since conservative papers had been silenced and the Legislative Assembly's communiqué had offered a very biased tale of the events that failed to mention the Paris Commune's role at all.[157] Once again the lack of declared candidates stating programs undermines any attempt to find political opinions in the voting, and both Malcolm Crook and Patrice Gueniffey note that patronage networks and kinship-based factional struggles often had more to do with voting in the provinces than did preferences among the rival groups in Paris.[158] Writing that "the opinion of the electoral assemblies does not reflect that of the primary assemblies, and the latter do not at all express the opinion of the country," Gueniffey concludes that "it is impossible to describe the state of opinion using electoral results."[159]

Despite these problems, it is possible to offer a few general comments on patterns of opinion in this period. One of the first points to note is that on many of the issues being debated in Paris, countless citizens probably did not have opinions. Recalling what Eugen Weber has told us about France's more remote areas as late as 1870, one may wonder how people speaking various languages and dialects, living in extremely isolated areas, and feeling resentful and inferior toward the overwhelmingly urban political class felt about trying to follow events that can be confusing even to modern historians. Although everyone in France was unquestionably affected by the Revolution, millions most likely had no opinions on many specific issues, and probably thought about the entire Revolution in ways that do not fit the categories and concepts familiar to revolutionary leaders and modern observers. Thus despite the enfranchisement of many "passive citizens" (raising the electorate from about 4.5 million to about 6 million out of a population of some 25 million), most adults did not use their political rights. The Revolution, in short, was in many ways a contest waged by minorities speaking for and posing as majorities.

Although the risks of voicing opposition to the Revolution make it especially hard to gauge that current of opinion, by late 1792 a significant number of the French opposed much, if not all, of what the Revolution had become. Offering a glimpse of the counterrevolutionary outlook, a group of rebels in the Vendée sent a message to the authorities in Paris, saying, "We have risen up to combat the disastrous principles with which you have overthrown the throne and the altar," and the group demanded "laws that are not without force and a religion that is respected." The rebels' statement that "France, formerly so flourishing, is now nothing more than chaos" exemplifies a way of judging the Revolution by comparing present and previous living conditions, and anyone who judged the Revolution that way may well have found it wanting in a time of war, severe shortages, high inflation, and chronic political turmoil.[160] The Vendée rebels were not the only ones staunchly opposed to the King's arrest and execution, and many historians believe that sympathy for the King rose during his imprisonment and trial.[161] And though deducing opinions from abstention rates is always hazardous, at least some who now abstained did so out of opposition to either the Revolution or its current path. Crook reports that "there are numerous examples of refusals to comply" with even the relatively bland oath voters had to take in 1792, as people appeared at the polling places only to turn around and go home rather than swear.[162] Finally, there is the evidence of the revolts breaking out throughout France. Whether these revolts were the tip of an iceberg would be hard to prove, but of course it takes more than a little discontent for people to risk their lives rebelling against their government.

Another way to assess opposition to this regime is to read the revolutionaries' own descriptions of opinion. Already in late August, a Jacobin reporting on the Tarn Department announced that "the public spirit, which the *journée* of 10 August had reinvigorated, seems to have changed greatly since then," and that one even heard Lafayette defended "in the public places [and] in the cafés."[163] Other Jacobins returning from their travels informed the Club that "the priests still reign over opinion in a large part of the Republic," that public opinion "is as corrupted as in 1791," that "opinion is lost in the departments," and that in the big cities "one almost finds nothing but corrupt and cowardly men."[164] A representative-on-mission reported that in Lyons "the public places resound with the most seditious cries, which are not rejected by public opinion," while one in Brittany found that "the public spirit in this department was deteriorating daily, that fanaticism was making great progress, [and] that the inhabitants of the countryside made daily processions from parish to parish, from chapel to chapel," proclaiming their support for monarchy.[165] Poor leadership and the lack of monarchist newspapers left this current of opinion relatively powerless, but these reports show that even the Jacobins doubted their own claims that only a handful of "aristocrats" opposed the regime.

Just as depressing to the left were reports of widespread support for the Girondins—including the support of many Jacobins outside Paris. One speaker just back from the provinces told the Club that "Roland is regarded as a God there," while another announced that "the departments are infected with the *virus brissotique*," and a third asked the Club's directors to "spare us the displeasure of constantly listening to diatribes sent to us by the [provincial] societies, which are patriotic no doubt, but totally misled."[166] In addition, one may interpret the Montagnards' rejection of various referendum proposals in part as a reflection of their estimation of how most people would have voted. These pessimistic views of provincial opinion were probably fairly accurate, and Michael Kennedy reports that even among the Jacobin Clubs, the Girondins had more supporters than the Montagnards.[167]

Nevertheless, it would be a mistake to accept the view, offered by the Girondins and some conservative historians, that the left only had the support of a band of determined militants. As historians have long argued, the abolition of the remaining seigneurial privileges earned the Revolution enormous gratitude in the countryside, and those reforms remained incomplete in August 1792. Several historians also see a leftward movement of opinion between August 1792 and June 1793; Kennedy, for one, sees the King's trial as a crucial moment but adds that the trend continued throughout the spring, in part because the Montagnard representatives-on-mission were doing a good job of spreading their party's viewpoint to people who often knew little of what was happening in Paris.[168] Nevertheless, a leftward movement of opinion is easier to demonstrate inside the National Convention—where the Plain was gradually shifting its support toward the Mountain throughout the spring—than in France as a whole, and as Kennedy notes, as late as spring 1793 most of the provincial Jacobin Clubs remained moderate.[169]

Although one cannot really speak of the Plain as a party, it may well be that this uncommitted center, the largest current of opinion inside the Convention, was also the largest current outside the Convention. Many citizens favorable toward the Revolution, that is, refused to side with either the Girondins or the Montagnards, and by spring 1793 the Convention was receiving a flood of letters urging the factions to end their quarrels and write a constitution. "The divisions that exist among you afflict all of the French," wrote one popular society, which also asked, "What do these words mean: Mountain, Valley, right side, left side?"[170] Another letter told the deputies, "You have lost sight of the important object of your mission," as "scandalous debates and constantly recurring quarrels have changed the sanctuary of the laws into an arena of gladiators."[171] Calling on the deputies to "impose silence on these insolent galleries that dare to interrupt your deliberation," a letter from Mayenne recognized "neither Plain nor Mountain," and a Club from Saint-Tropez complained that "your scandalous debates are the cause of the anarchy that is desolating France."[172] Also attesting to this pattern of opinion, Kennedy counted 130 Jacobin Clubs favoring the Girondins, 56 favoring the Mountain, and 583 favoring neither in spring 1793.[173] These patterns were not lost on the Girondins and Montagnards; Vergniaud, referring to "the state of discontent and exasperation that all spirits are now in," warned the deputies in April that allowing a national vote to recall unpopular representatives might lead to a massive purge of the Convention.[174] The Montagnards, despite their eagerness to see the Girondins removed, seem to have shared Vergniaud's perceptions and his reluctance to allow a recall vote. In short, if one takes the electorate and the individualist model of opinion it implied as a basis for assessing the distribution of opinions in France, it seems safe to say that opinion was highly fragmented, with a sizable group opposing the Revolution (or the Republic) altogether, another supporting the Girondins, a third backing the Montagnards, a fourth having some sympathies for the Revolution but refusing to back any party, and a fifth having no opinions at all on many issues.[175]

In seeking to explain this regime's ongoing legitimacy crisis, there is no need to dispute many familiar arguments, such as those emphasizing the effects of the economic crisis, but there are certain aspects of the political culture and the politics of public opinion that deserve greater emphasis than studies of this period have given them. One problem that grew worse in this period was the weakness of any distinction between legitimacy (in the sense of people accepting their leaders' right to govern) and popularity (defined as people liking or actively supporting those leaders). In many democracies, after all, leaders may retain a basic level of legitimacy despite lacking popularity, but the growing French insistence at this time on the citizens' right to revoke their representatives at their first moment of displeasure essentially nullified any distinction between these two concepts. Leaders, in short, had to remain popular at all times, a requirement that few modern democratic leaders could meet.

Also affecting the regime's quest for legitimacy was the republican antipersonalism noted earlier. That mistrust of popular leaders originated in the deputies' concerns over the reverence the King enjoyed, but suspicion soon surrounded any individual who grew too popular. Making frequent references to Caesar (and to Brutus), the deputies quickly rejected all proposals to allow popular election of a chief executive, or even to bestow certain honors on the president of the National Convention.[176] Just before one Jacobin complained that Roland was viewed almost as a god in the provinces, the Girondin deputy Jean-Baptiste Louvet had warned of Robespierre being viewed as an "idol" or a "god"; he reminded the deputies of their vow "never to consent to the substitution of the sacrilegious idolatry of a man for the holy love of the fatherland," and even some radicals voiced suspicions of Robespierre's popularity, as Hébert, for example, wrote that he was "not among those who regard Robespierre as an oracle and who [want] to make him their idol."[177]

This refusal to allow popular leaders probably contributed to the regime's legitimacy crisis. The French often stressed the need for authority to be vested in the executive in a time of war and internal crisis, but the Convention refused to yield its powers to an independent executive, and the resulting governmental inefficiency cannot have helped promote faith in this regime. The Convention did eventually create a powerful executive, but the Committees of Public Safety and General Security were never widely admired, in part because they were not directly elected, and in part because in creating them the Convention forced citizens to focus their affections on committees instead of individuals. As Marcel Gauchet has observed, governmental power "demands, in order to be perceived and recognized, a firm association with a person, quite unlike the acephalous image cultivated by the Revolution."[178]

Prevailing interpretations of the concept of sovereignty also had much to do with the ongoing legitimacy crisis, particularly the idea of sovereignty as a limitless authority that any group of citizens could use against their representatives at any time. Intertwined with that doctrine were specific ideas about representation, whose legitimacy now came under increasing attack. Some of the attacks came from outside the Convention, but many came from the deputies themselves. No better example of such attacks can be found than the following declaration by Marat, whom many Parisian militants adored:

> Friends, we are betrayed! To arms! To arms! . . . Your greatest enemies are in your midst, they direct your operations. O vengeance!!! . . . Yes, brothers and friends, yes, it is in the Senate that parricidal hands tear at your entrails! Yes, the counterrevolution is in the government . . . in the National Convention! . . . Make petitions rain down manifesting the formal wish for the instant recall of the unfaithful members who have betrayed their duty. . . . With their prompt expulsion the fatherland will be saved!!![179]

Although this speech used an unusually hysterical tone, these ideas could be heard regularly in Paris by early 1793.

Much of the deputies' attack on their own authority can be traced to the blatant opportunism that guided their rhetoric on representation. Historians have often pointed out that the Jacobins may be quoted speaking either for or against representation, a situation that reflects their desire to undermine representative authority when the Girondins controlled the Convention and to strengthen it when they began to take power there.[180] Yet the Girondins could be just as opportunistic, promoting ideas dangerous to representation in moments such as their campaign for a referendum on the King. So instead of a carefully formulated theory of representation presented at the outset, the parties offered a series of ad hoc arguments made to serve short-term partisan goals, and the cumulative effect of these arguments was to erode the citizens' belief in the deputies' right to make decisions for them.

As important as it is to examine legitimacy in terms of how citizens viewed their government, the deputies' habit of encouraging citizens to question their leaders' right to represent them indicates the need to view legitimacy in horizontal terms as well. Put simply, the Girondins and Montagnards did not accept each other's authority, and as Alison Patrick writes, neither "saw any need to accept inconvenient decisions [of the Convention] as legitimate, however arrived at."[181] This problem may be seen as a product of the insistence upon unanimity and consequent attitudes toward dissent. The Jacobins, often charged that the Girondins' opinions were not just mistaken, but even criminal—one orator insisted that "moderation is a crime in times of revolution"—and they acted on that idea by arresting the Girondins in June 1793.[182] Yet the Jacobins were not alone in such attitudes. In October

Roland issued a report stating that "a party of the opposition, so necessary against the despotism of one or the aristocracy of several, becomes disastrous in a regime of equality."[183] And just as Robespierre derided "the right to have a will against the general will," Barère called it "lèse-nation" to oppose an "expression of the general will."[184]

As in the previous period, some leaders did voice support for pluralism and the toleration of dissent. One deputy, for example, told the Convention, "I am far from wishing to imitate the example, all-too frequent today, of making a crime out of my colleagues' opinions and of slandering those who think differently from me," and another called it "impossible for us all to have the same opinion on the means of assuring the public good."[185] Even at the Jacobin Club, one orator criticized "the domineering spirit of certain members . . . who want their opinion and nothing but their opinion to be heard," and he urged his listeners "to get used to finding it good that others might not always be of their opinion and to allowing others to present opinions that at times differ from theirs."[186] And in reply to those who considered dissent against a majority decision criminal, Barère reminded his colleagues that "if the deputies who succeeded today persecute those of a condemned opinion, soon those roles could change."[187] Some of those pleading for freedom of opinion even alluded to the Inquisition, including one deputy, who opposed new press regulations by urging the Convention not to "reestablish censorship and the inquisition," and a speaker at the Jacobin Club, who opposed a colleague's idea of burning rivals' pamphlets by asking, "So are we in Salamanca?"[188] These speakers remained in a minority—the news that crowds had attacked a Girondin print shop in March brought applause from the left side of the Convention—but their pleas for pluralism show that the intolerant and unanimist path France took represented a conscious choice among thinkable alternatives.[189]

Historians have shown that before 1789 those interested in the formation of public opinion valued sociability, politeness, and civility. Such values also appear in this period, as many letters sent to the Convention begged for civility and admonished the deputies for their bitter personal attacks, and even some of the deputies agreed. Asking for calm, decency, and dignity, a deputy from the Plain proposed the censure of anyone who launched personal attacks in the Convention, and the deputies did eventually pass such a decree, barring any deputy from calling another a *factieux* (subversive) or a *scélérat* (scoundrel).[190] Yet Marat, who might have been speechless without such terms, called the decree the work of "traitors" and proclaimed, "I laugh at your decrees."[191] Indeed the resolution was soon ignored, and though the deputies who presided over the Convention's sessions kept trying to promote civility, they were often completely powerless, as order broke down and the deputies spent long periods screaming insults at each other.

As the art of invective reached new levels, many orators used medical and corporeal metaphors, such as when Robespierre demanded the amputation of "the gangrenous portion of the Convention," or when *Le Père Duchesne*, seeking the Girondins' expulsion, wrote that the Convention would only act forcefully once "it has vomited up this excrement."[192] At other times they turned to the animal kingdom for metaphors. The future terrorist Jacques-Nicolas Billaud-Varenne, for example, predicted that the Mountain "will crush the reptiles that crawl at its feet," and Jeanbon opposed new rules against Girondin journalists, urging the Convention simply to "let these vile insects croak in the mud and the slime."[193] Threats of violence also became common, as one Jacobin, for example, claimed, "We will not enjoy liberty until the conspirators have been exterminated," and Robespierre announced that "liberty will triumph when all the scoundrels I am denouncing are in their tombs"—a statement that brought "violent interruptions" from the right and center but applause from the left and the galleries.[194] In short, the abandonment of the search for civility and the use of hyperbolic, hateful, and violent personal attacks made it harder to create a viable political community or to form something recognizable as public opinion.

Unanimity being utterly unrealistic even in a far less dysfunctional political community than this, a more attainable goal would have been the kind of indirect consensus in which people agreed not upon specific leaders and policies but merely on the procedures used to choose leaders and policies and resolve disputes. Unfortunately, the French could agree neither on the basic principles of political life (beyond a few vague platitudes) nor on the procedures for granting or reconfirming leaders' authority, and inside the Convention the deputies continued to skirmish over parliamentary procedure, failing, after more than eight months, to agree on a constitutional draft.

Much of the problem had to do with the habit of proposing procedures that obviously favored one party's interests in a given conflict, but an even more fundamental problem involved lingering doubts about the very idea of legitimation by numbers. The Jacobins spoke confidently about their popular support at certain moments but turned deeply pessimistic at other times. Robespierre's famous comment that "virtue has always been in the minority on the earth" was but one example of this questioning of the foundations of democracy, as another Jacobin asserted that "patriots are not counted, they are weighed" and that "a patriot from the Mountain must weigh more than

100,000 *Brissotins*."[195] Speaking against the referendum on the King, one of
the Jacobins stated that if the people were to vote to spare the King, that
would simply be "proof that they do not see their true interests," and he
urged his colleagues to "make the people happy in spite of themselves if necessary."[196] Such statements, which contrast the reason and virtue of the few
with the ignorance and gullibility of the many, not only bring to mind prerevolutionary ideas (as well as later theories of the revolutionary vanguard),
but also point to a major cause of the ongoing legitimacy crisis. The deputies,
in short, disagreed not just on the means of resolving their disputes but even,
at times, on the very criteria of political legitimacy.

Under such conditions, it is not surprising that the rhetoric of public opinion did little to resolve political disputes. The frustrations that the participants in these debates voiced indicate that they knew their efforts were failing, and with the constant heckling and "murmurs" in the Convention one
could hardly have thought otherwise. Already on the eve of the 10 August
uprising an exasperated Jacobin had told the Club, "No more letters, no
more petitions; the French must turn to their arms, their cannons, and lay
down the law," and by late May 1793 the left had once again reached the
point of laying down its rhetorical weapons in favor of more efficient
ones.[197] Of course the leaders' ability to assemble a large armed force suggests that their rhetoric had at least helped mobilize their own sympathizers,
and it may even have swayed some of the uncommitted. As the historian Albert Mathiez wrote, the *fédérés* and others arriving in Paris often "abandoned their apprehensions and gradually passed over to the party of the
Mountain" once they came in contact with local militants—*Le Père Duchesne* wrote that they had been "*sans-culottisés*"—and though we have few
records of the words spoken in these encounters, it seems likely that invocations of popular sovereignty and public opinion helped persuade those arriving from the provinces.[198] The left's rhetoric may also have helped intimidate many deputies of the Plain through "third-person effects," as deputies,
though not personally persuaded by a message, assumed others would be
and adjusted their behavior accordingly.[199] It may also be that leaders, in
claiming the people's support for actions that often violated the law and
their own proclaimed principles, managed to convince *themselves* of the justice of their actions, though perhaps this was not such a difficult task. Nevertheless, the rhetoric of public opinion in this period appears not to have
convinced rivals or produced consensus, and indeed the more effectively this
rhetoric galvanized one's followers, the more deeply it alienated other parties and made broad legitimacy even more elusive.

Aware that they were facing a profound legitimacy crisis, many leaders, particularly the Girondins, tried to promote greater respect for the law and for the country's formal institutions. Alarmed at the actions of the new, more radical Paris Commune that had pushed aside its predecessor on 10 August, Roland insisted that "all insurrectionary powers must be temporary . . . and the regular functioning of laws must be reestablished promptly" once previous authorities have been toppled. Newly formed insurrectionary powers must thus "give the example of obedience to the laws," but he charged that the new Commune was leading people to "disdain and ignore constituted authorities." Insurrection, he concluded, was "a sacred duty against oppression but a damnable revolt in a state of liberty."[200] Once again, however, the efforts of one group of leaders to inculcate certain ideas among the citizenry were undermined by a rival group. Defending the new Paris Commune, Robespierre argued that Roland and others might as well condemn the primary and electoral assemblies and the sections as well, for before 1789 "all those things were illegal, as illegal as the Revolution, as the fall of the throne and the Bastille, as illegal as liberty itself." France's guiding principle, he claimed, should not be the law, but rather "public safety."[201] Unfortunately, that concept, unlike the law, was hopelessly vague and could not be used to settle disputes among political rivals. So whereas the events of 1789 had shown that a regime cannot rest solely on laws but must also have some degree of popular support, events were now demonstrating that regimes could not rest solely on a force as nebulous as "public opinion" but must also have laws and some means of enforcing them as well.

Explanations of why legitimacy remained so elusive throughout these months do not account for why it was the Mountain that eventually prevailed. For years French historians suggested that the Mountain gained control of the state because it had the support of "the people," but more recent studies have suggested that the Girondins probably had more supporters, and throughout most of this period they also controlled many of the levers of power within the National Convention and the government. Why, then, were they defeated?

A large part of the reason concerns the Girondins' many tactical blunders and other problems outside the scope of this work, but there are issues related to patterns of opinion that may help explain the Girondins' downfall. Although there were probably more individuals favoring them than backing the Mountain, the support of "the departments" ended up counting for very little in practical terms. This was true in part because of the issue of the intensity of opinions, for although passions did run high in some parts of the provinces, no one could really match the zeal of the Parisian militants who attended sessions of the Convention and their sections on a daily basis. Power, in other words, was not secured through a kind of electoral contest in which all opinions were equally weighted—though even in elections the Jacobins' ability to turn out their highly motivated followers helped them thrive amid very high abstention rates—but rather through a contest in which the intensity of opinions and the willingness to act and use violence counted for a great deal.[202] Aware of this problem, Roland complained of the sections being controlled by "ardent men whose fantastic imaginations or violent passions produce only excesses," adding that because of this "savage ferocity" and a "kind of tyranny that stuns or constrains good sense by its audacity . . . the weak or timid citizen is pushed aside."[203] Invoking a kind of silent majority against the Jacobins, Guadet declared, "Let the majority stand up and you will see this faction return to the void," and indeed the Girondins believed the departments would march on Paris if the Convention were attacked.[204] A few uprisings did take place when the Girondins were expelled from the Convention, but for the most part their supporters resigned themselves to defeat.

One reason why many of the Girondins' supporters failed to act concerns problems of communication, with news from Paris often taking up to two weeks to arrive in many departmental capitals and even longer to reach outlying villages.[205] As a result, by the time news arrived, people knew they were hearing about events that had happened quite some time ago, a situation that must have made many people feel helpless. An angry letter from Bordeaux read in the Convention on 14 May expressed concerns over the deputies from the Gironde, but the authors worried that "perhaps they are no more," and though this group swore to avenge their deputies if necessary, many others probably resigned themselves to the situation.[206]

As historians have pointed out, another reason why many of the Girondins' sympathizers failed to take up arms to defend them was their reluctance to rebel at a time when France was at war. Second, the fact that deputies did not legally represent the districts that had elected them may also have weakened the impetus for revolt. More importantly, however, the Girondins' support in the departments also amounted to little because the very concept of "the opinion of the departments" was only an abstraction. Not only was opinion divided in each department, but the departments as a whole had no positive common identity, no shared tradition of action, and only the most rudimentary channels of direct communication among themselves, so that their chances of acting in concert were virtually nil.[207] "The opinion of the departments" may have been a useful rhetorical device, but transforming a vast array of individuals and local organizations hostile to the Montagnards and the Parisian militants into an effective and coherent army was another matter.

What this situation shows is that "public opinion" simply did not determine the outcome of this period's main power struggle. Securing power ultimately remained a matter of using force effectively, and Paris had a clear advantage in that kind of contest. Whereas the Parisians, for example, could take part in an insurrection while missing little work and sleeping in their own beds at night, provincials seeking to overthrow the government had to abandon their work for weeks on end and undertake long and difficult expeditions facing numerous practical obstacles, and whereas the Parisians were already organized in military units based on the sections, the provinces had no such organizational basis or unified command. In short, with power resting on military force rather than a tallying of votes or opinions, the Parisian militants had enormous advantages despite their inferior numbers. For Cochin, the victory of *le petit peuple* over *le grand peuple* recalled the Lilliputians' victory over Gulliver, and he wrote that by June 1793 "the little people were now sitting in mastery on top of the huge body lying on the ground, and the bloodletting was beginning."[208]

V

❧

The Terror

If an advantage in physical force allowed the Jacobins and their allies to defeat the Girondins, they knew that the legitimacy of their actions remained very much in question, and they must have felt considerable anxiety as they waited to see how their fellow citizens would react. Fueling those anxieties were the realizations that not all of the Girondins had been arrested and that some of those arrested had managed to escape to the provinces, where they would soon be spreading unfavorable accounts of the events. One such account, by Gensonné, stated that "conspirators, after having seduced or misled a small part of the citizens of Paris, have subjugated most of the inhabitants of this city through the fear of arrests, have seized the powers of the constituted authorities, [and] have taken over control of the armed forces, the revolutionary committees, and all the sections."[1] The task of justifying the August 1792 coup had been hard enough, but this time one could claim neither that the target had been a hereditary monarch nor that the deputies expelled had been chosen by an electorate that excluded the poor.

At first, the movement's defenders did little more than declare the Girondins guilty, saying little about who had reached this verdict, what right they had to issue it, or what the evidence had been. A few days later, however, a communiqué from the Paris Commune sought to address provincial resentments, stating, "You have seen the people of Paris rise up as a whole . . . to do for you what you could no longer do for yourselves," and asking, "What have they done if not what the French people would have done had they been here?"[2] Another report then took a more theoretical approach, insisting that popular sovereignty included the people's right to recall their representatives at will. Asking the deputies, "By what right would you presume to prohibit the sovereign from revising or reforming its own work?" it claimed that "each part of the sovereign possesses not only the right of this initiative but also the right to pronounce definitively on your dissolution or total or partial expulsion." The report also called it impossible "for the same thought, the same proposal, the same wish to be manifested spontaneously at the same time, on the same day, at the same hour by all 85 of the departments," and because the sovereign could only express its will "through the successive wish of all [its] divisions, . . . one of these parts must be the first to propose the question and to declare its wish." Once again, Paris had shouldered the burden, and though the report claimed that Paris's acts awaited confirmation by "the majority of the other integral parts of the sovereign," the new leaders never held a referendum on the Girondins' fate.[3]

Before 2 June such claims would have provoked heated debate in the National Convention, but the lack of such debate this time underlined the significance of what had occurred. Many of the remaining deputies undoubtedly had grave doubts about the legitimacy of the recent events, but few dared to protest, and a kind of eerie calm descended on the Convention. The remaining deputies continued to meet, but records of their sessions show very few debates on political matters, as they now concerned themselves with administrative affairs. With power now mainly residing elsewhere — in the Committees of Public Safety and General Security, in the Paris sections and Commune, and in the Jacobin Club — the Convention did little more than rubber-stamp others' decisions, and even the new constitution drawn up in June gained rapid approval with little discussion. The spectators in the galleries also took a lower profile, with accounts of the sessions now containing few references to cheering or jeering from the galleries. Outside the Convention, the situation was more complex; the Girondin press had been largely silenced and many local affiliates of the Jacobin Club now abandoned their support for the Girondins, but in some provinces outrage over the events of 2 June soon produced a series of so-called federalist revolts.

French political theorists have long associated the doctrine of popular sovereignty primarily with this moment of the Revolution. The most prominent of these theorists, Carré de Malberg, defined popular sovereignty as a kind of direct democracy in which an actual collection of citizens exercised its will through voting, defined as a right. National sovereignty, on the other hand, involved the theoretical sovereignty of an abstract nation (in which voting was merely a function) and allowed representatives to use their discretion, amounting to a de facto sovereignty of the state.[4] This distinction has some value, as the 1793 Constitution called the people rather than the nation sovereign, and the ideology of direct democracy also asserted itself even more fully in 1793. Yet one should not overstate that distinction, for as we have seen orators routinely referred to popular as well as national sovereignty before June 1793, and after that date the Jacobins still used the terms "national" and "nation" in discussions of sovereignty. Also, as the previous chapters have shown, the theory and practice of direct democracy were hardly unknown from 1789 to 1793, coexisting uneasily with that of representative democracy throughout that period. Finally, whereas Carré de Malberg focused on the 1793 Constitution in his discussion of popular sovereignty, it must be noted that the rulers of that regime never put their own constitution into effect.[5] The language of the 1793 Constitution aside, then, how did the revolutionaries of this period interpret popular sovereignty?

Virtually all public voices in this period agreed that popular sovereignty meant the supreme and unlimited authority of an indivisible entity, the people, to act however it saw fit, including having the right (at least in theory) to remove "unfaithful mandataries" and to approve all their actions and laws. This definition was not new, but as several historians have noted, the Paris Jacobins, who dominated this regime, thought of sovereignty in less quantitative terms than some of their predecessors, attributing it not to the collection of all French citizens but only to a kind of vanguard of the virtuous.[6] Therefore, rejecting electoral definitions, the Jacobins, following Rousseau, saw the will of the people as an abstract, eternal, and necessarily virtuous general will rather than the fallible expressed desires of a majority of the current citizens. So whereas Carré de Malberg describes the sovereign people as an actual collection of individuals expressing their will through voting, R. R. Palmer writes that "Robespierre's 'people' was the people of his mind's eye, the people as it was to be when felicity was established," while Jaume speaks of "a future people," and Annie Geoffroy calls Louis Antoine de Saint-Just's idea of the people "the expression of an ideal" rather than "an objective reality."[7] Exemplifying this outlook was Saint-Just's October 1793 comment that "the people err, [but] they err less often than men do."[8]

Although an abstract, idealized notion of the people certainly figured prominently in the theories of this period, one also finds many more sociological characterizations. Of course one often encounters the old concept of the people as the lower classes, as in Saint-Just's comment that "bread belongs, by right, to the people" rather than to "the rich man."[9] The term "sans-culottes" also appeared frequently as a synonym for the people or the lower classes, even if historians from Soboul to Furet have shown that given the mixture of shopkeepers, small property owners, and wage-earners in that group, the term was more a political than a sociological designation. Sociological descriptions of the people could be simplistic, as in the Dantonist Louis Legendre's defense of an accused colleague as a man "born in the class of the people," or they could paint a more complex picture, as in Edme Bonaventure Courtois's statement that the Jacobins spread enlightenment "throughout all the classes of the people."[10] As the latter statement suggests, some speakers admitted that virtue could exist in the middle classes, but most held that it increased as one descended through the social hierarchy — an inversion of the prerevolutionary outlook.

The idea of the sovereign people as an abstract and idealized future entity produced ironic consequences. Despite writing a constitution that outlined a more direct democracy than ever, the regime's leaders, calling for "revolutionary government" to remain until war and counterrevolution ended, suspended that constitution indefinitely and prohibited the elections that were to have followed its adoption. Those actions were consistent with the idea that what guided the state was the theoretical will of an abstract people — that is, what the people *should* want, or *would* want once enlightened, rather than what they did want, or thought they wanted, at that moment. What resulted, however, was a system far closer to Carré de Malberg's idea of national sovereignty and "sovereignty of the state" than even the previous constitution had dared to create. Carré de Malberg's concept of parliamentary sovereignty (used to describe the Third Republic) also seems to apply here, even if it was primarily the Committee of Public Safety rather than the National Convention as a whole that exercised power at most times. So although references to popular sovereignty did not disappear from the government's lexicon in this period (as Soboul contends), the term now acquired a new meaning, and actual practice seemed even less "popular" than before.[11]

Although four years of egalitarian rhetoric had undoubtedly helped undermine belief in representation, there were still some who defended that concept after June 1793. In his newspaper, *Le Vieux Cordelier*, the Dantonist deputy Camille Desmoulins wrote that "a representative is no more infallible than he is inviolable," so "he must be allowed to be mistaken."[12] In the Girondin deputy Jacques-Charles Bailleul's view, it was "to the philosophe alone, to the man who reflects, that the faculty of arranging the means of government, of a system of legislation, belongs, for the philosophe has learned to reflect, as the artisan has learned the trade he exercises." The people, he insisted, lacked the qualifications to participate in the drafting of laws, and were "only a good judge of their effects." Drawing on an ancient idea, he argued that although one might tell a shoemaker whether a shoe fits, one would not try to tell him how to make that shoe.[13]

The Jacobins found themselves in a delicate position on this topic, for although they now had reason to promote belief in representation, they had come to power in part by attacking the practice. It helped somewhat that the Jacobins had also defended representation at certain points, and they now emphasized this aspect of their thought, with Robespierre even calling representation "sacred."[14] Representation was legitimate, the Jacobins argued, as long as the people chose truly virtuous men to represent them, and as long as there were mechanisms allowing the citizens to control and remove their delegates at any time. All such mechanisms were suspended, of course, under the emergency regime of "revolutionary government" (implemented in October 1793), but the Jacobins could at least point to their dormant constitution as proof of their good intentions, and as for virtue, Robespierre and his colleagues were hardly shy about proclaiming their own merits.

Of course with the advent of the Terror, denouncing the hypocrisies of France's new rulers, or even attacking the practice of representation, became extremely dangerous, but despite the risks, a few bold souls carried on that revolutionary tradition. Among the deputations from the Paris sections that still came to petition the Convention, a few continued to address the deputies as their subordinates, and the Cordeliers promised that their new version of Marat's *Ami du peuple* would publish "denunciations . . . particularly against unfaithful mandataries of the people."[15] Even bolder was Hébert, who complained in *Le Père Duchesne* of "the buggers who govern us," and of a Convention that seemed "to have forgotten it has promised the people, its master and sovereign, that it would no longer work with lawyers, officials, journalists, and clever wits."[16] Angry at the Convention for not doing more for the people, Hébert insisted that "when the entire people command, their servants must obey," and he even likened the powers of the Convention's ruling committees to the absolute power of kings. "Liberty is screwed," he concluded, "when all powers are conferred on inviolable men."[17]

The government naturally bristled at such attacks, and the terrorist Lazare Carnot, speaking for the Committee of Public Safety, warned that if people kept criticizing their representatives for "the inevitable errors of a large administration, it would make the rapid and robust action that all governments must have absolutely impossible."[18] Similarly, Barère complained that in Paris "people keep putting up posters directed against the National

Convention" and "agitating, misleading, fooling," and "stirring up" the people against their representatives.[19] The Jacobins found it hard to break their
old habit of sending deputations to the Convention to protest the government's actions, but now that Robespierre was in power he quickly grew irritated at this practice. Telling the Club it could not keep "sending deputations
to the Committee of Public Safety at every instant," he stated that "one must
suppose that the Committee is made up of men of intelligence and political
judgment and that it has some idea of how to use these qualities."[20]

The Club seems to have heeded his message. When a speaker in January
1794 attacked the Convention for one of its appointments, Robespierre, noting that "the Convention cannot be insulted," invited the Club to "swear
death to the traitors who would degrade the Convention," and the Club com-
plied.[21] He also told the Convention that "the fatherland is lost if the government does not enjoy unlimited confidence," and he warned the government's
critics that "they will go from being accusers to being accused."[22] That threat
proved real enough: when the Hébertists were arrested in March 1794, they
were charged with "degrading national representation."[23] Ironically, when
Robespierre himself fell from power in July 1794, his colleagues in the Committee of Public Safety charged him with "seeking to stir up movements
among the people" against their representatives.[24]

Yet the same speakers who tried to defend representation often helped undermine it at other times, as they answered their rivals' populist rhetoric with
even more populist assertions of the citizens' authority over those they
elected. In defending the Girondins' arrest, Fabre d'Eglantine stressed the
people's right to remove their representatives, reminding the deputies, "You
are here to represent [the people] because of the need for a concentration of
opinion and will, and not because of your wisdom," and telling them that "the
people are wiser than you."[25] Various speakers repeated the principle that the
Convention, in one Jacobin's words, "does not have the right to go against the
people's wish."[26] In September 1793 the president of the Jacobin Club told a
deputation from another club that "the sole existence of public misery suffices
to make criminals of those who are at the head of the state, and to authorize
the people to rise up and punish the guilty."[27] Perhaps just as harmful as these
assertions of the people's absolute powers over their representatives was the
rarity of positive arguments for representation, as orators mostly continued to
rely on the notion of the impossibility of assembling the nation.

One new way in which leaders addressed the dilemma of representation
being both inevitable and unacceptable involved trying to erase the very distinction between representatives and the represented, treating the two as in-

separable parts of a single body politic. One version of this theory made the sociological claim that those in government had been "born among the people" or "in the plebeian class," but because few deputies were really from the lower classes, that was a claim heard only rarely.[28] An even stronger version used organicist ideas of representation reminiscent of absolutism, with the government (or the Jacobins) considered the head, the voice, or the arms of what Jaume calls "the collective Person of the people."[29] Chabot, for example, admitted that the Jacobins had called for a given suspect's arrest, but he claimed that "the whole people accused him . . . [and] we have only been their voice."[30] Similarly, in April 1794 Collot d'Herbois declared that "the Convention . . . and the people themselves are but one," and in July he proclaimed, "The Jacobins are the Convention! The Convention is the people!"[31] In this outlook, the entire question of representation virtually disappeared, for governors and the governed were inseparable, even indistinguishable.

As for the structure of the country's representative institutions, many emphasized the need for more efficient and streamlined powers while France was facing invasion and civil war. Though the situation seemed to call for a strong executive, the executive outlined in the new constitution seemed far too independent and powerful to many, who perhaps shared Chabot's fear that "when one establishes an executive power, one sows the seeds of royalism."[32] With a separation of powers now out of the question, the Convention needed some way to act more efficiently, and it ended up vesting powers in the Committees of Public Safety and General Security (with the former gradually becoming dominant). In theory the committees' powers were limited and subject to frequent renewal but in practice were unlimited and renewed with little or no debate, so the committees, despite their denials, essentially became an executive branch. Rejecting a suggestion to rename the Committee of Public Safety the Government Committee, one of its members claimed it was merely "the advance-post of the Convention," and he insisted that "we are the arm it uses, but we are not the government."[33]

The denials notwithstanding, the Committee of Public Safety did govern, and its members brooked no interference from the Convention. The Committee identified itself as the arm of the people, but the head would have been a more accurate metaphor, for it essentially monopolized the tasks of thinking and speaking. Moreover, two heads not being better than one, that committee gradually pushed aside the Committee of General Security, usurping even its main function of supervising the repression of political opposition. The Committee also resented all intermediary powers such as local administrators, whom Saint-Just denounced as "functionaries who place themselves between the people and the national representation."[34] Even the Paris sections, which had done so much to create this order, now seemed more a threat than an asset, and though the committee wished to keep the sections at hand for use against the remaining moderates in the Convention, it soon passed severe restrictions on their right to meet and act. Doing so violated many of the leaders' proclaimed principles of representation, but as Soboul notes, "principles were subordinated to the demands of the policy of public safety."[35]

Contrary to some historians' claims, the terms "public opinion" and "opinion" did not disappear even in this period, as Robespierre and others still used them at least as frequently as they did terms such as "the public spirit." References to public opinion also became almost entirely unitary, so "public opinion" did not suggest division any more than "the public spirit" did. And indeed when Saint-Just proposed the use of the more egalitarian *conscience publique* in a speech on 15 April, the term he was proposing to replace was "the public spirit," not "public opinion." In his view, the public conscience originated in people's "hearts" or "consciences," where class-based advantages of education meant little, whereas "the public spirit is in people's heads," and "each person cannot have an equal amount of understanding and enlightenment."[36] Yet whatever misgivings he may have had about both public opinion and the public spirit, Saint-Just largely ignored his own plea to use the term "public conscience," using both of the former terms much more often. In her study of Saint-Just's rhetoric, Annie Geoffroy argues that the most common term in his political speeches was neither "the public conscience" nor "the public spirit" nor "public opinion," but rather "the people," a conclusion one could apply to political language as a whole at this time.[37]

This rhetoric also continued to employ a range of terms lacking consistently distinct meanings. Even the relatively common line between public opinion, a collective judgment, and the public spirit, a necessarily virtuous and revolutionary zeal, often disappeared. So while some defined the public spirit as a positive, if fragile, force that could disappear altogether — unlike public opinion, which always existed, for better or worse — the painter and Jacobin deputy Jacques-Louis David asserted that public opinion could not thrive under despotism, "or, more precisely, where one reigns, the other cannot exist."[38] And whereas those describing the level of revolutionary zeal in France often spoke of the public spirit rather than public opinion, one Jacobin proclaimed the need "to reanimate public opinion," and a deputy just back from the provinces claimed he had "revived public opinion" there.[39]

When speakers did propose distinct definitions, others often failed to embrace them. For example, ignoring Saint-Just's Rousseauian notion of an incorruptible public conscience, the Committee of Public Safety issued a decree in June 1794 that warned of those who were working "to corrupt the public conscience."[40] Therefore, as a group the revolutionaries had no clear sense of what each of these terms meant.

As for these terms' sociological referent, some speakers did use phrases that suggested differences between public opinion and the people's opinion. One source of such distinctions was the growing animosity toward the classes and groups whose opinions had once constituted public opinion, for as Bronislaw Baczko explains, "the Terror encouraged distrust of the cultural élite," including "scholars, 'artists,' [and] educated people in general."[41] Yet many continued to invoke "public opinion" and "opinion" and to equate those terms with the people's opinion, as in Saint-Just's contention that "opinion and the people have accused those I am accusing."[42] So whereas some distinguished between public opinion and the people's opinion, others did not, and even those making negative comments about public opinion could either have been referring to the suspect opinions of social elites or simply to the unfortunate current state of the opinions of a people still vulnerable to counterrevolutionary manipulation. Moreover, despite the growing nationalism and xenophobia of the time, some still invoked the opinions of "Europe," "the world," and "the universe." Yet if Desmoulins wrote that "the jury of the thinking universe" would judge the Revolution, and if Robespierre worried about what would happen "if we pass for imbeciles in Europe," at least one deputy dissented, asking, "What need do we have of a good reputation in Europe?"[43]

In characterizing public opinion and other such forces, many orators alluded to old, familiar qualities such as omnipotence, incorruptibility, and omniscience — the latter being especially useful in a time of rampant suspicion. "The sans-culottes," wrote *Le Père Duchesne*, "see everything [and] find out everything sooner or later," and one Parisian club warned conspirators "that the gaze of the people shines on all their conduct, that their ears seize their most secret words, that their wisdom uncovers their most hidden designs."[44] Yet others were more pessimistic, and many spoke of public opinion, the public spirit, or even the public conscience having been corrupted.[45] Some tried to distinguish between the incorruptible people and a corruptible public opinion, but that distinction was problematic, for if the people were incorruptible and public opinion was the opinion of the people, then how could public opinion be corrupted? Few speakers addressed this question, but one possible answer involved the idea of a distinction between the heart, which was presocial, and the mind, which was shaped by society; counterrevolutionaries, in this view, might poison the people's minds (and thus public opinion), but the poison could not reach their hearts or consciences, so the people remained pure. Another possible answer lay in the distinction between actual individuals and "the people" as an ideal, eternal entity. Finally, some references to public opinion being corrupted may have involved mere linguistic carelessness, as speakers overlooked Rousseau's distinction between the people being "corrupted" and "misled" or "mistaken."

Nevertheless, the idea of the people being misled was a remarkably common theme in this period. In Rabaut's words, the people of Paris were "easily fooled, misled, [and] stirred up," and he lamented that "one agitates them with false terrors" and "abuses them by flattering them."[46] Relative moderates such as Desmoulins might complain that "the French people as a whole" were not "enlightened and educated enough" to tell friend from foe, but even *Le Père Duchesne* despaired over the sansculottes' gullibility, calling them a "sheeplike species" and writing that they "cannot see farther than their noses."[47] Pursuing the myopia metaphor, the paper wrote that, especially in the provinces, people did not have "good enough spectacles to see what was happening in Paris."[48] Given these perceptions, it is not surprising that many were pessimistic about public opinion, complaining endlessly of the people being fooled and calling their opinions "vacillating" and "unstable."[49]

Enlightening the people thus remained a major concern, and the Convention now devoted considerable attention to plans for a national educational system. Underlying these plans was faith in the Enlightenment ideas of the universality of reason and the self-evident nature of truth. In Jeanbon's words, "The people of the Midi . . . may lack enlightenment, but when one shows them the flame of truth, they grasp hold of it," and Barère said that "a few rays of light are enough, and soon the people's reason grabs hold of it."[50] Still, complaints about public opinion and the people being gullible and fallible vastly outnumbered more optimistic assessments, leaving most leaders deeply reluctant to grant the people any real power, and ruthless repression of the press now sought to shield the people from dangerous words.

How one might ascertain public opinion remained another troubling question, now made all the more vexing by France's growing obsession with conspiracy and deception. Some supporters of the new regime found encouragement in the overwhelming vote in favor of the new constitution in June 1793, but one Jacobin questioned the authenticity of much of this support, arguing that "the aristocrats have agreed to support the constitution even in the

Vendée" simply as a ruse to protect themselves.[51] Making a common complaint about eleventh-hour patriots, Robespierre warned the Club that "today all the royalists are republicans, all the Brissotins are Montagnards."[52] Ironically, however, Robespierre himself eventually bore the brunt of this obsession with deception, as the men who overthrew him accounted for his previous popularity by explaining: "It is because the mask with which he was covered was almost impenetrable," and upon his arrest the Club proclaimed that "the mask has fallen."[53] While many warned of faces hidden by masks, others suggested that careful observers could spot false patriots by their faces. Barère, for example, claimed that in Paris one could "recognize the aristocrats by their long faces," and Couthon agreed, stating that "in times of revolution all the good citizens must become physiognomists."[54]

Those unskilled in physiognomy, however, needed other ways to gauge public opinion. The left had long equated spectators in the National Assembly with the people, defending their right to watch over their representatives and to applaud, jeer, and even heckle the deputies, but once in power the Montagnards refused to tolerate such behavior. On 5 August 1793, when a woman in the galleries merely called out, "Speak up," the deputies immediately reacted with "murmurs," and Chabot charged that "the cry that was just heard was a federalist cry." The Convention then voted to turn the woman over to the Committee of General Security.[55] But if the crowd in the galleries now lost its right to represent the represented, crowds in the streets of Paris and other towns might still claim or be accorded that right. Describing the scene at the Dantonists' execution, the *Moniteur Universel* wrote that "the unanimous cries of *'Vive la République!'* heard at the moment of the execution have proved that the jury's conviction" was indeed "the will of the people."[56] In addition to the reactions of crowds attending executions, the actions of crowds at revolutionary festivals were interpreted as expressions of public opinion. Desmoulins, for example, wrote that "the acclamations that the Convention received everywhere it passed on the day of the *Fêtes des Victoires* demonstrate the opinion of the people," and of course when a crowd invaded the Convention to demand the Terror on 5 September, some viewed these militants as the people.[57]

Many revolutionary leaders, then, considered crowds reliable indicators of public opinion, and with the Mountain's enemies now mostly silenced, such claims often passed unchallenged. Unfortunately, in rebellious areas crowds might offer unwelcome evidence. One Jacobin, for instance, concluded that opinion in the Jura opposed the government after he heard antigovernment crowds there cry out "Down with the Marats!" and "To the Guillotine!"[58] So to the extent that crowds' opinions were equated with public opinion, those who gained physical control of public spaces in effect acquired the power to articulate public opinion. Perhaps it is proper that only opinions expressed openly in the public sphere should qualify as public opinion, but it is by no means certain that the revolutionaries believed this, for their obsession with deception suggests that many remained deeply concerned about the opinions of the silent.

For the most part, objections to letting Paris represent France disappeared after June 1793, at least outside the areas in open rebellion. But if the bitter debates over Paris had disappeared, they had certainly not been forgotten, and various speakers could not stop rebutting their deceased or imprisoned rivals on that issue. "In a revolutionary tempest," insisted Robespierre, "there must be a rallying point," and because "the people en masse cannot govern themselves, this rallying point must be Paris."[59] For *Le Père Duchesne* Paris was not just any French city, but "the rendezvous of the universe," and because "its inhabitants were almost all born in the other departments," it was a true microcosm of French opinion.[60] So although the government continued to send agents to monitor opinion in the provinces, no one objected when one deputy offered proof of his descriptions of the opinions of "the people" by noting, "I have just toured a large part of Paris."[61]

Yet those who monitored talk in Paris's cafés and public places did not always like what they heard. Robespierre noted that if one believed such talk, he himself was "a moderate [and] a feuillant," and even *Le Père Duchesne* now called the Palais Royal "the rendezvous of all the impure and the scoundrels there are in the world."[62] Those now in power thus took a position like that of their predecessors, accepting Parisian opinion as a reliable gauge of French opinion when it was favorable and dismissing it when it was unfavorable, and few dared protest such inconsistencies.

Similar contradictions appear in the Convention's view of the Paris sections and the clubs. Deputies occasionally cited messages of support from the sections, but fears of their power led the state to impose restrictions on their right to meet and make public proclamations, and leaders also closed some of the more radical clubs that competed with the Jacobins in the provinces. Jaume cites a government document of December 1793 that called the clubs "the arsenals of public opinion" while also insisting that "the Convention alone gives [public opinion] the direction it needs, pointing out where it must strike." And despite admitting that the clubs "have, in a way, the initiative of public opinion," the document also asked, "Wouldn't their power, if usurped by conspirators, become dangerous for liberty?"[63]

Many statements suggest that officials considered the clubs' opinions note-worthy but did not equate them with public opinion. A deputy describing his visit to one town explained that "the people were heard from as well as the popular society," and another noted that representatives drew their strength "from public opinion and the opinion of the popular societies."[64] According to one Jacobin, the clubs played a useful role in the formation of opinion, for "the goal of these institutions is to enlighten the people."[65] Yet if clubs were distinct from both the state and the people, then their presence could seem unwanted at a time when leaders resented *corps intermédiaires*, and indeed leaders often seemed frankly hostile toward them. In December Robespierre charged that "a lot of conspirators" attend the clubs, "but the people are not there," and he unwittingly echoed conservatives in affirming that "while the idle and men of evil intent are deliberating in these societies, the people are in the workshops."[66] Another Jacobin said that "emigrés from Paris, men of the law, men of finance, [and] agents of the old regime . . . infiltrate the popular societies to mislead and corrupt the public spirit," and Saint-Just held that "the popular societies are filled with artificial beings" so "the people amount to nothing there."[67]

Yet if leaders generally refused to equate the clubs' opinions with public opinion, attacking them posed a problem for the Jacobins, who were after all members of a club. One way out of this quandary involved asserting a doctrine of Jacobin exceptionalism, which the deputy Jean Tallien did in urging the closing of all other clubs. Calling it "necessary that opinion have a focal point," he felt that France should have "a single society, which corresponds with the entire Republic, and which is the source of the good principles and of the public spirit."[68] Many Jacobins, however, were unsure about the Club's relationship to both public opinion and the government. Drawing a subtle (or unclear) distinction between the Club's opinion and public opinion, one Jacobin deputy stated that "public opinion has its base in this society, but opinion, in turn, reacts to it" as well, and Jacobins often denied that they were an unelected, behind-the-scenes government.[69] For the most part, they merely claimed to represent the represented, addressing the government in the name of the people and acting as "the eyes and ears of the people," but the almost total overlap between the leadership of the Club and the government, along with the Club's habit of speaking for the government in its public state-ments, made that idea hard to believe.[70] Designed to resolve the entire prob-lem was Collot d'Herbois's declaration, noted earlier, that "the Jacobins are the Convention" and "the Convention is the people." Though the parallel would have been unwelcome at the time, one might compare the Club's role to that which the parlements had claimed before 1789—simultaneously representing the people to the government and the government to the people.

With the Jacobins aspiring to monopolize the expression of public opinion, individuals could still send letters and petitions to the Convention. Yet most of the messages read aloud in the Convention came not from individuals but from local officials, the Paris sections, and the clubs, and the deputies rarely cited them as proof of public opinion. Perhaps the flood of angry letters and petitions the Convention received after the Girondins' arrest influenced their thinking, and indeed *Le Père Duchesne* wrote soon after 2 June that "all these petitions, all these threatening letters that are raining down upon the Convention from all sides are but smoke that will dissipate in the wink of an eye."[71] This skepticism toward letters and petitions also reflected the deputies' sense that their followers belonged to classes that rarely wrote letters, and orators often dismissed pro-Girondin letters and petitions as nothing more than the views of local elites. As for the regime's opponents, we have little evidence of their views about the letters and petitions read aloud in the Convention, but one written protest over the 2 June events probably expressed a common view in complaining that only progovernment messages now had any chance of being read in the Convention.[72]

As for election results, some speakers did cite the voters' overwhelming approval of the new constitution in June 1793, but such comments were rare.[73] Once again, low turnout made it hard to gauge public opinion, though a deputy who made the mistake of mentioning the recent abstention of 10 million citizens provoked "murmurs" in the hall and drew an official reprimand.[74] The very logic of elections, it seems, did not suit the prevailing concept of opinion; as Pierre Rosanvallon writes, "the vote as a manifestation of individual opinion . . . seemed an eminently suspect procedure in [the Jacobins'] eyes," and they preferred "that individual opinions fade away completely, melting into a single, unitary voice of the people."[75] Françoise Theuriot makes a similar point in writing that Saint-Just dreamed of "a harmonious fusion of the consciences of each member of society."[76]

Rosanvallon and Theuriot are right about the Jacobins' dislike of the individualism inherent in voting, but an even greater reason for their attitude toward elections during this period may have been, as R. R. Palmer writes, that "the ruling group knew that in a free election it would not be supported."[77] Of course the Mountain would not actually have lost any elections, having by now taken near-total control over the voting process in most areas, and the lack of secrecy of the ballot at this time made voting more a communal than an individualist exercise, but even the possibility of people registering their discontent now seemed intolerable. When one deputy proposed holding the elections that were supposed to follow ratification of the new constitution, Robespierre charged that this proposal "would only tend to replace the purged members of the current Convention with the envoys of Pitt and Cobourg."[78] And when another deputy recommended letting the voters elect their administrators, a colleague replied that "in a revolutionary government, entrusting the people with the election of public functionaries is a counter-revolutionary measure."[79] That statement did provoke "murmurs," but the objections probably had less to do with a desire to hold elections than with the speaker's decision to make such an undiplomatic comment.

Collot d'Herbois's claim that "the Convention is the people" suggests that some continued the tradition of equating government opinion with public opinion, as did the Convention's December 1793 decree that it alone had the right to speak "in the name of the people."[80] Yet the dismissal of any kind of public opinion outside the Convention continued to strain credibility, and though many deputies alluded to government opinion as public opinion, they rarely claimed that public opinion *only* existed inside the Convention or its committees. With the Jacobin Club available as a safe and reliable voice of public opinion, there was little need to use a theory that would be more likely to anger than convince even the regime's sympathizers.

As they looked for suitable methods of representing public opinion, the regime's leaders had an advantage their predecessors had lacked, namely, that those who might object to their ways of characterizing public opinion had either been executed, arrested, or otherwise silenced, and though the Montagnards must have been glad not to hear objections to their claims, that silence was not the sound of any real consensus. So the French, who had just barely begun the long and difficult process of developing and negotiating broadly acceptable standards for posing claims about public opinion, now essentially abandoned that task, as orators either cited evidence others had long questioned or presented no evidence at all. This lack of evidence made no difference insofar as speakers invoking public opinion had in mind not the actual opinions of living citizens but rather those of some abstract future community — what Palmer calls people's "fundamental, unrealized, inarticulate ultimate desires."[81] Nevertheless, if Robespierre, Saint-Just, and others certainly embraced the idea of a tiny elite monopolizing the right to speak for an imaginary future people, others undoubtedly harbored doubts about it, and even its true believers seem to have remained profoundly uneasy about having to ignore the opinions of actually existing citizens.

· · ·

However the French envisioned public opinion, and however they sought to invoke it, they still had to work out a theory of its role in the political system. The idea of public opinion as a tribunal or a jury judging cases brought before it remained common, but the idea of it as prosecutor ferreting out wrongdoers in advance of the formal authorities proved even more appealing in a political culture obsessed with the search for suspects. Desmoulins illustrated this idea in telling the Jacobins that "when a man is proscribed by public opinion, he is halfway to the guillotine," and after the arrest of the Dantonists, one of the Jacobins claimed that "public opinion [had] already struck down these criminals [and] anticipated the judgment of the Revolutionary Tribunal."[82] And lest anyone consider this authority less frightening than formal authorities, a speaker at the Paris Commune called "the sword of opinion . . . the most terrible and the surest weapon" any criminal could face.[83] This idea of public opinion as the accuser cooperating with the government recalls the role of the Inquisition, which merely accused and judged suspects before turning them over to princes for execution, and like those Inquisitors who could deny they had bloodied their hands, *Le Père Duchesne* denied that the Parisians had done anything wrong on 2 June by insisting that public opinion in Paris had merely accused the traitors.[84]

Within this unofficial diarchy, the question of which entity led and which followed remained unsettled. Some spoke of public opinion playing a reactive and supportive role, including Chabot, who declared that every "declaration of the Convention . . . is supported by public opinion," and one deputy, who assured his colleagues that "the people are there to support the energy of the Convention."[85] When Fabre d'Eglantine reported on plans for an annual *Fête de l'Opinion* to be held at the end of each year under the new revolutionary calendar, he also outlined a system in which public opinion would normally play a subordinate role. Envisioning a kind of carnivalesque annual inversion of authority, he explained that "on this single, solemn day of the Festival of Opinion, the law will open the mouths of all citizens regarding the morality, the composition, and the actions of the public officials," and "this single holiday will do a better job of keeping magistrates within their duties throughout the year than even Dracon's laws and all the tribunals of France could do." What he implied in the rest of his text was that for the other 364 days the public would remain silent and subordinate to governing officials.[86] Despite their assertions of public opinion's right to dictate to the country's "mandataries," then, these leaders seemed interested in finding ways to keep public opinion in a subordinate role.

Others, however, continued to portray the government as a passive, almost helpless entity that obeyed the dictates of public opinion. Robespierre, for example, praised a general recently rejected for a key post, but explained that "opinion was so much against him that the Committee did not dare appoint him," and he also called the minister of the navy "a man promoted to the ministry by public opinion."[87] Others made it clearer that they welcomed the idea of public opinion playing such a role. For the Cordeliers, "the unfaithful mandataries of the people" should be judged by this "irresistible tribunal," and one speaker at the Jacobin Club replied to a plea for even stricter regulation of the press by saying, "I do not believe that the deputies can allow themselves to direct public opinion, since it is public opinion that must direct them."[88] Nevertheless, the same orators who called for public opinion to rule over the state one day might complain of it having been "fooled," "perverted," or "corrupted" the next, and in such moments speakers usually said little about what role public opinion should play.

Those concerned about public opinion's influence on the state might have found reassurance in the Jacobins' idea of a pure identity between the government and the people, which offered possible grounds for the state to ban any public expression it disliked. The Committee of Public Safety, of course, often took such an attitude toward public expression. In his speech announcing the arrest of the Hébertists, for example, Saint-Just made the ominous pronouncement that any "resistance to the revolutionary and republican government . . . will be punished with death," and he justified that decree with the claim that "it is the people who reign today."[89] Unfortunately, this idea amounted to a denial of civil society's right to criticize its government, making the new system resemble the hated absolutism of the Old Regime. Public opinion, in other words, had originated in France as a tool civil society could use against its government, had then come to coexist uneasily with the government in an ill-defined relationship from 1789 to 1793, and had now essentially become a new name for the will of the government. In a way, though the rhetoric of power had changed dramatically since the prerevolutionary years, the government's intolerance of private citizens citing public opinion against it meant that France had come full circle, leaving the country with a crisis of absolutist legitimacy not unlike the one that had caused the Revolution in the first place.

Turning from the revolutionaries' ideas about the role public opinion should play to the ways in which the concept actually functioned during the Terror, it may be useful to recall Habermas's concept of "representative publicness." In characterizing the system of authority that preceded the rise of a true public sphere in Europe, Habermas described the typical lord or king who publicly "displayed himself, presented himself as an embodiment of some sort of 'higher' power," showing his power "not for but 'before' the people." In that system, rulers were the only legitimately public persons, though power remained "dependent on the presence of people before whom it was displayed." "The people" thus did not constitute a public (formulating and expressing its own critical judgments through free public deliberation) but rather an audience (merely watching and listening), or more precisely, both an audience and a group of extras participating in the pageantry and cheering on cue.[90]

Habermas did not use this concept of representative publicness in his brief comments on the Revolution, but it seems appropriate for analyzing this moment in the Revolution. For public opinion at that time was not the product of deliberation in an autonomous public sphere, but rather something only rulers were really allowed to articulate, and with the Jacobins shutting down newspapers and rival clubs, one could also say they had become the only legitimate public persons. As in prerevolutionary times, the people now played an important role as a supporting cast in a series of meticulously choreographed political rituals and festivals, but their participation did not involve the actions and functions of a public. In reporting to the Convention on a festival he was designing, for example, David read excerpts from his script, noting at one point, "All of a sudden, the people [will] raise their voices and cry out three times, 'they died for the fatherland!'"[91] Also telling the people what to say was a message the Jacobins sent to the departments after 2 June, which stated, "You will congratulate the Parisians," and "you will applaud the generous and peaceful insurrection."[92] And of course in addition to instructing the people what to say, these leaders routinely put words in the people's mouths, making up imaginary quotations.

To some extent, one could say that revolutionary orators in this period used their rhetoric less as a tool for gaining power — their previous proscription of their rivals having already given them a monopoly of the state's means of coercion — and more as a way to maintain that power, reminding all listeners of their political status by displaying their (exclusive) right to articulate public opinion. At times invocations of the people's will, supported by some well-timed cheering, might intimidate potential rivals, a useful function in a Convention still filled with mostly silent men of uncertain views; at other times those invocations might be part of the state's announcements of its will, a means of keeping all their supporters marching in step. At still other times they might serve to boost morale and rally the timid inside the Convention or the Jacobin Club.

Here it is worth noting that invocations of public opinion do not appear with uniform frequency throughout the debates of this period, but rather tend to cluster around moments when the government took its most politically risky steps, such as crushing a provincial rebellion or arresting members of a rival faction. At such moments, those in power often did their best to downplay their own role, using the concept of a pure identity between governors and the governed. Robespierre, always leery of accusations of his being a dictator, denied his responsibility for the Hébertists' arrest, insisting that "it is the fury of the people that crushed them" and complaining that although "one would like to have people believe that [the arrests] are the work of one man" they were in fact the work of "national opinion."[93] Similarly, one Jacobin orator proclaimed that "it is not to the Convention that we owe the decrees that have saved liberty, but to the energy of the people," and Jeanbon defended the Committee of Public Safety's actions by saying, "The Committee has deferred to general opinion, it has done its duty, for opinion is the queen of the world."[94] In making such statements, these orators were probably seeking not only to convince doubters, but also to persuade themselves of the legitimacy of actions they knew violated their own previously stated principles.

Assessing legitimacy becomes even harder in this period, when the epistemological problems already noted grew even worse. In short, the period's pervasive atmosphere of terror makes most evidence about public expression rather suspect. One indication of the problem is the behavior of crowds in Paris, which cheered Robespierre during his Festival of the Supreme Being in June 1794 but then also cheered his execution in July.[95] Of course the crowds on those two days may simply have been made up of different individuals, but it is also possible that people had learned to protect themselves against denunciation by zealous neighbors by feigning support for the regime and by going along with any opinion others were expressing.

The Terror, in addition to tainting evidence of popular opinion, also made many previous forms of public expression simply disappear. There were no elections held in this period, only the plebiscite on the constitution, and as Gueniffey notes, the rulers who organized that plebiscite used "the network of popular societies" under "the surveillance of representatives on mission" to assure a favorable result. Gueniffey calls the entire exercise "an organized mobilization, a controlled vote, . . . [which] does not constitute a photograph of the degree of popular support for the revolutionary government, but rather a sure indication of the capacity of the government and its local agents to supervise the country."[96] It is true that turnout rose in this plebiscite, but the pressure the government brought to bear undoubtedly had something to do with that, as did the practice of counting women and children among the voters in some areas.[97] Also, as Mathiez observes, "many voters had only voted for the constitution with the ulterior motive of getting rid of the Montagnards when it went into effect."[98] Thus with few other forms of expression available for examining voters' motives and intentions, it remains difficult to find messages in the plebiscite's results.

Serious problems also affect the representatives-on-mission's reports on local opinion. Many delegates painted implausibly rosy portraits of the local state of opinion, perhaps out of fear of being held responsible for any problems, or perhaps out of revolutionary zeal. "With palpable evidence to the contrary," writes Palmer, "they still believed the people enthusiastically behind them."[99] Rather typical was a report from the Aude department that the constitution "has been accepted unanimously by all the citizens in this department."[100] Ignoring issues such as the representativeness of their informants or the honesty of people's statements, representatives often reported hearing nothing but encouragement and praise wherever they went.[101] Oddly, however, the same representatives, once back in Paris, might well decry the pitiful state of public opinion or the public spirit in France. Their reports thus fit a general pattern in assessments of opinion in this period in that they alternated between extremes of despair and euphoria.

One reason for this inconsistency was the reporters' refusal to describe opinion as divided, but another concerned Jacobin ambivalence about the very nature and source of legitimacy. As Jaume argues, for the Jacobins "legitimacy did not reside in the law of numbers (voting) and conformity to constitutional norms; it was in virtue," that is, in the virtue of the leaders supposedly enacting the people's will.[102] Many an example supports Jaume's argument. *Le Père Duchesne*, for instance, complained that "seven-eighths of all men do not know what they want," making it necessary for a vanguard to take actions that a majority would dislike.[103] Similarly, one member of the Committee of Public Safety, Jean-Marie Collot d'Herbois, ridiculed the "mathematical calculations" of a colleague who had hesistated to attack a vastly superior number of rebels in Lyons; "What good are means of defense founded on a count of the number of patriots?" he asked, insisting that "even if there were only one patriot, . . . he would be heeded . . . because he has the entire people behind him."[104] And one Jacobin, dismissing a colleague's worries about the legitimacy of a Convention purged of so many of its members, called for the removal of even more "dead branches," asking, "What does it matter how numerous the branches are if they are diseased?"[105]

And yet one cannot portray the Jacobins' concept of legitimacy purely in terms of a belief in virtue over numbers, for their constant concerns about the large number of adverse opinions suggest some belief in quantitative legitimation. Illustrating this outlook, Saint-Just explained that "the difference between a free regime and a tyrannical regime is that in the former, force is used against a minority opposed to the general good," whereas in a tyrannical regime force is used against the majority.[106] Saint-Just, in other words, was claiming that the present regime had majority support and was merely using the Terror against a counterrevolutionary minority. Saint-Just was not alone in this kind of thinking, as his colleagues could not resist invoking majority opinion whenever it seemed favorable. Part of their belief in their own popularity rested on the syllogism noted earlier, in which they assumed that political opinions corresponded reliably with economic class, then noted that the poor vastly outnumbered the rich, and concluded that they must have majority support. As *Le Père Duchesne* wrote, "Almost all of the rich are aristocrats, all of the big merchants are thieves, . . . [but] fortunately, *foutre*, nineteen-twentieths of the nation are neither rich nor merchants" and "this mass is always pure."[107] Unfortunately, this regime's outlook on legitimation, a complex and inconsistent blend of quantitative and qualitative criteria, makes it hard to analyze the regime's level of legitimacy by the dominant standard of the time.

Historians who have grappled with this issue have inevitably taken some position in the debate over standards of legitimacy. Some have basically adopted the Jacobin view that legitimacy should be assessed in terms of the leaders' virtue — the debate between Mathiez and Aulard over Robespierre and Danton comes to mind — but for the most part historians have implicitly favored quantitative criteria, making individual opinions the basis of their judgments. Many historians have thus described this regime as "democratic" or "popular," implying that it indeed reflected the will of a majority of the French, but the evidence for such claims is quite thin, and in some cases historians seem merely to have adopted the revolutionaries' assumptions that political opinions and economic class correspond, and that a regime devoted to "the people" must have had majority support. One can indeed find evidence of support for the Revolution, the regime, and its leaders, including accounts of patriotic fervor in the war effort and messages the clubs sent the government thanking it for measures such as the *maximum* (a 1793 law limiting the prices of commodities). Again, some of these messages may merely reflect attempts at self-preservation or various other hidden motives, but it would be foolish to deny that some of the French sincerely backed a regime that may well have seemed to embody the Revolution's boldest hopes and accomplishments.

Nevertheless, even the most radical of the French were sometimes less than enamored of this regime, its rulers, and their policies. *Le Père Duchesne* undoubtedly reflected (and shaped) many Parisians' feelings as it repeatedly criticized the government for failing to crush counterrevolution and provide a steady supply of bread, and the Cordeliers' decision to cast a black veil over their copy of the Declaration of Rights reflected, among other things, anger at the government's dictatorial ways.[108] Historians of the sans-culottes have long emphasized their growing anger with the government by 1794; Mathiez, for example, noted that "beneath the apparent calm a profound discontent was brewing," and Rudé wrote that by summer 1794 Robespierre and his colleagues "had lost the support of the Parisian *sans-culottes*."[109] Rudé also reports an incident in which a group of Parisian workers, when told of Robespierre's arrest and asked to come to his defense, simply shouted *"Vive la république!"* and went back to work.[110] Some of the French did react angrily to news of Robespierre's arrest, but most contemporary observers and historians have stressed the weakness of the popular reaction on 9 Thermidor.

Discontent on the government's left was mirrored by what was probably an even larger (and growing) current of opposition on its right, comprising everyone from moderate republicans to constitutional monarchists and staunch opponents of the entire Revolution. Evidence of such opinions is naturally elusive, but Paul Hanson reports that messages of protest over the coup d'état of 2 June were drafted in forty-seven of France's departments.[111] Only in a few departments did "federalist" revolts erupt, and most of the rebels were local officials, but of course it is hazardous to gauge opinion by counting those willing to risk their lives in a revolt against a ruthless government.

Some evidence of moderate republicans' views appears in a set of statements from June 1793 that the Convention collected as evidence against the roughly seventy deputies who protested the Girondins' arrest. One petition called the Montagnards "conspirators" who appointed themselves "the sole organs of the general will" and "made the rest of the national representatives the passive instrument of their will," and it charged that only force and intimidation had allowed this faction "to extract from the Convention, or rather from the one-sixth of its members who [now] make it up," a decree authorizing the seizure of power. The text also denied that "Paris" had waged the attack, charging that "the majority of the inhabitants of this city"

had been "frightened by the proscriptions with which they had been inces-
santly threatened."[112] In another statement, Rabaut called the Paris Commune
"a usurping commune, which for the last year has enslaved two successive legislatures, and which governs through tribunes and commands through
pikes."[113] Several messages contested the rump Convention's legality and legitimacy. "The representation of the French people is no more," declared one
deputy. "It is not [the people] who have dissolved it, but rather a few brigands,
under the name of a section of the people."[114] The Convention did not permit
these messages to be read aloud, but several deputies sent such messages to
their departments, where others undoubtedly found them persuasive.

If dissenters could rarely voice their complaints publicly, the rulers and
their supporters sometimes inadvertently publicized their ideas in attacking
them. In April 1794 Legendre warned the Convention of "the intrigues of a
few counterrevolutionaries who want to make the people say, 'There is no
more national representation, no more freedom of opinion, since deputies are
arrested for motions made inside the Convention.'"[115] Another deputy cautioned that "the accomplices of the conspirators were saying yesterday,
'Today twenty deputies are going to the scaffold, tomorrow another twenty,
the day after yet another, and soon the Convention will be dissolved.'"[116] Still
another deputy reported that the disgruntled believed the Convention "was
worn out, that it needed renewal, that it was incapable of saving liberty, [and]
that those who governed so long with such great powers ended up wielding
tyrannical power."[117] And Hébert, reporting in *Le Père Duchesne* on the opinions he had heard during a recent tour of the provinces, wrote that some
claimed "that the Convention is enchained, that more than half of its members have been murdered, that it is surrounded by cannons and bayonets."[118]

The revolutionaries' own assessments of opinion thus attested, once again,
to a crisis of legitimacy. Some observers dismissed negative opinions as limited to the rich and powerful, but others disagreed. Immediately after the
Girondins' arrest, Robespierre spoke of the need to "reelevate the demoralized public spirit," and similar complaints continued to appear even when
the military situation improved in 1794.[119] Negative reports from the
provinces must have seemed endless. Couthon wrote from Lyons in October
that although the rebels had been defeated, "the public spirit is in ruins in
this wretched city" and "the patriots are in such an alarming minority that
we despair of ever rejuvenating them."[120] A Jacobin in the Gard department
reported that "the aristocrats are raising their heads" and "the people . . . are
indecisive," while another told the Club that "the situation in the Jura is truly
alarming."[121] Hébert informed the Jacobins that "in Rouen, as in all the large

commercial towns, the public spirit is very bad," and Robespierre lamented that "the public spirit has not changed in Marseilles" despite the defeat of a rebellion there.[122] Representatives-on-mission in Perpignan reported that "the people themselves are corrupted there," and a report from Vannes informed the Convention that out of twelve thousand inhabitants, only two hundred supported the Revolution.[123] Also indicating the leaders' sense of their own poor standing in France was their refusal to allow the election of the new assembly that was supposed to follow the completion of a new constitution. "The Committee," writes Mathiez, "was under no illusions about the real strength of the Montagnard party," and he adds that the Terror itself suggests a lack of popular support, for "only minorities, after all, have need of dictatorship and violence."[124]

So despite the difficulties of assessing opinion under such conditions, it appears that this regime was facing an even worse legitimacy crisis than those of previous revolutionary regimes. Nevertheless, if Palmer is right that "only a minority was even republican," it would probably be excessive to conclude that a majority was antirepublican.[125] For the number of *sans opinions* probably grew amid severe restrictions on the circulation of information and the dizzying series of events that saw men called heroes one day and led to the guillotine as traitors the next. Even in Paris, writes Mathiez, "the illiterate and miserable crowds . . . watched with bewilderment the events they did not understand."[126] Thus throughout France, though there were probably more opponents than supporters of this regime, both of those groups may have been outnumbered by those with a jumbled collection of conflicting opinions, emotions, and questions.

Explanations of this regime's legitimacy crisis have long emphasized the country's economic crisis, and though the link is real enough, it bears noting that much of this discontent reflected a disappointment of expectations that had been overinflated by demagogic rhetoric.[127] For in seeking to discredit their rivals, the men now in power had often blamed the country's economic ills not on the disruptions of the Revolution, but on the failures of France's leaders to crush counterrevolutionary hoarders and speculators. On countless occasions before June 1793, the Jacobins had attributed the economic crisis to the leaders' lack of political will or virtue, and they claimed they could end the crisis overnight if given full powers. Unfortunately, some of their allies persisted in making such arguments even after June 1793; in supporting the sans-culottes' demands during the 5 September invasion of the Convention, for example, Hébert wrote that with means of punishing "the enemies of the people" now in place, "in two weeks Paris and the whole Republic will have its subsistence assured for the entire year."[128] Insofar as people believed such promises, the anger they then felt over persistent shortages and inflation was not solely a product of economic circumstances.

Demagogic rhetoric also fueled unrealistic expectations of pure political equality. *Le Père Duchesne* wrote that "the republican constitution, in making all of the French equal, has destroyed forever the reign of the strongest," but the French soon found power even more concentrated.[129] Other problems included the new regime's intense centralization of power — which, according to Paul Hanson, played a major role in provoking the revolts of summer 1793 — while in Paris the government's harsh measures against the sections alienated some of the regime's most loyal supporters.[130] And for some, as we have seen, the forcible removal of some of the people's elected representatives undermined the Convention's legitimacy, while for others the Montagnards' refusal to implement the newly ratified constitution and to call new elections seemed to prove that they were bent on prolonging their own power.

The concentration of power in the Committee of Public Safety also elicited protests from the few voices still willing or able to criticize the government. *Le Père Duchesne* advised its readers, "Do not put up with your committees' meddling in the governing of the Republic," asking, "What good will it have done us to have destroyed our former tyrants if we let others take their place?"[131] Not long before his arrest, the Hébertist François-Nicolas Vincent attacked a decree increasing the Committee's powers, calling it "an assault on the people's sovereignty" and warning that the Committee was becoming "a monstrous power."[132] In defending the Committee's powers, Robespierre often used the syllogistic argument that because the Convention had the people's confidence, and the Committee had the Convention's confidence, the Committee had the people's confidence, but the indirectness of the Committee's popular mandate remained a problem that only worsened as its powers increased. Despite its members' rather disingenuous claims that the Convention could revoke their authority at any moment, that body in fact ruled France, and as many could see, it did so on the dubious basis of an extorted decree issued by a heavily purged assembly. For a regime so rhetorically committed to democracy, the vesting of nearly absolute powers in a committee not elected by the citizens must have cost it considerable support.

Given the revolutionary tradition of hostility toward personal power, Robespierre's rise to dominance also deserves mention. Clear evidence of resentment is naturally hard to find before Thermidor, but the outpouring of anger at Robespierre on 9 Thermidor points to long pent-up feelings. One deputy asked, "Will one man be the master of the Convention?" while Barère, insisting that "enormous reputations and equal men cannot coexist for long," declared that Robespierre had "gradually become the dominator of public opinion, and public opinion alone has the right to reign over a free people."[133] The *Moniteur*, which rarely made editorial comments in its reports from the Convention, could not resist writing that "the excessive influence of a single man is the most dangerous scourge of a republic."[134] The people, proclaimed Legendre, "will never again adore anyone," and when a delegation from one section then seconded that point by declaring, "We swear never to give a reputation to an individual," the deputies and the spectators in the galleries also swore to that oath.[135] Outside Paris, Robespierre's powers had certainly angered many officials, journalists, and political activists, who began voicing their complaints after 9 Thermidor.

Also weakening the regime's support were its policies on public expression. As Jaume explains, the Jacobins by this time favored a Rousseauian concept of liberty that valued a fusion of civil society and the state, as opposed to the liberal concept of guaranteed individual rights, and the application of this notion led to a dismantling of the barriers guarding the public sphere from state interference.[136] So whereas publicity had once been seen as a light shining on the government for the benefit of those deliberating in the public sphere, it now increasingly came to mean a light shining on the private lives of public figures and private citizens. In justifying censorship, speakers at the Jacobin Club insisted that a free press, though crucial under a dictatorship, was unnecessary in a republic, for a government of the people could not possibly oppress the people, and Chabot undoubtedly expressed the regime's outlook when he demanded that all writings "opposed to the principles of this government be exterminated along with their authors."[137]

But did these policies generate discontent, or did they simply reflect a general consensus in a famously illiberal period in French history? Here it must be noted that many complaints about censorship and repression did appear at this time, reflecting stronger currents of liberal thinking than one might expect. In the Convention, for example, Anne-Alexandre Thibault protested the government's policy of opening mail and searching travelers on the roads, and he also defended the deputies' right to express dissent, calling it unrealistic for "the 740 of us here . . . all to have the same opinion on any given decree."[138] Desmoulins also defended liberal ideas, and he charged in *Le Vieux Cordelier* that English journalists and members of parliament were freer than their counterparts in France—a virtually suicidal statement given the hatred toward England at that time.[139] He also wrote, "I no longer see anything in the Republic but the dull calm of despotism . . . [and] an equality of fear," and he demanded that liberty be something more than "this 46-foot high statue that David proposes."[140] Even Chabot, who had just demanded the extermination of dissenters, said there should not "always be a single opinion on all the decrees" in the Convention, adding, "If there is not a right side, I will form one by myself, even if I should lose my head, so that there will be an opposition and so one will not be able to say we pass decrees out of blind faith and without discussion."[141] One speaker at the Jacobin Club also praised free discussion, maintaining that "this society is the sanctuary of liberty and the place where one has the right to express all of one's opinions."[142]

If such protests over restrictions on public expression reflected the thinking of many others less willing to speak up, then the regime's repressive policies indeed contributed to its legitimacy crisis. Of course resentment over restrictions on public expression was probably stronger in the upper and middle classes, but people of all classes may have eventually grown weary of the denunciations, the atmosphere of fear, and the seemingly endless political violence, eventually coming to doubt the legitimacy of a regime that relied on such methods. That revolutionary terror and violence should become a source of legitimacy crisis was of course ironic, for the Terror had been conceived as a mechanism of legitimation, designed to create a regime of virtue by ridding the body politic of its impurities. But the Jacobin deputy Claude Basire was probably not alone in his misgivings about what he called "a system of terror which seems to herald the ruin of the patriots and threatens us with a new tyranny."[143]

Another crucial problem for the regime concerned the effects of the revolutionary penchant for excluding adversaries from the national community, a practice that now reached a new level. Ever since the publication of *What Is the Third Estate?* revolutionaries had identified undesirable groups whose exclusion would supposedly clear the way for a stable and legitimate political order. For Sieyès and others in 1789 it had been the privileged orders that stood in the way; in 1791 revolutionaries insisted that France could reach its goals if it could rid itself of Lafayette and his associates, the Feuillants; a year later it was the King and all royalists whom the revolutionaries wished to exclude; yet no sooner had the King been removed than the militants saw the Girondins obstructing the way. And with their removal, it was not long before the Jacobins found new enemies, arresting longtime colleagues such as the Hébertists and the Dantonists. Thus the exclusion of enemies, instead of bringing legitimacy and an end to the Revolution, became, as Rosanvallon writes, "a permanent motor" of the Revolution, a kind of mainspring that

propelled the Revolution forward without ever bringing it nearer to a conclusion.[144] Indeed, the series of exclusions, by shrinking the regime's political
base to an ever narrower portion of the spectrum of opinion, was making political stability and legitimacy even more elusive.

One way to see this problem more clearly is to consider the concept of
virtue, which figured so centrally in the regime's system of legitimation.
Given France's profound political divisions, the revolutionary vanguard's
references to virtue simply could not create authority or arbitrate political
conflicts. Indeed, unless any country already enjoys broad consensus on the
meaning of virtue (hardly the case in France in 1793), then its definition is
one of the key tasks of politics and public deliberation. But rather than en-
gaging their opponents in a dialogue about its meaning and the means of
identifying it in individuals, the regime's leaders chose to treat those opponents as traitors. Some of the French were undoubtedly so hostile to the Revolution that deliberation would have accomplished little, but many others
were not, so taking this approach toward all opponents cost the regime any
hope of securing broad support.

The choice of that approach, however, reflected much more than a tactical
miscalculation. It arose instead from the Jacobins' basic philosophy of democracy, which rejected liberal democracy's moral relativism and its willingness
to treat all individual preferences and opinions equally.[145] For the Jacobins,
democracy necessarily required the valuing of certain absolute, positive
moral principles that were beyond discussion and that had to be accepted at
the outset by all participants in the system. Yet in a community so deeply divided over the very nature of the good (or of "good citizens," to use a ubiquitous phrase), the Jacobins' philosophy of democracy simply could not work, a
point that may help explain the regime's reliance on terror and its lack of legitimacy. At least in this historical case, then, it may be true that democracy
demands a certain moral relativism and an essentially proceduralist and
quantitative approach to legitimation.

Like invocations of virtue, invocations of the authority of public opinion
also failed to give this regime the legitimacy it needed. With elections having
been suspended, and with the government operating without any democrati-
cally approved constitution, it was all the more crucial for France's leaders to
secure legitimacy through informal means. Yet the prevailing means of invoking public opinion, particularly the use of pure assertion, cost such rhetoric its
credibility, and the valuing of an abstract future popular will over people's actual opinions proved no more successful. At the beginning of this period, many
citizens, at least in Paris, may have found that rhetoric convincing, but it seems

highly unlikely that it did much to build ties or secure obedience from those outside the loyal core of followers, and even those followers began losing faith by summer 1794. By that time, it appears that the government was resting almost entirely on force and terror. Of course all regimes make some use of force and intimidation to guarantee their rule, but those that fail to persuade as well as to coerce — to *convaincre* as well as to *vaincre*— generally do not last for long, and this was surely a regime whose blend of persuasion and coercion was severely out of balance.

Nevertheless, this regime, despite having so many opponents, did not actually fall to an external attack by "public opinion" or any other force, but rather destroyed itself from within as its leaders turned on each other. At least in the short term, then, the problem lay not with the extent of opposition, but rather with the regime's obsession with that opposition, with its absolute refusal to tolerate or ignore it — indeed to see resistance where it did not even exist. In trying to do away with every last iota of opposition, the regime promoted certain forces that proved fatal to itself, namely, a pervasive attitude of suspicion designed to root out and destroy every last dissenter. One can cite no better indication of that force's damaging effects than the arrest of the Hébertists and the Dantonists, which cost the regime some of its most popular figures and alienated many of its most fervent supporters.[146] Throughout the Terror, citizens often heard warnings about treason in high places, such as when Saint-Just declared, "Citizens, all the enemies of the Republic are in its government," or when *Le Père Duchesne* cautioned that "false patriots are more to be feared than determined aristocrats" and told its readers to "mistrust everyone."[147] Such statements probably only made it easier for even the regime's staunchest supporters to abandon former heroes such as Hébert, Danton, and Robespierre. In seeking to promote its own legitimacy through denunciation and exclusion, the regime promoted a spirit that proved corrosive, even fatal, to that very legitimacy.

VI

❧

From Thermidor to Brumaire

One of the most troubling issues facing the leaders of the new regime after 9 Thermidor was their own complicity in the crimes they were now denouncing. The National Convention, after all, had repeatedly voted to authorize the actions of the committees and other institutions of the Terror, and many were on record voicing lavish praise for Robespierre and his fallen colleagues. Their shared complicity actually protected them somewhat at first, as most seemed wary of delving too deeply into each other's past, but as the repressive atmosphere abated and those who had not been part of the machinery of power during the Terror began speaking publicly, the Convention's complicity soon began to require some response.

An important part of their response included blaming public opinion, in effect arguing that although they had indeed backed Robespierre, so had the people. "The people were fooled," declared Barère on 14 Thermidor, and "public opinion was entirely misled, or rather taken over exclusively by Robespierre."[1] As that statement shows, however, public opinion's accusers ultimately blamed Robespierre for having "misled" or "corrupted" it. According to one speaker at the Jacobin Club, "for five years this crafty monster had thought of nothing but basing his absolute rule upon opinion," and another spoke of him having "seduced the people" and "taken over their votes, their opinions, their feelings, and even their thoughts."[2] The accusation then became official when the government announced that Robespierre and Couthon had been "charged with corrupting public opinion."[3]

But for some observers, Robespierre's manipulation did not exonerate public opinion for its role in the Terror. Barère and the others now put on trial took this position, asking, "Weren't the people themselves, by their error and their blind faith, the most active agents of the despotism exercised by this man?"[4] For conservatives, of course, the Terror seemed to confirm their repeated warnings about empowering the lower classes, but now such attitudes spread across the political spectrum. Though seeing the people as a malleable tool of tyrants, one deputy probably spoke for many in complaining that "for too long the opinion of a misguided multitude has had a fatal influence on France's destinies."[5] For France's leaders, then, creating a stable new order would require not only redesigning the country's political institutions, but also finding some way to tame the menacing power of public opinion.

With public opinion still being equated with the will of the sovereign people, these anxieties about public opinion naturally led many to rethink the idea of popular sovereignty. It was at this time that Joseph de Maistre wrote his famous counterrevolutionary attack on Rousseau and popular sovereignty, but even many revolutionaries now began to review the doctrine.[6] Sieyès, for example, criticized what he called the "exaggerated ideas with which one has chosen to surround what one calls sovereignty," and contending that "the sovereignty of the people is not unlimited," he complained that "the minds of the French, still full of royal superstitions, assumed the duty of endowing it with all the legacy of pompous attributes and absolute powers" of France's kings. He also challenged the hallowed principle that sovereignty's indivisibility meant it could only be delegated to a single power, proclaiming instead that it was "in the people's interest" to confer its exercise upon multiple powers.[7] The conservative newspaper *La Quotidienne* blamed the recent troubles on "the false application of the political dogmas of the sovereignty of the people and of equality," and Madame de Staël decried "the false application of the principle of the sovereignty of the people in representative government."[8] Although many were merely criticizing specific interpretations of popular sovereignty, some challenged the very principle itself, as royalists began to raise their voices very tentatively.

For those merely seeking to reinterpret popular sovereignty, one crucial question concerned its location, especially the claims that the Paris sections, the primary assemblies, and the popular societies had made. In his newspaper, *L'Orateur du Peuple*, the moderate deputy Louis Marie Stanislas Fréron chided a colleague who "dared to say that sovereignty existed immediately in the popular societies" rather than in "the people as a whole," and *La Quotidienne* derided the idea that the primary assemblies could each exercise sovereignty, "which can only belong to the combination of all of them."[9] A com-

mittee charged with revising the 1793 Constitution reported that it had removed passages that seemed "to give a turbulent and factious minority the
privilege of upsetting the peaceful and just resolutions of the majority of the
people, which alone must be sovereign," and the new text completed in 1795
replaced the statement that "sovereignty resides in the people" with a declaration that "sovereignty resides essentially in the universality of the
citizens."[10] Seeking to prevent future abuses, the committee also emphasized
the inevitability of the sovereign delegating its powers to representatives.

As the reference to sovereignty residing in "the universality of the citizens" suggested, many felt that avoiding a new Terror required formulating
and publicizing a proper definition of the people. The remaining Jacobins
adhered to a class-based definition, but as the left's power continued to ebb,
rival definitions reemerged. *La Quotidienne* was among those who defined
the people as "the collection of all individuals," and when Roederer later
wrote of public sentiment arising from "the lower classes of the people," he
was implying that the people included multiple classes.[11] For François Antoine Boissy d'Anglas, a leader of the new government, the people meant
"the mass of all men born on French soil," and in stating that "one part of the
people obtained property through inheritance, through purchase, or through
industriousness," he made it even clearer that for him the people included
property owners.[12] In addition to challenging class-based definitions of the
people, moderates and conservatives took aim at the Parisians' habit of posing as the people. "Can one use the term 'the people' for a small portion of the
people?" *L'Orateur du Peuple* asked, insisting that "the great majority of the
departments has formally rejected [that idea], and it is that majority that is
the people."[13] As they drafted a new constitution, the deputies essentially defined the sovereign people as the electorate—a group now composed, once
again, of men rich enough to pay a certain amount of tax. One deputy used
this definition when he referred to "the ability to place oneself on the list of
taxpayers, and thus on the list of the members of the sovereign."[14] Yet this definition led the pro-Jacobin *Journal des Hommes Libres* to scoff at "all of these
men proud of their supposed or real enlightenment," and "all these idle rich
property-owners who claim to be the sole sovereigns."[15] So despite movement toward definitions that had prevailed in 1789, controversy and confusion still surrounded this central term.

Despite their ambiguities, the concepts of the people and popular sovereignty continued to orient thinking about both formal institutions and the informal authority of public opinion, even among royalists. When the Executive Directory began nullifying royalist election victories in 1797, a royalist

pamphleteer could not resist telling the people that the directors "are ignoring your sovereign will," and *La Quotidienne* called the regime's leaders "enemies of the people" who were "in rebellion against the sovereign."[16] Another conservative pamphleteer echoed the Jacobins in arguing that the directors had no right "to dictate laws to these primary assemblies that make up the sovereign."[17] Although invocations of popular sovereignty by groups dedicated to a rival principle of sovereignty may have been little more than cynical attempts to embarrass their rivals, the longer they continued to invoke those principles, the more likely they became to internalize and accept them. If nothing else, the political struggles between republicans and royalists in this period were largely waged on the republican terrain of a politics of popular sovereignty, even if specific definitions and interpretations of popular sovereignty remained far from settled.

Just as the experience of the Terror led France's leaders to rethink popular sovereignty, it also led them to reconsider the theory and practice of political representation, paying particular attention to the powers that governors and the governed should have over each other. For many, the Terror had proven the need to check the authority of representatives even more closely. "We have seen the danger," deputy Edmond Dubois-Crancé announced, "of leaving power in the same hands for too long," and that concern led the Convention to begin rotating the membership of the committees and also to include in the new constitution a provision for the rotation of the directors.[18] Dubois-Crancé also told his fellow Jacobins that they should henceforth accept "neither kings, nor dictators, nor triumvirs, nor decemvirs," and the Club drafted a message demanding the immediate execution of "the first traitor who, behind the mask of a nefarious popularity, would dare to contemplate the ruin of the fatherland by elevating himself above the sacred level of equality."[19] Such thinking was understandable in light of recent events, but raising expectations for the perfect equality of all individuals would hardly make the creation of a stable new political system any easier.

While some contended that the Terror demonstrated the need to keep the authority of representatives under closer watch, others believed it showed the need to constrain the people, or more precisely, those who would claim to represent the people and exercise the right to control their representatives. Boissy d'Anglas denounced "the illusory principles of an absolute democracy and an equality without limits," calling instead for the pursuit of the more realistic goal of civil equality.[20] Though aimed specifically at the Jacobins, moderate deputy Jean François Reubell's statement that "the Convention must no longer be influenced in any way" suggested the emergence of new ideas about the public's role in France's system of representation.[21]

Concerns about safeguarding representatives' authority led to a search for new ways of shaping public opinion. One proposal in the Convention envisioned building as many amphitheaters as necessary to hold all the citizens in each electoral district; in this way the representatives "will communicate directly with each section of the republic" every ten days by means of messages read "to the citizens of every age and sex who will gather at a designated hour in each section's place of assembly."[22] While this plan would certainly have allowed representatives to address their constituents more effectively, it deliberately made no provision for allowing the assembled citizens to reply. Yet even the idea of assembling the people made many deputies nervous, and the proposal received no further consideration. One speaker opposed the whole idea of seeking to address the people, warning, "You are going to open up discussion with all of the drafters of messages in the republic," and he argued that it was instead "through good laws, through salutary measures, through vigorous government that the Convention should fix public opinion."[23]

Proposals to give the people ways to control and recall their representatives still appeared in this period, but they now mostly encountered hostility. The Jacobins made many of these proposals, so after the Convention voted to close the Paris Club in November 1794 such demands appeared less frequently; the Convention also omitted any reference to a right of insurrection in the new constitution. In August 1795 one deputy did defend the people's right to recall representatives from office at any time, but the Convention reacted with "murmurs" of disapproval, and when Boudin offered the more modest proposal to make a deputy removable only by the citizens of his own department, no one even seconded the motion.[24] As Boissy d'Anglas explained, because only the people as a whole could remove representatives, such a procedure would require "almost perpetual deliberation by 6000 primary assemblies in a country of 25 million, whose most numerous part must almost always devote itself to its labors." And because working men could not take time off for this purpose, letting these assemblies oversee representatives "would soon transfer all authority to idle and turbulent men."[25] So while leaders still acknowledged the people's theoretical authority over their representatives, their refusal to create concrete mechanisms amounted to a shelving of the idea.

The people's right to change their constitution at any time posed a more complex problem. Assertions of that right had been part of the package of ideas now being discarded, but in a kind of role reversal that became common in this period, the Jacobins and their allies opposed the idea in the hopes of preserving a constitution they had written—and one, they pointed out, that the voters had already approved. In response, moderates and royalists took up an old argument of their radical adversaries, insisting that to prevent the people from revising their constitution at any time would be to restrict their sovereignty. Although moderates had the votes to prevail on this point and to scrap the previous constitution (as well as to make any revision of their own text nearly impossible), it was not long before their defense of a perpetual right of revision came back to haunt them, when royalists began calling for yet another revision to create a monarchy. The Directory's annulment of royalist election victories, known as the Fructidor coup of 1797, led a royalist pamphleteer to protest that "the people, in France, can only be republican through their will, which they have the right to change" at any time.[26]

Throughout this period many leaders voiced concerns about an erosion of respect for representatives. One orator, for example, complained that "everyone wants to govern and no one wants to obey," calling this attitude "a contagious disease that has spread throughout all of France."[27] Another deputy, seeking to promote what he called "the habit of cherishing and respecting all the [representative] powers," proposed a law requiring that petitions be worded "in a decent manner," but his colleagues declined to legislate respect and deference toward representatives.[28] Indeed despite their concerns, the deputies did little to articulate a positive case for representatives' authority, and when they did try to do so, they often repeated arguments that had already proven highly contentious. "We must be governed by the best," declared Boissy d'Anglas, defining the best as "the most educated and those most interested in the maintenance of the laws," or, more bluntly, "the richest," an argument that would again prove offensive and controversial.[29]

Once again some of the fullest arguments for representation came from Sieyès, who reiterated his support for a social division of labor. Denying that "the people must only delegate powers they cannot exercise themselves," he contended that by that logic citizens wishing to send letters to Bordeaux would have to "carry their letters themselves."[30] Unlike most others, Sieyès portrayed representation as something desirable for the represented, but despite retaining a certain prestige among the deputies, he remained mostly an outsider, and after the Convention rejected his proposed constitutional ideas in 1795 he withdrew from an active public role for some time. Without his voice the case for representation lost much of its force, and many deputies reverted to treating representation as a necessary evil in a large republic. These leaders did nonetheless manage to resolve some of the problems that had plagued representatives, shutting down the Paris Commune, subjecting the Paris sections to stricter regulations, and taking control over the National Guard.

As for the structure of France's representative institutions, the Terror had revived interest in a separation of powers. Yet illustrating the ambivalence that many still felt about this principle, *L'Orateur du Peuple*, despite calling it essential "that any authority be checked by another authority," also insisted that "it is not within the powers of the people themselves to confer or to alienate to two parties a power that is one and indivisible."[31] Such ambivalence — or incoherence — marked the theory and practice of representation in this regime, which took some steps in the direction of a divided power (creating a bicameral legislature, for instance) but stopped well short of a true separation and balance of powers.

Although the Convention refused to create a judicial branch at all, it is the executive power that best reflects the framers' mistrust of a separation and balance of powers. Believing that the previous regime's lack of an independent executive had allowed the Mountain to dominate the state, many speakers now called for a truly independent executive, and a few added that the executive must have popular legitimacy to stand up to the legislature. As one lawmaker said in opposing the executive's election by the legislature, the executive needed "the moral force that opinion must give it," and the Committee of Eleven spoke of the need "to surround it with power, respect, and *éclat*."[32] But was this executive to be a representative rather than a functionary? Some insisted it was, including both *L'Orateur du Peuple*, which called the legislature and the executive "two sections of the national representation," and the Committee of Eleven, which held that the executive "is also the depositary of a considerable portion of the people's powers."[33]

Given memories of the King and Robespierre, a truly independent and powerful executive horrified many, and those memories, combined with visceral fears of political division and the institutional biases of men expecting to serve in the new legislature, resulted in an executive lacking the power and independence some felt it needed. The deputies thus created a "Directory" of five men, rotating its members annually and restricting its powers over the legislature. (The deputies had responded with "violent murmurs" to a proposal to give it an American-style veto.[34]) Most importantly, they denied it the legitimacy of popular election, allowing the legislature to elect its members. Popular legitimacy, in short, was to remain a monopoly of the legislature.

As for suffrage, the Convention reinstated a property qualification, a residency requirement, and indirect elections, and though the franchise was fairly broad for the primary assemblies, only about thirty thousand citizens were eligible for the electoral assemblies.[35] Despite all these safeguards, the government soon began annulling election results and promoting splinter assemblies in many districts to secure favorable results. Both in its design and its actual operation, then, France's new representative institutions reflected the twin fears of an unruly people and a tyrannical chief executive.

Orators in this period continued to use a staggering array of terms to invoke the sovereign's will, and they did little to clarify distinctions among them. Both "the public spirit" and "public opinion" (or simply "opinion") remained very common, and both terms most often conveyed unanimity, as speakers used the plural "opinions" when describing a state of division.[36] A contributor to *Le Journal des Hommes Libres* illustrated this outlook in writing that "we have no public opinion" because of "the divergences of individual opinions," and Madame de Staël claimed that "in an empire where two opposing parties wage a furious combat, there is very little public opinion."[37] In many cases "public opinion" and "public spirit" were used interchangeably, as in this passage from *L'Orateur du Peuple*: "In the city that made the Revolution, where does the public spirit stand, now that one boasts of having corrupted it, of having perverted opinion so thoroughly?"[38]

In arguing that "public spirit" replaced the less desirable term "public opinion," Ozouf cites the government's reports on "the public spirit" from this period, but even in those reports the terms overlap. In the Paris reports, for example, one finds under the heading *l'esprit public* countless references to opinion or public opinion, and the category headings often drift, with *l'esprit public* giving way to *moeurs et opinions*, or to *moeurs et opinion publique; esprit public*. One report from Paris did use *moeurs et opinion publique* and *esprit public* as separate categories, but the text under the latter heading refers to *l'opinion*, leading one to wonder whether there was any logic at all in the choice of terms.[39]

If there was any difference between these terms, it had less to do with division versus unanimity than with a dichotomy between thought and action. As in previous periods, "public opinion" often meant "what the people think," while "the public spirit" referred to people's willingness to take revolutionary actions. Roederer made this distinction in a treatise on public opinion, writing that "the public spirit is nothing other than opinion disposed to action."[40] And speakers discussing the public's morale or level of enthusiasm often used "the public spirit," as in the Directory's 1797 plea to the legislature to "revive patriotism [and] resuscitate the public spirit."[41] Nevertheless, such distinctions were far from consistent.

On the sensitive question of Paris's place in public opinion, during this period one still sees an unwitting bias among many observers in Paris, who continued to assess opinion based on quick tours of cafés and public places, but overt claims of Paris's special right to speak for the nation mostly disappeared. As for notions of class implicit in terms such as "the people" or "public opinion," one might assume that moderates using those terms had in mind an electorate now purged of the poor, while Jacobins were thinking of the lower classes, but these patterns did not always hold. For moderates might be thinking of the poor when disparaging public opinion, just as Jacobins anguishing over public opinion might have in mind the views of wealthy elites. At any rate, "public opinion" remained synonymous with "the people's opinion," and the two terms often appeared together, as in one Jacobin's warning that the rich would face "the indomitable mass of the people and the gleaming bayonets of public opinion," or *L'Orateur du Peuple*'s allusion to "the wish of the people and the work of public opinion."[42] Placing the two phrases alongside each other may suggest some cryptic distinction, but it may also involve a meaningless repetition, like the English phrases "ways and means" or "betwixt and between." A few speakers did distinguish between the two, depicting public opinion as an abstract entity shadowing the people—one deputy, for example, stated that on 9 Thermidor public opinion had "broken its chains and those of the people"[43]—but Madame de Staël illustrated a more typical outlook when she wrote of "the free choice of the people, that is to say, public opinion."[44]

There was at least one direct challenge to this association between public opinion and the people's opinion. In October 1794 an article in the newly revived *L'Ami du Peuple* complained that "for too long one has confused public opinion with the people's opinion," insisting that "the public is not the people, and rarely do the people think like the public." The paper had in mind a largely class-based distinction, as it explained in writing that "the public is the honorable million of which one speaks nowadays, and the people [are] these 24 million sans-culottes."[45] But others quickly scoffed at this distinction between public opinion and the people's opinion; Tallien, for example, maintained that if one went into "the workshops, into the suburbs, into the public squares," one would hear "a unanimous voice" saying that "public opinion is the people's opinion," and the moderate *L'Orateur du Peuple* simply dismissed *L'Ami du Peuple*'s ideas as "nonsense."[46]

There was another means of contrasting public opinion and the people's opinion that had little to do with sociological distinctions. That means treated public opinion as the collective opinion of actual individuals while

envisioning the opinion of the people as something more eternal and fundamental—an idea recalling Rousseau's distinction between superficial public
opinion and an infallible but disembodied general will. Echoing Saint-Just,
Fréron saw the opinion of "the entire mass of the people" as "less a calculation of the mind, which is changing, than a movement of the heart, which
never changes," while another deputy decried "the depravity of public opinion" despite declaring that "there is no part of the republic where the good
citizens . . . are not in the immense majority."[47] In much the same way, some
distinguished between "artificial public opinion" (the opinion heard in public) and "true public opinion" (a force that remained hidden). These ideas
had certain advantages—one could divine virtually any message in an opinion one never actually heard—but this *chassé croisé* of the real and the imaginary, in which actually existing opinions were considered illusory and purely
imaginary ones were called real, had the drawback of making one's claims
completely undemonstrable.

One of the more thorough attempts to specify public opinion's sociological
referent was Roederer's brief 1797 essay, *Théorie de l'opinion publique*.[48] For
Roederer, before public opinion could form, those at the bottom of society
first had to feel the effects of a problem, creating what he called "the general
sentiment." In his view, those classes lacked the necessary education and intelligence to formulate concrete opinions about a problem, but they helped
set the agenda of public concerns. Through conversations between husbands
and wives, masters and servants, employers and employees, this sentiment
gradually rose through the social hierarchy, passing through various social
strata until it gained the attention of a country's most brilliant and enlightened men. It was only at the peak of the social pyramid, where the enlightened could form opinions on the solutions required, that public opinion came
into existence; in Roederer's words, "Public opinion alone enlightens . . . regarding the cure and the remedies." For Roederer, then, "public opinion has
its source at the summit of the pyramid, and keeps descending continuously"
through countless conversations among the same social pairs that had trans-
mitted the general sentiment upward.[49]

Although Jaume rightly notes that for Roederer "opinion is constituted at
the meeting points between popular sentiment and the formulation given by
enlightened minds," in a strict sense public opinion only originates among
the upper classes, even if the lower classes begin the process and disseminate
public opinion once it is formed.[50] Reflecting his confidence in enlightened
minds, Roederer describes public opinion as "sound, strong, active, and
durable."[51] It must be emphasized, however, that this text had little to do

with others' views of public opinion, or with actual patterns of opinion formation in France. Not only is the theory too rigidly schematic to summarize the myriad sociological patterns and processes by which people came to hold common opinions, but its vision of an orderly and deferential society lacking divisions within its classes and its conclusion that a unanimous public opinion routinely arises make the text yet another exercise in fantasy about public opinion, albeit one providing a useful glimpse of how some members of the upper classes wished public opinion could be.

Roederer was not alone in taking such an optimistic view of public opinion. Distinguishing between mere "popularity" and "true public opinion," one deputy called the latter "as immutable as the truth, as unflinching as justice, as eternal as nature," and another called public opinion "a power that one never defies with impunity."[52] Several months after Thermidor, *L'Orateur du Peuple* wrote that "public opinion is no longer uncertain" and it now "thunders against the leaders of oppression and the executioners of France." The paper later added that plotters "no longer dare to struggle against the colossus of public opinion" or to oppose "the always pure and inalterable river of public opinion."[53] And of course orators continued to lavish praise upon the people, including one Jacobin who denied the people's gullibility by insisting they "will know the truth as soon as it is presented to them."[54]

Many others, of course, took a much dimmer view of public opinion, and the balance appears to have shifted in that direction. Speakers continued to describe public opinion as uncertain and fickle, and one deputy trying to portray the instability of the revolutionary paper money called it "as vacillating as opinion."[55] Similarly, *La Quotidienne* wrote that "if [public opinion] puts up 300 statues one day" for a popular hero, "it topples them the following day."[56] Others emphasized its foolishness, including Tallien, who demanded measures "to put an end to the depravity of the public spirit," and Jeanbon, who lamented that good men were often "condemned by public opinion without having been heard."[57] Once again fueling perceptions of public opinion's volatility and irrationality was the prominent role women had played in radicalizing the Revolution. Reubell was one of many to use gendered metaphors, referring to the "Furies of the guillotine" who still filled the galleries of the Jacobin Club and the National Convention, and the deputies, angry over women's role in the failed uprisings of Germinal and Prairial (April and May 1795), voted to bar women from attending future sessions.[58]

Women's presence in the public sphere also fostered a sense of public opinion's gullibility. *Le Journal des Hommes Libres* wrote that because royalist propaganda worked so well on "a sex whose exclusive sensitivity makes it so credulous, the public spirit has changed and given way to a thorough volatility."[59] And if women's presence in the public sphere created anxieties about public opinion, so did the presence of the poor, given their role in the Terror, the Germinal and Prairial uprisings, and Babeuf's conspiracy.* One deputy bemoaning the manipulation of public opinion noted that "one especially misleads the class of workers," and the royalist *La Quotidienne* concluded that "when an ignorant and crude multitude wants to deliberate on public affairs, nothing is easier for men greedy for fame and power than to lead it to fanaticism."[60] Such perceptions of gullibility were not limited to moderates and conservatives, as the Jacobin Jean-Marie Goujon told the Club, "One of the principal causes of our misfortunes is that the people's opinion has been manipulated in all directions."[61] Leaders continued to plan a national educational system that would make the people less gullible, but *La Quotidienne* dismissed these efforts, noting that enlightened men had been spreading their doctrines for over a century. "Are the people any more enlightened?" it asked, responding that "whatever one may do, it is doubtful that they will become more so." Few speakers openly echoed the paper's description of the people as "ignorant, credulous, and superstitious," but others often made similar points more delicately.[62] Consequently, many opposed resting political authority on public opinion, and for those who saw public opinion as a necessarily unitary force, there might be nothing at all to use as a foundation of power, only what a spokesman for the Committee of Eleven called "this prodigious variety of discordant views."[63]

The sense of public opinion's irresistible power, so notable up until the recent events, also came into question. Some still spoke of that overwhelming power—though often with considerable regret given doubts about the public's wisdom—but many others did not. As if to refute Roederer's portrait of the formation of public opinion, *La Quotidienne* wrote that because people living in republics disregard the advice of their former social superiors, opinion becomes atomized and "the power of public opinion is reduced to very little."[64] After the Fructidor coup, a royalist pamphlet claimed that public opinion favored royalism but noted "the impotence of the moral effort of opinion against a rampart of bayonets," and Mathiez reports that when

* In the Germinal uprising of 1–2 April 1795, several thousand Parisians invaded the National Convention demanding bread and a return to the 1793 Constitution. In the Prairial uprising of 20–23 May 1795, a similar uprising was met by organized forces protecting the National Convention, and the uprising ended in defeat. François Noël "Gracchus" Babeuf was a lawyer and political activist who demanded socioeconomic equality; his attempt to organize a movement to overthrow the government ended in his arrest in May 1796 and his execution a year later.

Frédéric-César de La Harpe, the Swiss political leader, attending a dinner party with Madame de Staël, said that the Convention could be toppled because public opinion was against it, she replied, "I ask M. de la Harpe what is the calibre of the cannons of public opinion?"[65] These comments suggest that the extensive use of physical force in French politics in recent years had begun to make many previous ideas about public opinion seem naïve.

Providing some relief from the manic-depressive outlook that marked views of public opinion were a few voices offering a more nuanced image. De Staël spoke of "a mass in the nation, always inert, always immobile, which, in times of confusion seeks only to recognize the stronger party in order to rally behind it," and claiming that "two-thirds of the French population . . . is made up of men who are only concerned about their monetary fortunes," she insisted that "the nation never wants anything but results and does not get excited about the means." Committed to neither the republicans nor the royalists, "this mass of the nation," she insisted, "wants rest above all."[66] A royalist pamphleteer writing after the Fructidor coup also contended that "what the people want today is rest."[67] Most of the French, in this view, were either apathetic, or, to borrow a twentieth-century term, *attentiste*, reserving judgment until the course of events became clearer.

As for perceptions of public opinion's texture, the penchant for describing opinion in unitary terms persisted, but again it bears noting that some favored pluralism and individualist notions of opinion. Tallien, for one, complained that "the liberty of opinions has long been smothered" in the Convention, and Legendre asked "that none of us regard a colleague as an enemy of the public good just because he holds a different opinion."[68] One speaker even defended fools' right to voice their opinions, insisting that the bar of the Convention, where citizens read petitions, was "not only a place for congratulations, but also complaints," and that "one must listen to everything there, even nonsense."[69] Jeanbon reminded his colleagues of their duty to learn the public's wishes and declared that the only way to do so was "to allow it to express itself freely."[70] The Convention used an individualist concept of opinion in its laws on the right of petition, which Boissy d'Anglas called a right "one must be sure not to let be usurped by any kind of corporation, which then replaces individual opinion with that of a false majority."[71] Echoing Le Chapelier's 1791 attack on the clubs' collective petitions, Roederer charged that "the formation of a collective opinion in the political societies is a tyranny exercised against the opinions of their members," and he also called it a tyranny "exercised over public opinion, which can only be composed of the majority of the citizens' individual opinions."[72] As one pamphleteer put it, "What is the will of the people if not the wishes of individuals?"[73] Yet if individualist notions of opinion seemed to be gaining strength, pluralist impulses remained weak, as the plea to hear even foolish petitions brought "violent murmurs" in the Convention, and Dubois-Crancé warned that because "if we argue here one will argue everywhere, . . . there can no longer be any difference of opinions here."[74]

As for the problem of how to know public opinion, many speakers continued to ignore the issue, making sweeping assertions about the public's views, but because rivals routinely contradicted those assertions, the search for evidence went on. And because this regime periodically outlawed or repressed opponents on both its right and left, clandestine opposition was common in this period, making it hard to take expressions of opinion at face value. In 1799 the Directory warned of royalist *agents provocateurs* infiltrating arenas of popular expression, explaining that these royalists "dress themselves in many forms, mask themselves in many disguises, [and] make use of all manners of speaking."[75] As the French sought reliable voices of public opinion, one new addition to the list was the army, whose political role continued to grow in this period. Leaders occasionally cited messages sent in from army units as evidence of public opinion, as Barère, for example, prefaced a message from one unit by saying, "Hear how public opinion speaks in the frontier districts."[76] Others, however, doubted that men busy fighting on the frontiers could express themselves on political matters, and some even denied that elections could be held as long as citizens were away on military service.[77] So while some invoked the army's opinions, others were skeptical of them.

A much older candidate to articulate public opinion was the press in its various forms. "It is the people as a whole who speak to you through our organ," claimed Fréron's *L'Orateur du Peuple*, "it is their sentiments that we interpret, it is their thoughts that we proclaim." In the Convention Fréron added that through the press "all the citizens, if they do not make their thoughts enter into the laws, can make them enter into the minds of the legislators" so that "representatives and the represented tend continually to blend into one."[78] In his *Théorie de l'opinion publique* Roederer urged leaders to study the press to learn public opinion, though his faith in this method rested on his belief that only the educated could form public opinion, and those who did not share that view were more skeptical about using the press this way.[79] Even those who valued newspapers did not always consider them a voice of the public. In asking "how, in a nation of 33 million men, public opinion could be enlightened other than by newspapers," one deputy saw a vital role for the press, but only in providing information and insight for a public that would have to find some other means of expression.[80]

When the government once again began subsidizing sympathetic newspapers, suspicions about the press's claims to speak for the public only increased. One deputy charged that journalists "have appointed themselves the magistrates of opinion," and that "newspapers have never done anything but pervert and corrupt" the public spirit.[81] Similarly, Jeanbon asked the deputies: "Will you call public opinion that which, prepared in the dust of an office . . . comes back to you after having originated, so to speak, from within your midst, and offers you only the product of the speculation of a few men, repeated by a multitude of others who are fooled, seduced, or intimidated?"[82] Fears of journalists' willingness to write whatever their patrons wished was even clearer in Legendre's typical observation that "whoever pays for a text makes the mercenary who sells him his pen say anything he wants."[83] The press, in short, remained an object of too much disdain and suspicion to serve as a broadly credible indicator of national opinion.

Some argued that the clubs offered a unique form of popular expression, for unlike the sections, which were now restricted to periodic meetings, the clubs could meet at will. One Jacobin even described them as "part of the people," while another referred to them as "this eye of the people," and *Le Journal des Hommes Libres* called them "the one and only means the people have to express and publicize their thoughts."[84] Yet for many observers clubs meant the Jacobin Club, and widespread anger at the Jacobins' role in the Terror led the government to shut down the Paris Club in 1794. Contesting clubs' right to speak for the people, one moderate deputy charged that they "pull the people in all directions" and "make them the instrument and the victim of their ferocious passions," and he added that although the Jacobins "claimed they were the sovereign people," in fact they "never stop tyrannizing opinion."[85] Fréron's *L'Orateur du Peuple* charged that because the Paris Club was "the center and the throne of the opinion" of all their affiliates and "the Paris Jacobins themselves were always dominated by three or four ringleaders, it followed that opinion as a whole was at the mercy of three or four men."[86] In 1799 the legislature, seeking allies against royalism, allowed a new version of the Jacobin Club to reopen, but the Directory soon protested that "the French nation should not have to fear the return of a monstrous power that it has seen as a bold rival and an audacious overseer of legitimate and constitutional powers," and in late July the Club was shut down again.[87]

Ironically, royalists' efforts to develop their own clubs and to take over existing ones eventually led the Jacobins to cry foul and to make arguments that had long been used against them. Criticizing a proposal to give more power to local clubs, a Jacobin orator denied they reflected the people's true opinions now that "aristocrats" and "plotters" had infiltrated them and seized "sole possession of the right to speak in the popular societies," and another sounded a familiar theme in charging that royalists were using shady tactics to monopolize the floor and dominate the clubs.[88] In short, now that all sides had some negative experiences with the clubs, there was little chance of their being accepted as a legitimate voice of public opinion.

Some of those who disliked the clubs suggested that the sections, being officially regulated institutions without ideological membership requirements, could serve as a channel for the expression of public opinion. But for most, memories of the fraud, manipulation, and strong-arm tactics that had allowed militants to comandeer the Paris sections were simply too strong for the sections to elicit much confidence. And in case memories had faded, several Paris sections again played a key role in the Germinal and Prairial uprisings, the second of which saw the murder and decapitation of one deputy inside the Convention. After Prairial, the *Moniteur* printed the rebels' *plan d'insurrection*, bringing to light the kind of control over expression that made many wary of the sections; in that document the movement's leaders told participants exactly what words to chant and to write on their signs, adding that any other sign or saying was "absolutely forbidden and prohibited."[89]

As for the primary assemblies, those who felt that a truly national will could only be formed through deliberation in a single national arena saw no way for several thousand assemblies to form such a will. In rejecting the primary assemblies' right to approve all legislation, *La Quotidienne* claimed it would require some means to "gather them together [and] establish a discussion among them," some procedure "in which each one can judge and give its view, in which the assemblies of the north [can] enlighten the assemblies of the south" and vice versa, until "one can finally manage to discover the truth."[90] If such elaborate national deliberation was out of the question, so was deliberation within each primary assembly, now that the new constitution had forbidden it.[91] In one moderate deputy's words, "one abuses principles in presenting as the wish of the French people that of the envoys of the primary assemblies."[92] And though radicals initially defended the primary assemblies, they turned against them when royalists and moderates began returning to them after Thermidor, and when the "gilded youth" and other royalists based in Paris's wealthier sections mounted their own insurrection against the Convention on 13 Vendemiaire IV (5 October 1795). At that

point, many Jacobins began echoing conservatives' earlier charges of manipulation and strong-arm tactics within the assemblies.

As the preceding references to uprisings in Germinal, Prairial, and
Vendemiaire show, crowds still played a vital role after Thermidor, and some
continued to view them as authentic expressions of the popular will. In Prairial, for example, the rebels issued a document that began with the phrase
"The people decree the following . . ." and they also repeated the old claim
that "it is up to the portion of the people that is closest to the oppressors to recall them to their duties."[93] In retelling the Germinal events, several deputies
themselves could not help calling the crowd "the people," but by now most
deputies refused to accord these crowds any legitimacy at all, and when one
deputy recalled something he had said to "the people" on 12 Germinal, the
minutes state that "a great number of voices" interrupted him, shouting, "It
was not the people who violated the Convention." Another deputy then
questioned the authenticity of the crowd's expressions by charging that he
had heard "14-year old children repeating phrases they could not understand," and he concluded that this *journée* was not an "insurrection of men,
but one of toddlers."[94] And amid the din of the crowd on Prairial, Louvet
could be heard declaring, "We here are the representatives of 25 million men;
50 subversives will not lay down the law to us."[95]

Similar hostility greeted attempts by spectators in the Convention to influence their proceedings. One deputy recalled how those in the galleries had
long "interrupted, jeered, threatened, [and] insulted those who did not speak
in the sense of their patron," and another repeated the charge that they "have
no other trade" than to attend the sessions.[96] Focusing on women, *L'Orateur
du Peuple* charged that the galleries were "full of *applaudisseuses* and
hurleuses" (female applauders and screamers) and that "nods, winks, and reciprocal gestures" allowed the deputies of the left to give these women instructions.[97] And though some seemed confident that the deputies could now simply ignore any pressure from the crowds, Fréron's paper probably expressed
a common fear when it wrote that "murmurs and applause always influence
the opinions of the members and the deliberations of the assembly."[98]

Based on these fears and memories, the moderates who now dominated
the assembly often took action against crowds claiming to speak for the people. A committee report issued after Prairial warned of "a tiny portion of the
people wishing to dictate to the majority of the nation," and the Committee
of Eleven recommended that the size of the audience henceforth be limited
to half the number of the deputies.[99] Showing unprecedented resolve, the
Convention reacted to the Germinal uprising by ordering its security force,

now armed with whips, to clear the galleries, and on the very first day of the new legislature the representatives showed their intolerance of interruptions from the galleries by voting to eject a citizen who had dared to applaud.[100] Though the deputies' rejection of crowds' claims to represent public opinion was not new, their willingness to use force against them was, and it showed that France's leaders were now learning from their experiences and taking steps to create a more stable order.

Once again, a role reversal took place when conservative militants started forming their own crowds, leading the horrified Jacobins to adopt their rivals' old arguments. In Germinal, a change in the rituals of insurrection occurred when crowds from conservative sections arrived in the Convention to support the embattled deputies, and in the following months records of the Convention occasionally noted applause from the galleries for moderate and conservative speakers as well as for Montagnards.[101] During the trial of the terrorist Jean-Baptiste Carrier, who had overseen the mass drowning of suspected rebels in the Vendée region, *L'Orateur du Peuple* noted the spectators' hostility toward the defendant, writing that "lively applause showed the assembly how much the people were thirsting for justice."[102] At the same time, one Jacobin seemed shocked that "the galleries of the Convention were occupied by people we do not know," and another angrily proclaimed that "the elegant people who fill the galleries were proof that one had not chosen the spectators among the good sans-culottes of the faubourg Antoine."[103] Unconsciously echoing the moderates of 1792, another Jacobin protested that "scarcely does a Montagnard open his mouth than the galleries try to silence him with their cries."[104] As for the anti-Jacobin mob that assaulted the club's headquarters in November 1794, whereas *L'Orateur du Peuple* referred to that crowd as "the people," the Jacobin *Journal des Hommes Libres* wrote that they were only "a band of raging madmen," and when a deputy reporting on the events alluded to "the people" besieging the Jacobins, several voices on the left shouted, "They were not the people!"[105] This turnabout may not have led the French to agree on any method of ascertaining public opinion, but at least the rivals now had a more similar set of experiences.

In the absence of consensus on so many representations of opinion, one deputy called elections "the only legal, the only legitimate means . . . to learn the wish of our constituents," and after the referendum on the new constitution, the relieved *Moniteur* wrote, "Finally the oracle has spoken! The will of the sovereign has manifested itself."[106] Elections indeed remained the most credible manifestation of opinion at this time, serving as what one deputy called "our common compass," but arguments about how voting should take place still created problems.[107] The question of when to consult the people was one such issue; whereas many on the left, for example, felt that because the voters had already spoken in approving the 1793 Constitution it was unnecessary to ask them if they wanted a new constitution, others questioned the conditions under which voting had taken place. *La Quotidienne* insisted that the lack of deliberation before the 1793 referendum had ruined the whole undertaking, writing that "anyone bold enough to want to discuss it was put to death," and Boissy's report stated that "France as a whole, in admitting that it had been tyrannized, has sufficiently nullified this supposed acceptance that one alleges today."[108]

Even under the best of conditions, elections seemed to many a rather blunt instrument for learning the people's will. Taking issue with those who cited a vote on the constitution as clear proof of support for each provision in it, one deputy saw the referendum answering only one question: "Is the constitution accepted by the majority, yes or no?" To answer more than that question, he added, six thousand primary assemblies would have had to debate all 159 of its articles, and "there is no means of calculation sufficient to bring together the number of the voters and that of the points discussed."[109] For others, low turnout remained a problem, as Babeuf, for one, denied the new constitution's legitimacy on the grounds that only one million people had voted for it.[110] When the Convention submitted its constitution to the voters, it also gave them the opportunity to approve the controversial "two-thirds" decree, which would reserve two-thirds of the seats in the new legislature for (moderate republican) incumbents of the Convention. The Convention took heart in the measure's passage, seeing a kind of tacit consent in the silence of those who abstained on the two-thirds decree (not to mention the even larger number who declined to vote on either measure), but a deputation from the Halle-aux-Blés section voiced a common view in stating that "silence is a formal rejection of the decrees."[111] With only about a million voting in the referendum, and some three hundred thousand voting on the two-thirds decree, the problem of how to interpret abstention hampered attempts to ascertain public opinion from voting.

Compounding the problem in elections for the new legislature was the continuing reliance on indirect election, for as Baudin asked, "Who among us does not know how frequently the choice of the electoral assemblies has not matched that of their constituents?"[112] For some, the problem had to do with the electors being manipulated and pressured by the leaders of powerful factions, while for others it had to do with the electoral rules, which forced voters to pick electors from a pool of about thirty thousand of France's richest men. Moreover, Roederer noted that election results became "obsolete" very quickly, suggesting that there was often a significant difference between the "legal majority" in parliament and the current opinions of the citizenry.[113]

Finally, many observers did not even believe the election results the government posted. One Paris section doubted an official announcement that only ninety-five thousand had voted against the two-thirds decree, noting that Paris alone had seventy-five thousand voters, "of whom almost all had rejected the decrees."[114] And after the government's so-called Floréal coup, which annulled Jacobin election victories in 1798, one deputy justified the coup by charging "that the anarchist conspiracy had influence throughout the Republic and that no department was able to carry out the elections freely."[115] At the same time, a pamphlet published by local officials in the Eure department repeated the familiar charges that "the most peaceful citizens have been kept away from the primary assemblies," and it concluded that because of "fraud and violence," the election results did not reflect "the people's choice."[116] Similar allegations had arisen several months earlier, when the government had cancelled royalist victories. In backing these measures, a parliamentary report ended up painting a dismal picture of elections:

> The royalists lured into the primary assemblies foreigners, men taking bribes, . . . domestic servants, deserters, [and] refractory priests, and they had the same individual cast several ballots. Priests crossed the countryside forcing their flocks to go to the assemblies, and they gave them [prewritten] ballots, while others distributed them in the confessional.[117]

And yet the royalists also considered elections incapable of capturing the national will, given the republican oath voters had to swear and the many other ways in which authorities pressured and intimidated royalists. Profound doubts about the fairness of the procedures and the conditions in which campaigns took place thus weakened elections' ability to serve as a broadly satisfactory indicator of national opinion.

Dissatisfied with elections, some revived the old idea that only France's elected representatives could legitimately articulate national opinion. "It is here," one deputy told his colleagues, "it is in the midst of the National Convention that one must come to consult opinion."[118] But although the Convention eventually drafted a statement calling itself "the center of public opinion," few voices outside it seemed to agree.[119] Even inside the Convention the idea did not go unchallenged, as one speaker drew applause for a statement that "none of us arrives here with a seal of infallibility, and the Convention as a whole does not claim to have one."[120] Also distinguishing between the opinions of the nation and its representatives, Fréron argued that until the nation makes its views known, the laws "still only represent the thinking and the wish of eight hundred members of a national assembly."[121]

How, then, could public opinion possibly be known? In moments of frustration, some essentially concluded it could not, or at least doubted that there was any means of ascertaining it that rivals would find convincing. For some, the problem had to do with current circumstances such as restrictions on expression, which spoiled all supposed manifestations of opinion. Others felt that the problem lay in the vast numbers of individuals involved. Denouncing "a despicable charlatanism" that "speaks endlessly of the people's sovereignty and will without offering any means of knowing it," *L'Orateur du Peuple* wrote, "First show us some practical means of letting 25 million men participate in the making of the laws that must guide them, of establishing discussion among them, . . . [and] of making their opinions known."[122] And *L'Ami du Peuple* complained that public opinion "makes a great noise" while the people "stay silent," but its claim that "the people disavow" those who claim to speak for them did not explain how one could know what the people thought if they stayed silent and disavowed all spokesmen.[123] Not surprisingly, many simply ignored the entire problem of ascertaining public opinion, but those who grappled with it simply could not find any solution in these years.

The idea that this regime lacked legitimacy has remained almost beyond question since its demise, and though that picture is probably correct, it is worth noting certain problems that make definitive conclusions difficult. As historians have often noted, the Terror did not end immediately with Robespierre's arrest, and the habits of dissimulation and circumspection it had promoted continued well past 9 Thermidor. Such attitudes call into question the value of sources such as the messages the Convention soon began receiving congratulating it for toppling Robespierre. The previous regime had, after all, received its own share of such mail after arresting the Girondins, and as historian Bronislaw Baczko notes, although the messages sent after 9 Thermidor probably express a great deal of authentic relief, they also reflect the lingering "political conformism" of the time.[124]

Political expression did flourish somewhat as repression ebbed, but the government's closure of the Paris Jacobin Club and its subsequent measures against other clubs illustrate the limits of the regime's tolerance for opposition. At times, there was a vigorous press that reveals much about the content (if not the distribution) of opinions, but at other times, as Aulard observed, opposition papers practiced self-censorship and used "allusions so discreet that for us they are almost indistinguishable."[125] Election returns become somewhat more useful in this period, especially when the government's decision to allow declared candidacies cleared the way for voters to make informed choices between rival "parties," but the government, perhaps fearing the rise of popular opponents, soon revoked that policy.[126] Moreover, the tendencies of the regime's opponents to hide their true colors (as in the case of royalists swearing to support the republican constitution), along with many assemblies' failure to report vote totals or record minutes, also make election returns a very imperfect source.[127]

While these problems affected virtually all forms of public expression, the government's secret reports on "the public spirit" contain other kinds of flaws. The reports, compiled mostly from eavesdropping in public places, are full of vague and impressionistic statements such as "one says" and "people are saying," and they ignore many important topics and key events. The observers also show a fierce bias in their allusions to "anarchists" and "fanatics," and their disdain for these groups often prevents them from taking their opinions seriously. So although the reports have some value for establishing a chronology of public grumbling over certain issues, they have many limits for the assessment of people's views of the regime and its leaders.

Yet as in the Revolution's previous phases, the most serious obstacle to assessing the regime's legitimacy remains the country's continuing failure to settle upon one definition of public opinion and one clear standard of legitimation. Does "public opinion" include the views of those who did not voice their opinions publicly? Should one consider the opinions of those now disenfranchised, including women and the poor, or of those in exile? Should all opinions be equally weighted? Should one even count individual opinions? As in earlier periods, the historian answers these questions at the risk of imposing standards the contemporaries themselves had not agreed to accept. The rest of this chapter, then, will merely offer a few comments on patterns of support and opposition before proceeding to the somewhat easier question of why the regime encountered discontent and why it eventually fell.

The starting point for any such inquiry must be to note that this regime outlasted all its predecessors since 1789, so that despite its poor reputation, it must have enjoyed someone's support to last for over five years. Furet pointed to the military, purchasers of *biens nationaux* (the church property nationalized early in the Revolution), and members of the growing bureaucracy as the regime's three main pillars, while others have simply called property owners the foundation of this "bourgeois" regime.[128] But if it was indeed a regime of property owners, the number of citizens who owned enough property to worry about losing it to a Jacobin resurgence or to a restoration of the monarchy was probably larger than many historians have suggested. The regime, in other words, may not have been particularly well loved, but fear of the alternatives probably earned it a substantial measure of at least reluctant support.

Reluctant it was, however. From de Staël's observation that "nothing voluntary happens between governors and the governed" to the comments of virtually all historians, the picture of a discredited regime emerges.[129] The regime's leaders themselves seemed equally convinced of this—one deputy told his colleagues "this sad truth" that they lacked the people's confidence—and there can be no better proof of their perceptions than their decision to place two-thirds of the seats in the new legislature beyond the reach of the voters.[130] Yet several historians have also echoed de Staël's emphasis on French apathy, which calls for a more complex conclusion blending images of indifference and more active discontent.[131] That many people felt little enthusiasm for this regime should not be surprising, for after years of being promised imminent prosperity only to find ongoing economic hardship, after hearing predictions of rapid military victory only to endure a seemingly endless war, after watching one national hero after another fall from power amid charges of treason and corruption, after watching one constitution after another proclaimed as France's salvation only to be torn to pieces, the French had reason to feel emotionally drained, apathetic, and cynical.

Whether people felt mostly apathetic or mostly hostile, it seems that the opinions of "the people" or "the public" ended up counting for remarkably little in the regime's demise, for the regime did not succumb to something as abstract as "public opinion" or even to anything as "popular" as an uprising of sans-culottes, but rather to a military coup. As an important article by Lynn Hunt, David Lansky, and Paul Hanson pointed out, it was the regime's own leaders who "called in the generals" in Brumaire, so that the coup "only became possible when the majority of deputies themselves gave up on parliamentary government."[132] The most serious legitimacy crisis this "liberal republic" faced, then, was the one that existed within the structures of power, among members of the government as well as opposition leaders. The leaders' perceptions of the citizens' opinions undoubtedly affected their thinking, but the events of this period again suggest that in the French Revolution it was legitimacy's horizontal dimensions that mattered most.

Those who have sought to explain why many citizens disliked the regime have stressed problems such as the economic crisis, the effects of the war, and the state's heavy-handed efforts to replace traditional religion and culture with new revolutionary ways, and there is no need to revise those arguments. Of more direct relevance here are certain elements of France's political institutions and culture, as well as some of the mistakes the regime's leaders made. In the 1795 Constitution, for example, the return to a property qualification for voting certainly generated considerable resentment. It would be easy to overstate this point, for the threshold was low enough to give France an electorate relatively large for that era, and as Isser Woloch notes, "no masses of disfranchised citizens were clamoring for the right to vote."[133] The stated rationale for the rules, however, proved unconvincing to some, including Thomas Paine, who refuted the claim that the poor had no interests or stake in the existing order by pointing out that they did the bulk of the work and paid most of the indirect taxes. Noting that the propertied were to be called citizens, Paine asked "what name the rest of the people would have?"[134] So although there was no mass movement of the disenfranchised, the decision created significant resentment among leaders, journalists, and militants of the left.

Other constitutional provisions also created problems. As Lefebvre noted, holding elections every year proved "prejudicial to the efficiency of both government and administration, making them unstable and monopolizing their attention."[135] Similarly, the near impossibility of revising the constitution helped lead both branches of the government to violate some of its provisions. The most commonly noted constitutional flaws, however, concern the executive, which Aulard believed "was without unity or stability," and which Rosanvallon calls devoid of any "margin of initiative in relation to the legislative power."[136] Some historians have disagreed, noting that despite its limited powers the Directory could still act using methods such as annulling election results, but reliance on such dubious methods probably harmed the regime's legitimacy.[137] An equally serious problem concerned the executive's election by the legislature rather than the voters. It is true that the legislature was also elected indirectly—though not without some cost for its own legitimacy— but the extra step separating the citizens and the executive created an imbalance of the branches and may well have weakened the executive's standing with the citizens. Indeed one deputy underlined that problem, asking, "Will the people see as their chief magistrates men who were not their choice?"[138] The Committee of Eleven admitted the executive's need for prestige, but its proposals, which included giving the directors special costumes, a guard of their own, and residence in a national palace, could hardly make up for the disadvantage of being elected by a rival branch.[139]

Just how much the executive's indirect election harmed its standing with the citizens would be hard to establish, but the legislators certainly looked down on the executive, denying that the directors were representatives of the people. So although the framers, recalling the abuses of the committee system during the Terror, chose to give the executive considerable powers and independence, the deputies' institutional biases and their dislike for any true separation and balance of powers soon led them to doubt the legitimacy of the Directory's authority. That attitude, when combined with the directors' own institutional biases and resentment of the legislature's condescension, led to a virtual war between the branches, each of which used highly questionable means against the other in episodes such as the Fructidor coup, the Floréal coup, the Prairial coup, and the 18 Brumaire coup.* This was partly a constitutional problem, as the lack of proper checks and balances (and the lack of an independent judiciary or an arbiter such as Sieyès's proposed *juré constitutionnel*) had much to do with each branch's recourse to illegal means, but at root it was really a problem of political culture, for it seems that despite some of their statements, most of France's leaders simply did not believe in divided government.[140]

Another problem the regime faced concerned the conditions under which France had become a republic. Revolutionaries often insisted that the toppling of the monarchy in 1792 had reflected the people's will, but when the deputies themselves began to impugn the legitimacy of violent uprisings such as that of June 1793, the legitimacy of the August 1792 uprising also came into question. And although some cited the 1793 referendum as proof of people's desire for a republic, we have seen that the fairness of that referendum remained in serious doubt. In both cases, action had been taken with little or no prior national deliberation, and when Roederer sought to show that ideas will not take root in society if imposed from above without proper discussion, the example he chose was France's founding of a republic in 1792.[141] Moreover, one could argue that so much had changed since June 1793 that a new popular consultation was needed on such a fundamental question, particularly given the often-stated idea, now taken up by royalists, that the people

---

* In the Fructidor coup of September 1797, the directors arrested several dozen right-wing deputies, closed down many right-wing newspapers, and annulled the right's recent election victories. In the Floréal coup of May 1798, the directors, after rigging the elections for the National Convention in many districts, annulled the victories of several dozen Jacobin candidates. In the Prairial coup of June 1799, the legislature forced two unwanted directors to resign. On 18 Brumaire, Napoleon, with the assistance of the upper house of the legislature, took control of the government by force.

had the right to change their minds at any time. The two-thirds decree of 1795 only deepened suspicions that a republic was being imposed on the citizens. Republican leaders, in short, might have gained from holding a truly fair referendum to settle the debate between republicans and royalists. Of course some royalists, if defeated, would have rejected the result, but their position would have been significantly weakened. As it was, however, lingering questions about people's desire for a republic remained a significant problem for the regime's legitimacy.

It is hardly surprising that the government's constant revision of the electorate's decisions provoked a flood of accusations that it had infringed upon the people's sovereignty and, as *La Quotidienne* wrote, had "declared a brazen war on public opinion."[142] Among the main justifications leaders gave was that democracy could not be instituted by democratic means. One speaker claimed that "an assembly charged with making an empire as vast as France pass from a monarchical state to a democratic state must have in its hands all the means of doing so," and the Committee of Eleven, in defending the two-thirds decree, issued a statement asking "that one stop contesting the legitimacy of this measure" because "the only legitimate [measure] is the one that will save the fatherland."[143] Here, once again, was the "public safety" argument, but it does not seem to have been any more convincing this time than it was during the Terror, and one typical pamphlet wrote that "the pretext of the public good is always the most dangerous scourge of the people."[144] A more promising argument consisted of charges that royalists and Jacobins had broken electoral laws, but in many cases the government presented little evidence, basically treating the mere presence of royalists or Jacobins in the assemblies as sufficient grounds for dismissing the returns. Given the ideological gulf between the government and its rivals, a scrupulous respect for electoral procedures was probably France's best hope of finding some means to settle these disputes without force, but the regime was anything but scrupulous in this regard.

Some historians have suggested that the regime's leaders had no choice but to manipulate elections against opponents who rejected the regime's very principles and thought only of destroying it.[145] As *Le Journal des Hommes Libres* wrote in supporting the Directory's actions against royalists, just as "fire and water destroy each other, . . . it is impossible that royalists and republicans can ever live peacefully together."[146] That these two conflicting principles of sovereignty could not coexist may be true in theory, but in practice many royalists seemed willing to compromise with new ideas and to compete on the new terrain of public opinion and legitimation by numbers. Countless royalists could not resist invoking public opinion and the will of the people as they attacked the Directory, and even Louis XVIII told his followers to "expect from public opinion a success that it alone can render durable and solid."[147] Of course some royalists remained firmly opposed to the new politics, but according to Lefebvre constitutional royalists outnumbered their staunchly absolutist colleagues.[148] Moreover, the regime probably could have tolerated a royalist presence within the system, counting on the deep divisions among royalists to weaken them, but the idea of tolerating any kind of legal opposition was more than many leaders could bear.

Suggesting that the regime overreacted to its opposition, Aulard wrote that the "peril of the Left" was overestimated, and Woloch contends that "the Jacobins remained a small minority of the electorate (not to mention the population) and had little to hope for at present in genuinely free elections."[149] Indeed some urged toleration of the opposition, including one deputy who asked, "What do I care if there are still a few scoundrels, partisans of Robespierre?" and another who, while admitting there were still royalists in France, asked: "But are these men numerous?" and "Where are their armies?"[150] Yet as Baczko notes, "the emergence from the Terror was certainly not a period which encouraged evolution toward political pluralism," and the regime's leaders were generally as hostile to pluralism as their opponents were.[151] Still, the leaders' intolerance of opposition, while understandable, led it to take actions that eventually helped destroy the regime.

While focusing on eradicating opposition, these leaders failed to put much effort into developing their own organizational network, which might have produced a powerful party of the center.[152] Such a strategy, combined with an attempt to divide moderates from extremists on both the left and right (and a willingness to tolerate moderate opponents' presence in the system), might have made the regime stronger. The government also might have been wiser to increase rather than decrease participation in elections — by making it easier and quicker to vote, for example — particularly had it devised some mechanism to break the rural patronage ties that would benefit royalists. As Lefebvre noted, because the highly cumbersome voting methods were least likely to discourage devoted militants, "these methods benefited the extremist parties."[153] By seeking to crush all opposition by even blatantly illegal means, and by restraining rather than promoting political participation, the regime ended up undermining its own proclaimed principles, thus weakening its own legitimacy.

The government's antidemocratic measures appear to have rested on a serious misdiagnosis of the previous political crisis. These leaders, that is, seemed to view the Terror as a result of the poor being able to vote, and as they wrote the new constitution, they let loose an outburst of class hatreds to justify the franchise restrictions. "Who among us," asked Lanjuinais, "could still bear the hideous spectacle of political assemblies falling prey to crass ignorance, to vile greed, to depraved drunkenness?"[154] For another deputy, it was vital not "to allow into the primary assemblies all these men who are always in the cabarets and places of disorder, and who will behave in the people's assemblies as they do in their taverns." He concluded that it was "these men who have caused all our troubles throughout the Revolution."[155] In 1795, then, France had no Jules Ferry (the late nineteenth-century republican leader who believed in cultivating mass electoral support for the republic), no one who could imagine a republic in which massive political participation would produce moderate outcomes safeguarding order and property.

Although such an idea may seem anachronistic, it was not unthinkable at the time. Indeed many of the same men who voted to restrict the franchise had also denied the left's claim that the Parisian militants were the people, or that they represented the thinking of millions outside Paris. As one deputy reminded the Convention, it was a minority that had ruled France in 1793–1794, and that minority had come to power only with the support of the Paris Jacobin Club, the Paris Commune, and armed militants under the Commune's control—all of which were now gone.[156] One suspects that in theory most of the deputies agreed with this point, but it seems that the impulse to exclude undesirable elements was one few leaders could resist. Their decision to exclude the poor, of course, also reflected the prevailing political philosophy of that century, but it also reflects their own visceral fears of men and women who dressed and spoke so differently from them, as well as the skewed perspective that led them to judge all the poor by the actions of a handful of highly politicized urban militants.

As a result of this misdiagnosis, the new regime ended up oversolving the problem. The Convention, that is, resolved the problem of the threat from Parisian militants by taking control over the sections and clubs, by closing the Paris Commune, by disarming the *faubourgs*, by creating a constitutional mechanism for moving the legislature out of Paris in emergencies, and by creating a security force under the assembly's control. In addition, as we have seen, these leaders also abandoned most of the inflammatory rhetoric about sovereignty and representation that had helped inspire earlier uprisings. Especially given the use of indirect election, the regime probably did not need to take the politically costly step of disenfranchising the poor, any more than it needed to cancel its rivals' election victories in various districts. Of course there would have been some risk in letting the poor vote and in accepting moderate opposition parties on the left and right, but there was also much to be gained from winning more fairly. At least one deputy seemed to sense this point; believing firmly that most people favored a republic, he advised against tampering with elections by asking what good it would do "to give the French a form of government they would not want?"[157]

Few of the regime's leaders, however, showed much faith in the voters, in pluralism, in public opinion, or indeed, in democracy. Such attitudes were of course quite common in the eighteenth century, and are especially understandable given the country's recent experiences. Moreover, the Jacobins and royalists, who indeed used fraud and violence to further their aims, also had much to do with the regime's downfall. Nevertheless, if one is to explain the crisis that eventually toppled this regime, its leaders' own hypocrisies and misgivings about their own stated principles deserve considerable emphasis, for if a regime's own leaders do not believe in the system they created, it seems unlikely that others would either.

Once again, the weakness of the country's laws and formal institutions placed even greater weight on legitimation by the informal authority of public opinion, but as this chapter has argued, that mode of legitimation was in no better position to support a stable political order than the formal institutions were. As with the formal political processes, the politics of public opinion remained plagued by too much confusion and disagreement for references to the public's will to secure authority and resolve conflicts. The rhetoric of public opinion did continue to play some role in boosting morale within each political camp, but behind the apparent confidence of many invocations of public opinion, orators and journalists felt a profound despair over the nation's fragmentation and over their own inability to persuade others. "It is sad to speak only to the deaf," wrote *La Quotidienne*, adding, "We do not hope to convert anyone."[158] Echoing that sentiment, *Le Journal des Hommes Libres* made its arguments for letting the poor vote, but then asked, "What can reason alone do against these enemies of all that is reasonable and just? How can we persuade the rich man that the poor man is his equal solely because he is a man?"[159] These observers seemed to doubt the effectiveness of rhetoric itself, and to regret the absence of any national arbiter, whether in the legal form of the country's political institutions or in the informal realm of invocations of public opinion.

In the absence of any such arbiter, it is not surprising that the upper house of the National Convention turned, in 1799, to a new kind of power, granting Napoleon unspecified new powers. In his initial public statements on 18 and

19 Brumaire, the soon-to-be dictator pointed to a great national emergency, recalled the many violations of the constitution that had taken place, and spoke repeatedly about his own importance, but he made only one brief allusion to the people and one to the nation, and he did not use the phrases "public opinion" or "the public spirit" at all.[160] So although Napoleon later borrowed heavily from the Revolution's languages and practices of legitimation, his utterances on 18 and 19 Brumaire attested to the failure of France's attempt to build a new order on the foundation of public opinion, making it clear that a new kind of politics was now taking over.

Conclusion

✣

In the history of public opinion in France, there has been no more important moment than the proclamation of national sovereignty in the summer of 1789. Before the Revolution, the French often called public opinion more powerful than even kings, but they continued to envision it as a power clearly separate from the official authority of royal sovereigns. By 1790, however, to invoke public opinion was usually to invoke the will of the new sovereign. In defining national sovereignty, then, the French were in effect redefining public opinion, although given the paucity of serious and sustained deliberation on the new doctrine of sovereignty, it might be better to say that in failing to define sovereignty, they were failing to define public opinion as well.

Historians of French political culture have often called attention to certain problems in the concepts of sovereignty that the Revolution inherited from absolutism—particularly claims of sovereignty's indivisibility and limitless power—and those traits, which had already affected thinking about public opinion before the Revolution, continued to do so after 1789. In theory, the idea of indivisibility seems reasonable, for if the point of sovereignty is to have a final arbiter capable of resolving potentially crippling disputes, then it makes little sense to have multiple sovereigns. Yet this study has sought to distinguish between the concept of a single supreme authority and the idea that indivisible sovereignty demands indivisible representation. Although speakers occasionally hinted at the useful fiction that the sovereign people might *want* plural representation as a means of checking their representatives' authority, few speakers pursued that idea, and despite provisions for a separation and balance of powers in every revolutionary constitution, what resulted in practice were halfhearted and failed attempts at such a system. Belief in indivisible sovereignty also promoted a unitary conception of public opinion, whose consequences will be noted below.

It was also logical to envision sovereignty as an unlimited authority, for if one defines a sovereign as the highest power in a political system, then it would be hard to imagine it being subject to any limits. But once again problems surrounded the application of that idea, namely, the transfer of unlimited authority from the sovereign to its representatives. Those who considered the Constituent Assembly and the National Convention infallible representations of the sovereign people naturally insisted that those bodies have unlimited powers, but many others doubted that infallibility. Here was a profound dilemma, for many (perhaps inspired by Rousseau's hostility toward representation) rejected the Assemblies' claims to exercise the unlimited authority of the sovereign people, but others, aware that the sovereign people could not govern directly, wondered what would become of the unlimited authority of the sovereign people if neither the people nor their representatives could actually exercise it.

This problem had its roots in the transition from royal to national (or popular) sovereignty, which involved shifting sovereignty from a human being capable of coherent speech to an abstraction unable to utter complete sentences. In other words, despite countless claims attributing complex demands and opinions to "the people," the new sovereign, a collection of millions of individuals whose simultaneous and unorchestrated expression would only produce noise, could play little more than a reactive and passive role, answering questions posed by others and speaking in a cumbersome binary language as it voted for or against propositions placed before it. Of course this problem affects all democracies, but the leaders of many democracies rarely mention sovereignty, whereas the revolutionaries invoked and asserted the idea on a daily basis. The problems of public opinion and legitimacy in the French Revolution, in short, owed much to the revolutionaries' excessive investment in a highly problematic fiction.

France's leaders had some sense of this sovereign's inherent limitations, but their hasty proclamation of national sovereignty in August 1789 and their subsequent failure to define it carefully or to work out just what it meant to "alienate," "delegate," "transfer," or "exercise" sovereignty resulted in great confusion over the nature and source of their authority. And when militants in the clubs and the Paris sections took it upon themselves to act as France's sovereign and to issue orders to the country's representatives, some leaders, instead of explaining why no club or section could act that way, encouraged the militants with thundering assertions of the people's unlimited powers over their representatives. Yet if nearly every orator treated the people's sovereignty as something sacred, belief in that doctrine eventually turned out to be weaker than it appeared. Some royalists of course rejected the idea — despite invoking it repeatedly when it served their purposes — but moderates eventually grew disillusioned as well, and even the Jacobins appeared to back away from the idea once in power, questioning the very principle of legitimation by numbers and proposing to replace it with a kind of sovereignty of a virtuous minority. In thus favoring government "for the people" but not "by the people," these revolutionaries were proposing a system strangely similar to the absolutist system they had destroyed. So despite the general taboo on questioning the concept of national sovereignty during the Revolution, the idea had relatively shallow roots, and it remained a source of profound disagreement. Indeed Furet was probably right to argue that the Revolution did not truly end until the last part of the nineteenth century, when nearly all of the French abandoned rival visions of sovereignty and settled on the idea of national sovereignty.[1]

If the deputies as a whole did a poor job of conceptualizing and explaining the doctrine of popular sovereignty, the same could be said of their treatment of political representation. Much of the problem had to do with their public statements suggesting that there was some alternative to representation, as in the article of the Declaration of Rights that said that citizens "have the right to participate personally or through their representatives" in the making of the laws.[2] Leaders did often note the impossibility of direct democracy in a nation of some twenty-five million, but they rarely went into much detail about *why* it was impossible, and their endless claims that one could not assemble the people apparently did not convince those who were assembling and voting in sections and districts.

One leader who did make a sustained positive case for representation was Sieyès, but few others joined him in doing so. Moreover, although Sieyès did at times defend the importance of expertise, at other times he undermined the force of his argument for a division of labor by associating political capacity less with experience or training in technical fields than with the ownership of property, an idea that many perceived as base, selfish, and incompatible with the Revolution's fundamental principles. It is true that barring the poor from voting was hardly unusual in the eighteenth century, but if most theorists of that era believed in linking property ownership and political rights, dissenting voices invoking the idea of equality were influential enough that the exclusion of the poor earned leaders a significant amount of animosity. Those angry over this exclusion soon came to question not only the existing representative forms, but the very idea of political representation as well.

Regarding the specific structures of representation, the problem of the executive must figure in any account of the Revolution's legitimacy crisis. Although one can point out flaws in the specific forms each constitution gave the executive, it is probably better to view the problem as a reflection of a basic tension between two competing schools of thought. On the one hand, that is, theorists such as Montesquieu had taught the revolutionaries to favor a separation and balance of powers, but the ideas about indivisible sovereignty and representation noted above also led many to resist granting any real authority to an independent executive endowed with a popular mandate equal to the legislature's. One indication of the problem was the persistent confusion over whether the executive was a representative of the people or simply a functionary or an agent of the legislature. As some pointed out, if the executive was not a representative, then there would be no real separation and balance of powers, leaving parliament as the only branch that could claim to represent the people. Yet if the executive *was* a representative of the people, then why were the people not allowed to elect it? The Revolution never resolved this problem, and the executive remained a major focal point for political discontent and a persistent obstacle to ending the Revolution.

In accounting for problems in the design of the executive, it is important to note that the legislative branch of the new government wrote all three constitutions. The members of the Constituent Assembly, like the members of the National Convention in 1793 and 1795, wrote a constitution that reflected a severe institutional bias—a problem, by the way, that Charles de Gaulle had in mind when he refused to let legislators write France's new constitution in 1958. Indeed, the leaders' biases and their tendency to act opportunistically also affected a range of other issues of representation. It is easy to see bias and self-interest, for example, in an assembly of property-owning men disenfranchising women and the poor, and historians have often noted the Jacobins' inconsistencies on the question of representation, as they spent their time in opposition asserting the citizens' right to oversee and recall their representatives at will but then shifted abruptly to defending representation once they came to power. So although the language and tone of the Revolution's constitutional debates often seem part of a highly philosophical age, actual practice was deeply opportunistic and hypocritical, as many bitter contemporaries pointed out. In sum, instead of a political class united on the need for representative authority and divided simply over which faction would wield that authority, France had a political class whose members were willing to endanger the entire structure of authority to harm a rival faction. It was, in short, France's representatives who were primarily responsible for undermining belief in representation.

The weakness of the Revolution's formal political institutions and the severe questioning to which they were subjected inevitably placed even greater weight on informal modes of legitimation, bringing the politics of public opinion to the center of revolutionary power struggles. As we have seen, Furet noted this problem, arguing that a crisis of confidence in France's formal representative institutions led to "rule by opinion," but if Furet was right that the weakness of formal institutions made legitimation by public opinion all the more essential, it is another matter whether public opinion became the true power in the Revolution. As this study has argued, references to public opinion encountered far too much skepticism and confusion to play a major role in the legitimation of authority.

That skepticism, however, like the skepticism that surrounded France's formal institutions, was perhaps even stronger among French leaders and journalists than among its ordinary citizens, and this study has argued that the crisis of confidence affecting elites was far more consequential — in part because they were more powerful and in part because their dissatisfaction led them to encourage citizens to rebel. As for public opinion, this view of France's legitimacy crisis means that the most serious problem was not revolutionary writers' and orators' failure to convince "the people" but their failure to convince each other. From this perspective "the people" were not so much an audience for political rhetoric as a kind of stage prop. Nevertheless, because those hearing references to public opinion in the National Assembly and other arenas judged the truth of those claims in part based on their own impressions of popular opinion, one cannot completely ignore the opinions of ordinary citizens. Therefore, instead of viewing attempts to secure legitimacy as a project involving two groups, leaders and citizens, it may be best to imagine a triangular arrangement in which competing factions are not only addressing the citizenry but also each other.

Even to analyze the revolutionaries' uses of the term "public opinion" can be hazardous, for that phrase quickly lost its prerevolutionary specificity, blending into a cluster of ill-defined terms and neologisms intended to invoke the will of the sovereign people. A few voices objected to this linguistic chaos, with some trying to maintain distinctions between public opinion and the people's opinion or the general will, but such voices were simply ignored. Very much at stake in this process was the issue of whose opinions constituted public opinion, and while many were alarmed at the public sphere's opening to poor and uneducated men and women, others (including those who distinguished between "the public" and "the people") felt that the public still remained too exclusive. Overall, this sudden broadening of public opinion's sociological referent altered perceptions of its characteristics, as prerevolutionary images of public opinion's rationality and reliability soon gave way to perceptions of its irrationality, volatility, and gullibility—even among those who would never admit resenting the expansion of France's public sphere.

As for public opinion's texture, the prerevolutionary pattern of describing opinion in unitary terms remained prevalent during the Revolution, although individualist descriptions of opinion never disappeared. Claims that everyone held a given opinion may have sounded convincing to some timid or indecisive listeners, but people's tendency to be surrounded by like-minded individuals suggests that such sweeping claims probably seemed ridiculous to anyone who did not already hold the opinion in question. In other words, one reason why many people disbelieved claims about public opinion was that those claims failed to acknowledge the existence of competing views. Moreover, insofar as assertions of national unanimity were actually believed, they may have created unrealistic expectations and led to frustrations over the persistence of dissent, perhaps also exacerbating the existing atmosphere of intolerance toward those of a different opinion.

As the previous chapters have shown, the lack of any widely credible means of ascertaining the citizens' opinions kept the rhetoric of public opinion from contributing much to the legitimation of power. Some have argued that France could not possibly have resolved its disputes peacefully given the incommensurability of rival principles such as royal and popular sovereignty, and there is undoubtedly some truth to that argument. Yet people across the political spectrum, including many royalists, did believe quite strongly in the authority of "public opinion," if only out of resignation before a seemingly irresistible force. The lack of any universally recognized voice or representation of public opinion must therefore be considered a major reason why references to public opinion proved so ineffectual. It was as if the French stood before a kind of oracle, believing firmly in the existence of the god but quarreling endlessly over the oracle's accounts of its cryptic pronouncements.

Given the revolutionaries' tendency to act opportunistically and to view constitutional principles almost entirely through the prism of their own immediate political interests, it is not surprising that representations of public opinion were also evaluated that way. The Jacobins, for example, saw crowds in the streets and in the galleries of the National Assembly as authentic manifestations of the popular will only so long as those crowds backed them, whereas moderates and conservatives suddenly began to consider crowds' opinions representative after Thermidor, when their supporters began massing in and around the National Convention. What this suggests is that rival groups' views of each method of ascertaining opinion would only begin to converge when each method had worked both for and against them, which did not happen before 1794 and had only barely begun to happen by 1799. This is not to deny other reasons why many representations of opinion lacked credibility. Newspaper circulation figures and petitions, for example, raised doubts about the possibility of inferring national opinion from information that was so partial (in both senses of that word), and concerns about hidden oligarchies within groups expressing opinions also elicited skepticism, as those on the left dismissed the cahiers and letters from local officials as reflections of elite opinion while moderates dismissed petitions and the demands of crowds on the grounds that the rank and file had been manipulated into backing ideas they did not understand. But each group's indulgence toward flaws in desirable portraits of opinion and skepticism about messengers bearing unwelcome news suggests that the tendency to think opportunistically had much to do with France's failure to find broadly credible representations of public opinion.

Insofar as competing factions believed in incommensurable principles of sovereignty, the lack of suitable procedures for the formation and observation of public opinion or the resolution of political disputes probably mattered little. But was it inevitable for the French to wait another hundred years for political violence to result in the victory of one principle of sovereignty? Perhaps not, for although some royalists rejected any kind of compromise with the new politics, we have seen that many other royalists did not, and the latter group had good reason to doubt the republicans' assertions about public opinion and their claims that the people had clearly and freely proclaimed their preference for a republic. Moreover, many of the revolutionary conflicts, such as those between the Girondins and Montagnards, had little to do with rival principles of sovereignty. Here it is worth considering Habermas's suggestion that carefully designed procedures of deliberation and decision making may allow the formation of viable political communities where consensus on specific political principles, ends, and institutions does not already exist. In this view, regimes, leaders, and policies need only legitimacy, not popularity; the citizens, in other words, do not all need to support a given government, but only to accept the fairness of the procedures by which it gained and exercises its authority.

One can certainly see a search for a procedure-based legitimacy in the French Revolution, even if the efforts to design widely acceptable constitutions and electoral procedures were badly flawed. But if the French put great effort into designing formal political institutions, they put far less into creating procedures for the formulation and verification of public opinion (other than seemingly endless and fruitless debates on freedom of the press). Yet if the French rarely held direct discussions on procedures for ascertaining public opinion, their views on the subject can be found scattered throughout debates on other issues. Based on this study's survey of those views, it seems that the ideals for deliberation and legitimation that Habermas portrayed in *The Structural Transformation* did indeed have some relevance in revolutionary France. For at least some of the French wished for rational and critical debate in a public sphere that allowed various viewpoints to be heard regardless of a speaker's status. Habermas's portrait of that era does need qualification on the grounds that reason was often less valued than virtue and will, and there were also many who did not believe in disregarding speakers' statuses or in hearing all viewpoints. It is also true, of course, that in practice rational-critical deliberation often gave way to gushing sentimentalism, melodrama, hyperbole, ridicule, sarcasm, heckling, shouting matches, ad hominem arguments, character assassination, denunciation, intimidation, and physical violence, so that the French Revolution often bears little resemblance to Habermas's sanguine, if brief, portrait of it. Yet it is important to note that violations of the *ideals* Habermas outlines did often cost the system and its leaders much-needed legitimacy.

Violations of barriers between the government and the public sphere also led some to question the legitimacy of the public opinion subsequently produced there. Royal subsidies for certain newspapers outraged many on the left, as did those offered during the Republic's first year by Roland's Interior Ministry. Such practices led one deputy to complain that "all the committees for formation of the public spirit have only been committees for its deformation," but moderates and conservatives found it equally outrageous that the Mountain's representatives-on-mission were working, as one speaker said, "to subjugate public opinion."[3] As usual, people's positions were rarely consistent; Robespierre, for example, demanded at one point that the government execute writers who criticized the Parisians, and he also repeatedly urged the Convention to "direct" public opinion, but he also protested Roland's press subsidies and declared that "it is for public opinion to judge the men who govern and not for the latter to master and create public opinion."[4] So although Habermas's general point that state intrusion into the public sphere harms legitimation has some relevance to the revolutionary period, it would be more precise to say that the French of that time believed firmly in government intervention when it helped them or harmed their enemies but found it scandalous when the reverse was true.

Another characteristic of revolutionary France's public sphere that helps account for this legitimacy crisis is the lack of a national network of communication. Individual parties and groups such as the Jacobins and the Cercle Social had some connections among their local chapters, but nothing really linked these competing groups in one national forum. In the absence of any dominant national newspaper containing a broad panoply of ideas and opinions that all could read, many became suspicious of expressions of opinion on the grounds that people had only heard one side of a given argument (which was often true). Some political leaders perceived this problem and concluded that a true "public opinion" or "national will" could only form in the National Assembly, where a unified arena for deliberation existed, but the idea that public opinion could not exist outside the National Assembly seemed unacceptable to many. Nevertheless, in attempting to operate a kind of direct democracy in the absence of any national forum for deliberation, the French were in effect acting as if they had a unified national public sphere without actually having one, and the gap between this poor infrastructure of communication and an ideology of direct democracy (combined with a fierce rejection of any kind of federalism or decentralization) created a serious problem for political legitimation. That gap also explains the bitter battles over Paris's role, with one side insisting, quite understandably, that provincial opinion be valued, and the other claiming, also with good reason, that people in the provinces were not as well informed as the Parisians.

Although Habermas primarily warns of governments crossing the barrier with the public sphere, the events of this period also point to the damage to legitimacy caused by incursions from the public sphere into the realm of the government. Letters to the National Assembly and Convention often expressed outrage over spectators in the galleries interrupting the deputies' work and seeking to intimidate and influence them; more than once, militants even "invaded" the deputies' portion of the hall, seating themselves among the deputies of the left after presenting petitions and remaining there (over the other deputies' protests) while that body was still at work. In short, perceptions that the deputies were acting under duress created doubts about the legitimacy of many of the state's actions.[5]

Moreover, just as incursions from the public sphere into the realm of the government produced resentment, so did incursions into what Habermas calls the "intimate sphere." Many a recent study of prerevolutionary France has pointed to growing public concern over private virtue; as Simon Schama writes, "wholesome domesticity was officially considered a necessary attribute of patriotism," and "in this scheme of values there could be no distinction between the private and the public realm."[6] Throughout the Revolution's first years, the insistence on private virtue and transparency continued to intensify, becoming nearly irresistible when combined with belief in Rousseau's more explicitly political ideas such as popular sovereignty and an omnipotent general will. By the time of the Terror, the growth of these values and ideas culminated in the opening of mail, the searching of private residences, and other similar actions, eventually producing a backlash and a rejection of the legitimacy of any regime that would use such means. Therefore, if the French did not always envision the public sphere in quite the way Habermas suggests, many people did resent invasions of both the intimate sphere and the realm of the state, and that resentment exacerbated the legitimacy crisis of the time.

For Habermas, the "structural transformation" of Europe's public sphere and the cause of Europe's modern legitimacy crisis arose after 1870, when the entry of the proletariat into a public sphere previously occupied only by the bourgeoisie created a clash of incommensurable class interests that no rational deliberation could resolve, thus leading to a vastly expanded state role. Can this idea be applied to the Revolution? In other words, did a similar scenario not take place in the 1790s, with a new class entering the public sphere and producing a stalemate of class interests, in turn leading to greater state intervention? Many of the problems with portraying the Revolution as a class struggle are too well known to repeat here, but if it makes little sense to speak of a clash of incommensurable objective class interests, there may indeed be grounds to speak of a clash of more or less class-based political cultures at this time, and the legitimacy crisis and political stalemate of this period may be traced in part to difficulties of communication and political coexistence between the highly educated and wealthy deputies and the less educated and poorer sans-culottes.

An incident in the National Convention in April 1793 may illustrate this problem. A "citoyenne," angry that rich men were not volunteering for military duty, read a petition urging the state to send them to the front while holding their wives and children hostage and slitting their throats at their husbands' and fathers' "slightest treason." That demand produced a "general movement of horror" among the deputies, suggesting that this was more than just a policy disagreement.[7] As this incident shows, one can routinely see fundamental differences between the deputies and the sans-culottes in everything from patterns of speech and interpretations of terms to attitudes toward individualism and dissent, respect for the law, and the political use of violence. The growing presence of the sans-culottes in France's public life at this time may thus help explain why so many of the Revolution's debates were little more than dialogues of the deaf, ending in stalemate between moderates and the radicals who either came from the lower classes or, more often, simply embraced their demands and outlook. Given their attitudes toward dealing with political opponents and their dissatisfaction with existing arrangements, the sans-culottes' entry into the country's public life also helps explain much of the Revolution's violence.

But given the dominant attitudes among the sans-culottes, is it even appropriate to speak of an opposition between violence and legitimacy, treating violence as an indicator of legitimacy crisis and a consequence of the failure of the politics of public opinion? Offering an important argument that few specialists in the Revolution have addressed, Simon Schama rejects the idea that revolutionary violence was "an unfortunate side-effect from which enlightened Patriots could selectively avert their eyes." Outbursts of incredibly savage violence, he contends, were not mere parentheses, but were "the Revolution's source of collective energy" and the foundation of the new leaders' power. In his words, violence "was what made the Revolution revolutionary."[8] Considering how much time the participants spent demanding and threatening violence before it was used, and how much time and effort they then devoted to recalling and celebrating moments of violence — commemorating some of the Revolution's bloodiest *journées* through festivals and an extensive iconography — there is much to be said for Schama's claim that episodes of violence were neither aberrational nor tangential to the course of the Revolution. To a certain extent, then, it may be best to portray violence as an *expression* of public opinion and to describe it not as a consequence of legitimacy crisis but as a deliberate means of legitimation by purification.

Yet one might wish to qualify Schama's thesis by noting that the French Revolution was not a coherent and unitary whole, but rather a complex quilt woven by many artisans with strikingly different visions. The Revolution that the sans-culottes and their elite allies envisioned and implemented did often seem to value violence (even if Robespierre, who had no stomach for it, preferred to avert his eyes), but for many other French citizens this use of force was appalling, depressing, and deeply embarrassing. So although the Revolution produced countless scenes of horrific violence and repulsive practices such as the joyful display of severed heads, it also produced the Declaration of Rights and other similarly liberal decrees. Moreover, although Schama is right that many revolutionary leaders condoned and justified even the worst examples of mob violence, many other leaders and citizens condemned this violence, demanded the punishment of its perpetrators, and rejected the legitimacy of regimes and leaders that used it so extensively. Even many Jacobins seem to have felt profoundly ambivalent and insecure about their use of violence and their violations of liberal principles, and one suspects that Jacobin orators defending the justice of their actions were often seeking to convince themselves as well as their rivals. For many of the French, the occasional recourse to violence, as in the taking of the Bastille, might be tolerable, but once violence began to appear a systematic and permanent means of political action against more than just a handful of "aristocrats," it became increasingly objectionable to a growing number of people. Therefore, though it is true that violence was an indispensable feature of one important system of legitimation in the French Revolution, that system was only one of several competing systems, and given the breadth and depth of hostility toward it there are indeed grounds for viewing violence as an indicator and a consequence of a major legitimacy crisis in revolutionary France.

Because so many of the French found it outrageous when others used violence to gain political power, one must consider violence a cause as well as a consequence of the country's legitimacy crisis. Even verbal violence hampered efforts to form a broad political community, for the utter collapse of civility—which historians have shown was crucial to the formation of public opinion before 1789—certainly made it harder for participants in the Revolution's debates to forge any common understanding. But if the lack of civility did undeniable damage, one could argue that it simply reflected a more fundamental problem: a rejection of the very idea of pluralism. As political theorists have sometimes noted, pluralism and democracy involve a kind of moral relativism that treats all opinions, speakers, and positions indifferently, and that idea was simply unacceptable to many in France, particularly the Jacobins. Any attempt to unite a nation through deliberative and political procedures, that is, presumes that the competing groups recognize each other's membership in that nation, and that was not always the case in the Revolution. Once again, however, it would be misleading to conclude that the French were all too illiberal to live in a pluralist democracy, for this study has noted considerable support for liberal principles even during the Terror. Rather than concluding that the French rejected pluralism, then, it would be better to say that those favoring a pluralist democracy were defeated at several key moments by minorities using force. This problem underlines the point that although governments need some measure of legitimacy, they also need laws, and sometimes they must also use force or intimidation in support of the laws to remain in power, a point that liberal thinkers in general, and the National Assembly in particular, did not seem to grasp sufficiently at the time. And yet if pluralists relied too much on persuasion, their rivals on the left relied too much on force and intimidation during their time in power, making their regime just as unstable as those of their predecessors.

One final problem to note concerning public opinion was the confusion surrounding its role and its relationship to legal authorities. Once the Revolution began, many jubilantly declared that rulers would henceforth heed the dictates of public opinion, but the same speakers also claimed that France's government was now a faithful reflection of the will of the people. These dual claims constituted a serious dilemma, as people in effect asserted both that the government was an infallible expression of public opinion and that governments would now obey public opinion. For the government to claim that its opinion *was* public opinion seemed to replicate absolutism by denying the legitimacy of any other public voice, and yet if one did *not* claim that the government was an expression of public opinion, then its right to rule at all or to resist expressions of public opinion would remain very much in question, particularly given leaders' constant assertions of the people's powers over their representatives.

The problem might have been resolved by making more modest claims about the government's relationship to the will of the people, by presenting representation in a more positive light, and by treating public opinion as a force that advised but did not dictate to elected rulers. Opposition deputies and journalists, however, could not resist scoring political points against incumbents by constantly asserting the people's unlimited right to dictate to their representatives, to recall them from office at will, and even to launch insurrections against them. Given the combination of the revolutionaries' intense investment in the concept of public opinion and the lack of any practical and credible means of its expression, one could say that public opinion in revolutionary France ended up as a theory without a practice, creating considerable disappointment. But if public opinion was a theory without a practice, the inevitable use of representation in a system whose leaders made no clear and consistent case for it meant that France's representative system was a practice without a theory, also creating serious problems for the system's legitimacy. Add to this the confusion and discord over whose opinions constituted public opinion and the frequent demands that the public speak unanimously, and it is not hard to see why public opinion never really became the true power in the French Revolution, remaining only a highly contested set of proposed fictions and means of legitimation.

These problems, then, suggest that the roots of revolutionary France's legitimacy crisis lay not only in familiar areas such as the war and the economic crisis, but also in the politics of public opinion and other aspects of the political culture that much of the existing literature has not sufficiently recognized. In seeking to explain these problems, it seems essential to mention Rousseau's influence, for although some historians have sought to downplay the influence of *The Social Contract*, there seems little doubt that Rousseau's ideas—particularly his remarks on popular sovereignty, his concept of an infallible general will, his denigration of representation, and the overall utopianism of much of his political commentary—had an enormous and often unfortunate influence on the revolutionaries, even on those who only knew those ideas from hearing others quote (and misquote) them.[9]

Setting aside the entire question of influences, however, it is possible to explain some of the problems examined here by emphasizing the old concept of the revolutionaries' political inexperience. Tocqueville's version of this argument, which held that the inexperience and naïvety of the philosophes led them to pursue utopian experiments at the expense of time-tested political arrangements, has long been criticized, but if posed somewhat differently, the concept of inexperience may yet prove useful. Several historians have pointed out that both the philosophes and the revolutionaries of 1789 actually had far more practical political experience than Tocqueville acknowledged, but it bears noting that they gained their experience under a completely different kind of political system.[10] The experience the revolutionaries really needed was that of running a political system based on popular sovereignty, and that kind of experience no one in France possessed.

The French, then, had little choice but to serve a kind of unguided apprenticeship, working out the problems of popular sovereignty and public opinion with little directly relevant experience and no store of memories of past mistakes to help them plot their course. Difficult questions such as whose opinions should count, how public opinion should be ascertained, and what its relationship to formal political institutions should be simply could not be settled using theories learned from books, particularly since some of the most appealing theories were so utopian. Already by 1795 one can see a nascent accumulation of useful memories and lessons, as deputies responded much more decisively than before in dealing with issues such as crowds' claims to speak for the people. Nevertheless, resolving the immense problems inherent in the attempt to generate stable and legitimate authority from abstractions such as "the people" and "public opinion" would take much more than a decade. So although Furet may have been right that it took a full century for France to end the Revolution by settling the question of sovereignty, it would take at least another century after that for the French to reach even a basic working consensus on the profoundly problematic but ultimately irresistible concept of public opinion.

Notes

❦

Introduction

1. Jürgen Habermas, *The Structural Transformation of the Public Sphere: An Inquiry into a Category of Bourgeois Society*, trans. Thomas Burger and Frederick Lawrence (Cambridge, Mass.: MIT Press, 1989).

2. For a review of French historians' comments on Habermas's work, see Jon Cowans, "Habermas and French History: The Public Sphere and the Problem of Political Legitimacy," *French History* 13 (June 1999): 134–60; see also Benjamin Nathans, "Habermas's 'Public Sphere' in the Era of the French Revolution," *French Historical Studies* 16 (1990): 620–44.

3. Keith Michael Baker, "Public Opinion as Political Invention," in *Inventing the French Revolution* (Cambridge: Cambridge University Press, 1990), 167–99.

4. Baker, *Inventing*, 168.

5. Mona Ozouf, "'Public Opinion' at the End of the Old Regime," *Journal of Modern History* 60 (September 1988): 7; Jürgen Habermas, "Concluding Remarks," in *Habermas and the Public Sphere*, ed. Craig Calhoun (Cambridge, Mass.: MIT Press, 1992), 465; see also William H. Sewell, Jr., *A Rhetoric of Bourgeois Revolution: The Abbé Sieyes and* What Is the Third Estate? (Durham, N.C.: Duke University Press, 1994), 29–33; Vivian R. Gruder, "Whither Revisionism? Political Perspectives on the Ancien Régime," *French Historical Studies* 20 (spring 1997): 252–54.

6. Sarah Maza, *Private Lives and Public Affairs: The Causes Célèbres of Prerevolutionary France* (Berkeley and Los Angeles: University of California Press, 1993), 315.

7. Baker, *Inventing*, 168.

8. Arlette Farge, *Subversive Words: Public Opinion in Eighteenth-Century France*, trans. Rosemary Morris (University Park: Pennsylvania State University Press, 1995); Maza, *Private Lives*; Dena Goodman, *The Republic of Letters: A Cultural History of the French Enlightenment* (Ithaca, N.Y.: Cornell University Press, 1994); Daniel Gordon, *Citizens without Sovereignty: Equality and Sociability in French Thought, 1670–1789* (Princeton, N.J.: Princeton University Press, 1994); David A. Bell, *Lawyers and Citizens: The Making of a Political Elite in Old Regime France* (New York and Oxford: Oxford University Press, 1994); Roger Chartier, *The Cultural Origins of the French Revolution*, trans. Lydia G. Cochrane (Durham, N.C.: Duke University Press, 1991), chapter 2. For a review of four of these works, see Dale K. Van Kley, "In Search of Eighteenth-Century Parisian Public Opinion," *French Historical Studies* 19 (spring 1995): 215–26. There is also Kenneth Margerison, *Pamphlets and*

Public Opinion: The Campaign for a Union of Orders in the Early French Revolution (West Lafayette, Ind.: Purdue University Press, 1998), but that book is not a study of the concept of public opinion.

9. J. A. W. Gunn, *Queen of the World: Opinion in the Public Life of France from the Renaissance to the Revolution* (Oxford: Voltaire Foundation, 1995).

10. Philip P. Wiener, ed., *Dictionary of the History of Ideas* (New York: Scribner, 1973); *Dictionnaire historique de la Révolution Française* (Paris: Presses universitaires de France, 1988).

11. Mona Ozouf, "Public Spirit," in *A Critical Dictionary of the French Revolution*, ed. François Furet and Mona Ozouf, trans. Arthur Goldhammer (Cambridge, Mass.: Belknap Press of Harvard University Press, 1989), 771–80.

12. François Furet, *Interpreting the French Revolution*, trans. Elborg Forster (Cambridge: Cambridge University Press, 1981).

13. The sources used for the parliamentary debates are the *Archives Parlementaires de 1787 à 1860, première série (1787 à 1799)*, 99 vols.; vols. 1–82 (Paris: P. Dupont, 1879–1914); vols. 83–99 (Paris, 1961–1995) henceforth AP; *Réimpression de l'ancien Moniteur*, 32 vols. (Paris: Plon frères, 1858–1863) henceforth *Moniteur*; *Gazette Nationale, ou Le Moniteur Universel*, 7 vols. (Paris, 1794–1799) henceforth *Gazette Nationale*. For a very critical study of the *Archives Parlementaires*, see Jules Guiffrey, "Etude sur la collection publiée sous le titre de Archives Parlementaires," *La Révolution Française* 16 (1889), 5–29; for a more nuanced view, see Patrick Brasart, *Paroles de la Révolution. Les assemblées parlementaires, 1789–1794* (Paris: Minerve, 1988), 189. On the operations of the National Constituent Assembly, see André Castaldo, *Les methodes de travail de la Constituante* (Paris: Presses Universitaires de France, 1989).

14. F.-A. Aulard, ed., *La Société des Jacobins. Recueil de documents pour l'histoire du Club des Jacobins de Paris*, 6 vols. (Paris: Jouaust, 1889–1897).

15. Furet, *Interpreting*, 49.

Chapter I: Public Opinion and the People in Prerevolutionary France

1. Bernard Faÿ, *Naissance d'un monstre: L'opinion publique* (Paris: Librairie Academique Perrin, 1965); Joseph Klaits, *Absolute Monarchy and Public Opinion: Printed Propaganda under Louis XIV* (Princeton, N.J.: Princeton University Press, 1976).

2. Elisabeth Noelle-Neumann, *The Spiral of Silence: Public Opinion—Our Social Skin* (Chicago and London: University of Chicago Press, 1984), 64–65; see also David A. Bell, *Lawyers and Citizens: The Making of a Political Elite in Old Regime France* (New York and Oxford: Oxford University Press, 1994), 5; Patrice Gueniffey, "Les assemblées et la représentation," in *The Political Culture of the French Revolution*, vol. 2, *The French Revolution and the Creation of Modern Political Culture*, ed. Colin Lucas (Oxford: Pergamon Press, 1988), 241.

3. J. A. W. Gunn, *Queen of the World: Opinion in the Public Life of France from the Renaissance to the Revolution* (Oxford: Voltaire Foundation, 1995), 4. In a 1936 essay, Paul Palmer surveyed ancient and medieval versions of the concept of public opinion, but concluded that the term originated in the eighteenth century; see Paul A. Palmer, "The Concept of Public Opinion in Political Theory," in *Essays in History and Political Theory: In Honor of Charles Howard McIlwain*, ed. Carl Wittke (Cambridge, Mass.: Harvard University Press, 1936), 230–57.

4. Gunn, 105.

5. Baker writes that "the term *opinion publique* was not entirely unknown before the last decades of the Old Regime"; see Keith Michael Baker, *Inventing the French Revolution* (Cambridge: Cambridge University Press, 1990), 168; Maza writes that "appeals to 'the public' and to 'public opinion' . . . can be traced back to struggles over Jansenism in the 1720s and 1730s"; see Sarah Maza, *Private Lives and Public Affairs: The Causes Célèbres of Prerevolutionary France* (Berkeley and Los Angeles: University of California Press, 1993), 314. As Ozouf notes, "first attribution is a risky affair"; see Ozouf, " 'Public Opinion' at the End of the Old Regime," *Journal of Modern History* 60 (September 1988): 2.

6. Jacques Necker, "De l'administration des finances de la France," in *Oeuvres complètes*, vol. 4, ed. Auguste Louis de Staël-Holstein (Darmstadt: Scientia Verlag Aalen, 1970), 49.

7. Gunn, 134.

8. Necker, 9, 52–53.

9. Ibid., 56, 19.

10. Jacques Peuchet, "Discours préliminaire," in *Encyclopédie méthodique: Jurisprudence*, vol. 9, *La police et les municipalités* (Paris: Chez Panckoucke, 1789), ix.

11. Ibid., x.

12. M.-J.-A.-N. Caritat, marquis de Condorcet, "Vie de M. Turgot," in *Oeuvres de Condorcet*, vol. 5, ed. A. Condorcet O'Connor and M. F. Arago (Paris: F. Didot Frères, 1847), 123. See also Baker, *Inventing*, 163, 189.

13. See Dena Goodman, *The Republic of Letters: A Cultural History of the French Enlightenment* (Ithaca, N.Y.: Cornell University Press, 1994); Dena Goodman, "Governing the Republic of Letters: The Politics of Culture in the French Enlightenment," *History of European Ideas* 13 (1991): 183–99; Anthony J. La Vopa, "Conceiving a Public: Ideas and Society in Eighteenth-Century Europe," *Journal of Modern History* 64 (March 1992): 79–116.

14. This is not to suggest that Habermas was alone in eliciting such interest; long before Habermas, Augustin Cochin and many others studied prerevolutionary and revolutionary social institutions and practices.

15. François Furet, *Revolutionary France, 1770–1880*, trans. Antonia Nevill (Oxford: Blackwell, 1992), 14. For examples of such arguments, see Dale K. Van Kley,

The Damiens Affair and the Unraveling of the Old Regime, 1750–1770 (Princeton, N.J.: Princeton University Press, 1984); Jeffrey Merrick, *The Desacralization of the French Monarchy in the Eighteenth Century* (Baton Rouge: Louisiana State University Press, 1990); Roger Chartier, *The Cultural Origins of the French Revolution*, trans. Lydia G. Cochrane (Durham, N.C.: Duke University Press, 1994), 122; Roger Chartier, "Culture populaire et culture politique dans l'Ancien Régime: quelques réflexions," in *The Political Culture of the Old Regime*, vol. 1, *The French Revolution and the Creation of Modern Political Culture*, ed. Keith Michael Baker (Oxford: Pergamon Press, 1987), 255; Baker, *Inventing*, 227–28.

16. Habermas, *Structural Transformation*, 21; Bell, *Lawyers and Citizens*, 12–13.

17. Baker, *Inventing*, 172, 232.

18. Thomas E. Crow, *Painters and Public Life in Eighteenth-Century Paris* (New Haven, Conn.: Yale University Press, 1985); Maza, *Private Lives*, 6; Baker, *Inventing*, 171.

19. On this subject, see chapter 3 of Baker, *Inventing*; Bell, *Lawyers and Citizens*, 11; Chartier, *Cultural Origins*, 43; Arlette Farge, *Subversive Words: Public Opinion in Eighteenth-Century France,* trans. Rosemary Morris (University Park: Pennsylvania State University Press, 1995), 163; Reinhardt Koselleck, *Critique and Crisis: Enlightenment and the Pathogenesis of Modern Society* (Cambridge, Mass.: MIT Press, 1988), 138.

20. See, for example, David D. Bien, "Offices, Corps, and a System of State Credit: The Uses of Privilege under the Ancien Régime," in *Political Culture of the Old Regime*, 89–114; Gail Bossenga, "City and State: An Urban Perspective on the Origins of the French Revolution," in *Political Culture of the Old Regime*, 115–40; Bell, *Lawyers and Citizens*, 12–13.

21. See François Furet, *Interpreting the French Revolution*, trans. Elborg Forster (Cambridge: Cambridge University Press, 1981), 38–39.

22. Jacques-Bénigne Bossuet, "Politique tirée des propres paroles de l'Ecriture sainte," in *Oeuvres choisies de Bossuet*, vol. 2 (Paris: Hachette, 1892), 70.

23. Necker, 47; Ozouf, "Public Opinion," 10.

24. Furet, *Revolutionary France*, 17; see also Furet, *Interpreting*, 39; Baker, *Inventing*, 198.

25. Quoted in Pierre Rosanvallon, *Le sacre du citoyen: Histoire du suffrage universel en France* (Paris: Gallimard, 1992), 152; see also Ozouf, "Public Opinion," 14; Maza, *Private Lives*, 121.

26. Ozouf, "Public Opinion," 17; Goodman, *Republic of Letters*, 240.

27. Baker, *Inventing*, 186; see also Keith Michael Baker, "Defining the Public Sphere in Eighteenth-Century France: Variations on a Theme by Habermas," in *Habermas and the Public Sphere*, 192.

28. M.-J.-A.-N. Caritat, marquis de Condorcet, "Réflexions sur le commerce des blés," in *Oeuvres de Condorcet*, vol. 2, 201; Lezay-Marnezia, quoted in Rosanvallon, 158.

29. Condorcet, "Vie de M. Turgot," 112.

30. D'Alembert, quoted in Ozouf, "Public Opinion," 9; Condorcet, "Réflexions," 201, 197; see also Maza, *Private Lives*, 76–77; Baker, *Inventing*, 116, 189; Peuchet, x.

31. Necker, 60, 50.

32. Daniel Roche, *The People of Paris: An Essay in Popular Culture in the Eighteenth Century*, trans. Marie Evans and Gwynne Lewis (Berkeley and Los Angeles: University of California Press, 1987), 197–233; Chartier, *Cultural Origins*, 69; Françoise Weil, "La notion de 'peuple' et ses synonymes de 1715 à 1755 dans les textes non littéraires," in *Images du peuple au dix-huitième siècle. Colloque d'Aix-en-Provence, 25 et 26 octobre 1969* (Paris: Armand Colin, 1973), 31. A study of book ownership using death inventories in eighteenth-century Grenoble, however, shows both that book ownership was fairly rare among the "popular classes" and that the books owned were not very scholarly; see Jacques Solé, "Lecture et classes populaires à Grenoble au dix-huitième siècle: le témoignage des inventaires après décès," in *Images du peuple*, 95–102. For a discussion of commoners using the term "the public" in Louis XV's reign, see Lisa Jane Graham, "Crimes of Opinion: Policing the Public in Eighteenth-Century Paris," in *Visions and Revisions of Eighteenth-Century France*, ed. Christine Adams, Jack R. Censer, and Lisa Jane Graham (University Park: Pennsylvania State University Press, 1997), 79–103.

33. Quoted in Baker, *Inventing*, 192.

34. Quoted in Baker, *Inventing*, 129.

35. Maza, *Private Lives*, 253.

36. Daniel Gordon, *Citizens without Sovereignty: Equality and Sociability in French Thought, 1670–1789* (Princeton, N.J.: Princeton University Press, 1994), 201.

37. See Alexis de Tocqueville, *The Old Régime and the Revolution*, trans. Stuart Gilbert (Garden City, N.Y.: Doubleday and Company, 1955), part 3, chapter 1; see also Chartier, *Cultural Origins*, 9–10.

38. Ozouf, "Public Opinion," 5; see also Rosanvallon, 156; on French horror over political division in England, see Baker, *Inventing*, 179–85, 196.

39. Condorcet, "Vie de M. Turgot," 112; Necker, 8, 21.

40. Necker, 12.

41. For a brief account of the term's history in France, see Judith N. Shklar, "General Will," in vol. 2 of *Dictionary of the History of Ideas*, ed. Philip P. Wiener (New York: Scribner, 1973), 275–81.

42. Jean-Jacques Rousseau, *The Social Contract*, trans. Maurice Cranston (Harmondsworth: Penguin Books, 1968), 150, 72.

43. Ibid., 150.

44. Ibid., 72.

45. Jacques Julliard, *La faute à Rousseau. Essai sur les conséquences historiques de l'idée de souveraineté populaire* (Paris: Editions du Seuil, 1985), 18; Jean Roels also mentions the statement; see Jean Roels, *Le concept de représentation politique aux dix-huitième siècle*

français (Louvain: Editions Nauwelaerts, 1969), 13; see also Harry C. Payne, *The Philosophes and the People* (New Haven, Conn.: Yale University Press, 1976), 173.

46. Baker, *Inventing*, 186.

47. Rousseau, 73. On the concept of deliberation, see Bernard Manin, "Volonté générale ou délibération? Esquisse d'une théorie de la délibération politique," *Le débat* 33 (January 1985): 72–93.

48. François Furet and Mona Ozouf, "Deux legitimations historiques de la société française au dix-huitième siècle: Mably et Boulainvilliers," *Annales ESC* 34 (May–June 1979): 438.

49. See Furet, *Interpreting*, 32–36.

50. On the parlements and their notion of national sovereignty, see Roger Bickart, *Les parlements et la notion de la souveraineté nationale au XVIIIe siècle* (Paris: F. Alcan, 1932).

51. David A. Bell, "The 'Public Sphere,' the State, and the World of Law in Eighteenth-Century France," *French Historical Studies* 17 (fall 1992): 923; see also Baker, *Inventing*, chapter 2; Keith Michael Baker, "Representation," in *Political Culture of the Old Regime*, 474.

52. Necker, 21, 53.

53. Bossuet, 60, 45.

54. Ibid., 58; see also Chartier, "Culture populaire," 246.

55. Bossuet, 44, 59.

56. Ibid., 44.

57. Ibid., 113; see also Lucien Jaume, *Le discours Jacobin et la démocratie* (Paris: Fayard, 1989), 376.

58. See Rosanvallon, 22–29.

59. Necker, 70.

60. Keith Michael Baker and Anthea Waleson, trans. "Remonstrance of the *Cour des aides* (6 May 1775)," in *The Old Regime and the French Revolution*, ed. Keith Michael Baker (Chicago: University of Chicago Press, 1987), 65; see also Maza, *Private Lives*, 55.

61. "Remonstrance," 53.

62. Ibid., 65.

63. Charles Loyseau, "A Treatise on Orders," trans. Sheldon Mossberg and William H. Sewell, Jr., in *The Old Regime and the French Revolution*, 28; Louis de Jaucourt, "Le Peuple," in *The Encyclopédie of Diderot and D'Alembert: Selected Articles*, ed. J. Lough (Cambridge: Cambridge University Press, 1954), 173.

64. Jaucourt, 173; see also Payne, 7–8. On Jaucourt's debt to Coyer, see Jean Fabre, "L'article 'Peuple' de l'Encyclopédie et le couple Coyer-Jaucourt," *Images du peuple*, 11–24.

65. Quoted in Payne, 96.

66. Necker, 70.

67. *Dictionnaire universel, contenant généralement tous les mots françois tant vieux que modernes*, quoted in Payne, 8; Holbach, quoted in Payne, 20; see also Chartier, "Culture populaire," 245.

68. Voltaire, quoted in Payne, 19; Diderot, quoted in Roland Mortier, "Diderot et la notion de 'peuple,'" *Europe* 405–6 (January–February 1963): 82, 84.

69. See Payne, 96, 112–13, 184; on denigration of the people at this time, see also Chartier, *Cultural Origins*, 27–30.

70. Jaucourt, 175; see also Payne's comments on Diderot in Payne, 33; Roche, 40–41; William H. Sewell, Jr., *A Rhetoric of Bourgeois Revolution: The Abbé Sieyes and What Is the Third Estate?* (Durham, N.C.: Duke University Press, 1994), 183.

71. Quoted in Jean-Jacques Clere, "L'emploi des mots nation et peuple dans le langage politique de la Révolution Française (1789–1799)," in *Nation et république. Les elements d'un débat. Actes du colloque de Dijon (6–7 April 1994)* (Aix-en-Provence: Presses Universitaires d'Aix-Marseilles, 1995), 53; on Condorcet's distinction between *peuple* and *populace*, see Isabelle Vissière, "L'émancipation du peuple selon Condorcet," in *Images du peuple*, 205–6.

72. Ozouf, "Equality," in *A Critical Dictionary of the French Revolution*, ed. François Furet and Mona Ozouf, trans. Arthur Goldhammer (Cambridge, Mass.: Belknap Press of Harvard University Press, 1989), 671.

73. Letter to Linguet, 15 March 1767, in *Voltaire's Correspondence*, vol. 65, ed. T. Besterman (Geneva: Institut et Musée Voltaire, 1953–1965), 47–48.

74. Condorcet, "Réflexions," 206; see also Vissière, 206–8.

75. Quoted in Mortier, 81, 84.

76. Mortier, 87.

77. Harvey Chisick, *The Limits of Reform in the Enlightenment: Attitudes toward the Education of the Lower Classes in Eighteenth-Century France* (Princeton, N.J.: Princeton University Press, 1981), 52; Payne, 106; see also Weil, 32–33. On eighteenth-century views on the wisdom of trying to educate "the people," see Jean Biou, "Est-il utile de tromper le peuple?" in *Images du peuple*, 187–99.

78. Payne, 42; see also Shelby McCloy, *The Humanitarian Movement in Eighteenth-Century France* (Lexington: University of Kentucky Press, 1957).

79. Maza, *Private Lives*, 91, 215.

80. Ozouf, "Equality," 672.

81. Quoted in Darline Gay Levy, *The Ideas and Careers of Simon-Nicolas-Henri Linguet: A Study in Eighteenth-Century French Politics* (Urbana: University of Illinois Press, 1980), 121.

82. Payne, 149. On Condorcet's humanitarian view of the laboring classes, see Vissière, 201–13.

83. Ozouf, "Equality," 672; see also Corrado Rosso, *Mythe de l'egalité et rayonnement des Lumières* (Pisa: Editrice Libreria Goliardica, 1980), 104.

84. On this trend, see Chartier, "Culture populaire," 252; Chartier, *Cultural Origins*, 168; Farge, *Subversive Words*, 160, 198.

85. Furet, *Interpreting*, 40.

Chapter II: Sovereignty and Representation, 1789–1792

1. See Maurice Cranston, "The Sovereignty of the Nation," in *Political Culture of the French Revolution*, vol. 2, *The French Revolution and the Creation of Modern Political Culture,* ed. Colin Lucas (Oxford: Pergamon Press, 1988), 102; Lynn Hunt, "The 'National Assembly,'" in *The Political Culture of the Old Regime*, vol. 1, *The French Revolution and the Creation of Modern Political Culture,* ed. Keith Michael Baker (Oxford: Pergamon Press, 1988), 407–9, 413; François Furet and Mona Ozouf, "Deux legitimations historiques de la société Française au dix-huitième siècle: Mably et Boulainvilliers," *Annals ESC* 34 (May–June, 1979): 438–50; François Furet, *Interpreting the French Revolution*, trans. Elborg Forster (Cambridge: Cambridge University Press, 1981), 34. On the origins and development of the idea of national sovereignty in France, see J. K. Wright, "National Sovereignty and the General Will: The Political Program of the Declaration of Rights," in *The French Idea of Freedom: The Old Regime and the Declaration of Rights of 1789*, ed. Dale K. Van Kley (Stanford, Calif.: Stanford University Press, 1994), 200–10.

2. Michael P. Fitzsimmons, *The Remaking of France: The National Assembly and the Constitution of 1791* (Cambridge: Cambridge University Press, 1994), 42; Sewell writes that the events of 10–17 June "began the decisive transfer of sovereignty from the king to the nation"; see William H. Sewell, *A Rhetoric of Bourgeois Revolution: The Abbé Sieyes and* What Is the Third Estate? (Durham, N.C.: Duke University Press, 1994), 17–18.

3. P.-J.-B. Buchez and P. C. Roux, eds., *Histoire parlementaire de la Révolution Française*, vol. 2 (Paris: Paulin, 1835), 309–11; AP 8:285ff.

4. His proposed draft appears in François Furet and Ran Halévi, eds., *Orateurs de la Révolution Française*, vol. 1 (Paris: Gallimard, 1989), 1016–18.

5. AP 8:463; see also Buchez and Roux, vol. 2, 311–16. Kent Wright notes that Mounier got his wording from a draft by Lafayette; see Wright, 226.

6. AP 29:266; see also Marcel Gauchet, "Rights of Man," in *A Critical Dictionary of the French Revolution*, ed. François Furet and Mona Ozouf, trans. Arthur Goldhammer (Cambridge: Cambridge University Press, 1981), 818; Marcel Gauchet, *La révolution des droits de l'homme* (Paris: Gallimard, 1989), 9.

7. Gauchet, "Rights of Man," 818.

8. *L'Ami du Roi*, 25 September 1790; see also Gauchet, *Droits de l'homme*, 16–19.

9. *Le Journal de Paris*, 9 August 1792.

10. Jean Bodin, *Les six livres de la république,* 3d ed. (Paris: Chez Iacque de Puys, 1578), 96, 161; see also Keith Michael Baker, "Sovereignty," in *Critical Dictionary*, 844–45.

11. In Furet and Halévi, 351 (29 May 1789).

12. See Malouet's speech in AP 8:535–37 (1 September 1789).

13. Baker, "Sovereignty," 852.

14. Furet and Halévi, 1021 (7 September 1789).

15. Ibid., 1022, 1027.

16. AP 8:204 (7 July 1789).

17. Ibid., 183 (2 July 1789).

18. Furet and Halévi, 895 (5 September 1789), 1157 (16 May 1791).

19. Jacques Godechot, ed., *Les constitutions de la France depuis 1789* (Paris: Garnier Flammarion, 1970), 38.

20. AP 29:326 (10 August 1791).

21. Ibid., 327.

22. Ibid., 328.

23. Ibid., 327.

24. Ibid.

25. See, for example, AP 8:214 (9 July 1789), 530 (1 September 1789), 535 (1 September 1789), 538 (1 September 1789), 543 (2 September 1789), 550 (3 September 1789).

26. AP 8:260 (21 July 1789), 583 (5 September 1789); see also Jean-Jacques Clere, "L'emploi des mots nation et peuple dans le langage politique de la Révolution Française (1789–1799)," in *Nation et République. Les éléments d'un débat. Actes du colloque de Dijon (6–7 April 1994)* (Aix-en-Provence: Presses Universitaires d'Aix-Marseilles, 1995), 62.

27. Colin Lucas, "The Crowd and Politics," in *The Political Culture of the French Revolution*, 260. Lucas has also pointed out that the term had both a political and a sociological meaning; see Colin Lucas, "Revolutionary Violence, the People, and the Terror," in *The Terror*, vol. 4, *The French Revolution and the Creation of Modern Political Culture*, ed. Keith Michael Baker (Oxford: Pergamon Press, 1994), 64.

28. AP 8:154 (24 June 1789).

29. AP 8:110 (15 June 1789); for objections to Mirabeau's phrase, see Target, AP 8:114 and Thouret, AP 8:118 (both 15 June 1789); see comments on this episode in Etienne Dumont, *Souvenirs sur Mirabeau* (Paris: C. Gosselin, 1832), 76; Clere, 61.

30. *L'Ami des Patriotes*, 12 March 1791.

31. AP 8:228 (13 July 1789); on the social composition of the militia, see R. B. Rose, *The Making of the Sans-Culottes: Democratic Ideas and Institutions in Paris, 1789–92* (Manchester: Manchester University Press, 1983), 49–50.

32. François Furet, *Revolutionary France, 1770–1880*, trans. Antonia Nevill (Oxford: Blackwell, 1992), 63.

33. Le Vicomte de Noailles, AP 8:233 (14 July 1789).

34. Barnave, ibid., 155 (24 June 1789).

35. Ibid., 312 (31 July 1789); "Les héroïnes de Paris, ou, L'entière liberté de la France par les femmes" (Paris, 1789) [French Revolution Research Collection 6.2/955].

36. *Le Patriote Français*, 28 September 1789.

37. Timothy Tackett, "Nobles and the Third Estate in the Revolutionary Dynamic of the National Assembly, 1789–1790," *American Historical Review* 94 (April 1989): 279; see also Timothy Tackett, *Becoming a Revolutionary: The Deputies of the French National Assembly and the Emergence of a Revolutionary Culture (1789-1790)* (Princeton, N.J.: Princeton University Press, 1996), 169.

38. AP 8:126 (16 June 1789).

39. Ibid., 118 (15 June 1789).

40. Ibid., 146 (23 June 1789).

41. Ibid., 530 (1 September 1789).

42. Mounier, in Furet and Halévi, 894 (5 September 1789).

43. Pétion, AP 8:583–84 (5 September 1789).

44. See, for example, the comments of Barrère de Vieuzac, AP 26:225 (19 May 1791); see also Clere, 64.

45. AP 9:479 (22 October 1789).

46. *L'Ami du Roi*, 12 August 1791.

47. *L'Ami des Patriotes*, 15 January 1791, 7 May 1791.

48. AP 29:264 (8 August 1791); on Malouet's status as a pariah, see Dumont, 249.

49. See the description in AP 45:414.

50. Ibid., 417.

51. Ibid.; the document continues on page 438.

52. George Rudé, *The Crowd in the French Revolution* (Oxford: Oxford University Press, 1959), 44–46, 196; Albert Soboul, *Les sans-culottes parisiens en l'an II. Mouvement populaire et gouvernement révolutionnaire* (Paris: Editions du Seuil, 1968), chapter 3.

53. Quoted in Tackett, *Becoming a Revolutionary*, 141.

54. AP 45:419.

55. Cambon, AP 47:459.

56. Ibid., 128 (25 July 1792).

57. See Title VII of the constitution, in Godechot, 65–66.

58. Isnard, AP 47:128 (25 July 1792); Goujon, ibid., 129.

59. Terrasson, in Aulard, *Jacobins*, 4:4 (17 June 1792).

60. Emmanuel-Joseph Sieyès, *Qu'est-ce que le tiers état?*, in *Ecrits politiques*, ed. Roberto Zapperi (Paris: Editions des Archives Contemporaines, 1985), 162. He later repeated that point in the National Assembly; see AP 8:260.

61. Choudieu, AP 47:646.

62. Ibid., 651 (10 August 1792).

63. Quoted in Maurice Genty, *Paris, 1789–1795. L'aprentissage de la citoyenneté* (Paris: Messidor/Editions Sociales, 1987), 178.

64. Keith Michael Baker, *Inventing the French Revolution* (Cambridge: Cambridge University Press), 226.

65. At least since the time of Daniel Mornet, historians have argued that Rousseau's influence has been overstated and that *The Social Contract* was barely known at the Revolution's outset; see Mornet, *Les origines intellectuelles de la Révolution française (1715–1787)* (Paris: Armand Colin, 1933); see also Joan McDonald, *Rousseau and the French Revolution* (London: Athlone, 1965). For a recent example of such views, see Timothy Tackett, "The Constituent Assembly and the Terror," in *The Terror*, 39–54.

Roger Barny has given the fullest rebuttal to such arguments; see Barny, *Prélude idéologique à la Révolution française. Le Rousseauisme avant 1789* (Paris: Les Belles Lettres, 1985); *Rousseau dans la Révolution. Le personnage de Jean-Jacques et le début du culte revolutionnaire* (Oxford: Voltaire Foundation, 1986); *L'éclatement révolutionnaire du Rousseauisme* (Paris: Les Belles Lettres, 1988).

The argument that Rousseau's political ideas had little impact becomes harder to sustain with each month of the Revolution, as interest in the book grew rapidly; Patrice Higonnet reports that in 1789 *The Social Contract* had not been reprinted for seventeen years, but was then reprinted twenty times between 1790 and 1800; see Higonnet, *Goodness Beyond Virtue: Jacobins during the French Revolution* (Cambridge, Mass.: Harvard University Press, 1998), 319. Also, though many revolutionaries may not have read *The Social Contract*, Gary Kates's report that the Cercle Social studied a chapter from *The Social Contract* in each of its meetings, and Soboul's contention that ideas such as Rousseau's concept of popular sovereignty made their way "as if by osmosis" from the literate to the illiterate sans-culottes suggest that *The Social Contract* influenced more than those who actually read it; see Gary Kates, *The* Cercle Social, *the Girondins, and the French Revolution* (Princeton, N.J.: Princeton University Press, 1985), 80; Soboul, 226.

Rousseau came to accept representation when he designed the Polish constitution, but it was his negative comments in *The Social Contract* that the revolutionaries cited endlessly. On the evolution of Rousseau's thinking on representation, see Richard Fralin, *Rousseau and Representation: A Study of His Concept of Political Institutions* (New York: Columbia University Press, 1978).

66. See Baker, *Inventing*, 244.

67. Furet and Halévi, 1040, 1038.

68. Lameth, AP 8:551 (3 September 1789).

69. Furet and Halévi, 1040 (7 July 1789).

70. Sieyès, *Dire sur la question du veto royal*, in *Écrits politiques*, 237; Sieyès, *Tiers état*, 159.

71. Ibid., 164, 159–60; see also his speech in AP 8:592–601 (7 September 1789); Lucien Jaume, *Le discours Jacobin et la démocratie* (Paris: Fayard, 1989), 258, 285.

72. Mirabeau, AP 8:166 (27 June 1789); Malouet, AP 23:535 (21 February 1791).

73. Furet and Halévi, 1025 (7 September 1789).

74. Sieyès, *Tiers état*, 262; see also Keith Michael Baker, "Sieyès," in *Critical Dictionary*, 320; Sewell, *Rhetoric*, chapter 3.

75. AP 8:530 (1 September 1789).

76. Furet, *Revolutionary France*, 88; Baker points out that from roughly 1750 to 1789 various French reformers articulated what he calls a "social theory of representation," which held the preservation of property to be the aim of society and the basis of a common interest; see Baker, *Inventing*, 238–43.

77. AP 29:331 (10 August 1791).

78. Briois-Beaumetz, ibid., 362 (11 August 1791).

79. Barnave, ibid., 365.

80. Sieyès, *Tiers état*, 164.

81. Jeremy Popkin, *Revolutionary News: The Press in France, 1789–1799* (Durham, N.C.: Duke University Press, 1990), 2; the idea is also mentioned in *Révolutions de Paris*, 7 November 1789.

82. *Révolutions de Paris*, 7 November 1789, 6 December 1789.

83. *Révolutions de Paris*, 7 July 1792.

84. On the rules and procedures for voting, see Rosanvallon, 45, 78–79, 84, 94, 170, 185–86; Isser Woloch, *The New Regime: Transformations of the French Civic Order, 1789–1820s* (New York: W. W. Norton, 1994), 65; for a more detailed account, see also Patrice Gueniffey, *Le nombre et la raison. La Révolution française et les élections* (Paris: Les Editions de l'Ecole des Hautes Etudes en Sciences Sociales, 1993).

85. AP 29:365 (11 August 1791); see also Démeunier's comments, AP 9:479 (22 October 1789).

86. Briois-Beaumetz, AP 29:362 (11 August 1791).

87. Ibid., 357.

88. Ibid., 360.

89. Prugnons, AP 26:120 (16 May 1791).

90. D'Antraigues, AP 8:543 (2 September 1789); Mounier, in Furet and Halévi, 890 (5 September 1789). For a fine overview of ideas about a separation of powers and their intellectual origins, see Wright, 216–22.

91. Michael L. Kennedy, *The Jacobin Clubs: The Middle Years* (Princeton, N.J.: Princeton University Press, 1988), 239, 244.

92. AP 8:535–36 (1 September 1789); see also Keith Michael Baker, "Constitution," in *Critical Dictionary*, 488.

93. Duport, AP 28:264 (14 July 1791); Barrère de Vieuzac, AP 26:224 (19 May 1791); see also Baker, *Inventing*, 248.

94. De Bousmard, AP 8:579 (5 September 1789).

95. Sieyès, *Dire sur le veto royal*, 238.

96. Thouret, AP 29:326 (10 August 1791); Robespierre, AP 29:326 (10 August 1791).

97. Mounier, in Furet and Halévi, 900 (5 September 1789). For examples of deputies claiming it was the nation's will to delegate its powers to both a legislature and a king, see Thouret, AP 29:330; Pastoret, AP 45:446.

98. Roederer, AP 29:323 (10 August 1791); Rabaut, AP 8:569 (4 September 1789).

99. See, for example, Comte Stanislas de Clermont-Tonnerre, AP 8:283 (23 July 1789); Rhédon, ibid., 509 (29 August 1789); Malouet, ibid., 536 (1 September 1789).

100. Barnave, AP 8:242 (16 July 1789); Lally-Tollendal, AP 8:244 (16 July 1789).

101. AP 8:538.

102. Alexandre de Lameth, AP 8:572.

103. AP 8:545 (2 September 1789).

104. Ibid., 543.

105. See Genty, 37, 42–54.

106. *Révolutions de Paris*, 6 December 1789.

107. *Révolutions de Paris*, 6 December 1789, 21 November 1789, 28 November 1789.

108. *Le Publiciste Parisien* 3 (14 September 1789), in Jean-Paul Marat, *Oeuvres politiques, 1789–1793*, vol. 1, ed. Jacques de Cock and Charlotte Goëtz (Brussels: Pole Nord, 1989), 131.

109. Genty, 24.

110. Ibid., 53.

111. The petition appears in John Hall Stewart, ed., *A Documentary Survey of the French Revolution* (New York: MacMillan, 1951), 218–19.

112. AP 46:384.

113. AP 25:697.

114. Rouyer, AP 47:458 (4 August 1792).

115. Maximilien Robespierre, *Oeuvres complètes*, vol. 4, ed. Gustave Laurent (Paris: Societé des Etudes Robespierristes, 1939), 145.

116. Lafont, AP 47:693 (10 August 1792).

117. See Denis Richet, "Revolutionary Assemblies," in *Critical Dictionary*, 534.

Chapter III: Public Opinion and Legitimacy, 1789–1792

1. On this point, see Lucien Jaume, "Les Jacobins et l'opinion publique," in *Le modèle républicain*, ed. Serge Berstein and Odile Rudelle (Paris: Presses Universitaires de France, 1992), 58.

2. *L'Ami des Patriotes*, 1 January 1791; Le Pelletier de Saint-Fargeau, AP 8:616 (12 September 1789).

3. AP 26:208 (18 May 1789); for other examples of this view, see Mounier, in François Furet and Ran Halévi, eds., *Orateurs de la Révolution Française,* vol. 1, *Les*

constituants (Paris: Gallimard, 1989), 888, 900 (5 September 1789); Robespierre, AP 26:124 (16 May 1791).

4. Timothy Tackett, *Becoming a Revolutionary: The Deputies of the French National Assembly and the Emergence of a Revolutionary Culture (1789–1790)* (Princeton, N.J.: Princeton University Press, 1996), 242.

5. On this subject, see Jon Cowans, "Wielding the People: Opinion Polls and the Problem of Legitimacy in France since 1944" (Ph.D. diss., Stanford University, 1994).

6. AP 23:531 (21 February 1791).

7. *L'Ami du Roi*, 23 June 1791.

8. AP 26:124 (16 May 1791).

9. *L'Ami des Patriotes*, 5 March 1791.

10. AP 8:110 (15 June 1789).

11. Aulard, *Jacobins*, 4:6.

12. Crenière, AP 8:550 (3 September 1789); Malouet, AP 23:531 (21 February 1791); see also Pierre Rosanvallon, *Le sacre du citoyen. Histoire du suffrage universel en France* (Paris: Gallimard, 1992), 170; Kenneth Margerison, *Pamphlets and Public Opinion: The Campaign for a Union of Orders in the Early French Revolution* (West Lafayette, Ind.: Purdue University Press, 1998), 12. Dena Goodman points out that among the members of the Cercle Social distinctions between public opinion and the people's opinion, and between public opinion and the general will, disappeared; see Dena Goodman, *The Republic of Letters: A Cultural History of the French Enlightenment* (Ithaca, N.Y.: Cornell University Press, 1994), 297; here I am arguing that that erosion of distinctions was taking place across almost the entire political spectrum.

13. See J. A. W. Gunn, *Queen of the World: Opinion in the Public Life of France from the Renaissance to the Revolution* (Oxford: Voltaire Foundation, 1995), 342.

14. Furet and Halévi, 681 (1 September 1791).

15. *Révolutions de Paris*, 7 November 1789; AP 31:620 (29 September 1791).

16. Mona Ozouf, "Public Spirit," in *A Critical Dictionary of the French Revolution*, ed. François Furet and Mona Ozouf, trans. Arthur Goldhammer (Cambridge, Mass.: Belknap Press of Harvard University Press, 1989), 774.

17. *L'Ami des Patriotes*, 4 December 1790.

18. In J. Gilchrist and W. J. Murray, eds., *The Press in the French Revolution: A Selection of Documents Taken from the Press of the Revolution for the Years 1789–1794* (New York: St. Martin's Press, 1971), 47.

19. AP 47:458 (4 August 1792); Barrère de Vieuzac, AP 26:225 (19 May 1791); Mirabeau, AP 8:243 (16 July 1789).

20. *Le Journal de Paris*, 8–9 August 1792.

21. *Le Patriote Français* #66 (10 October 1789).

22. *Le Journal de Paris*, 9 August 1792.

23. AP 8:541 (1 September 1789).

24. *Le Patriote Français*, 28 September 1789; AP 8:566 (4 September 1789).

25. *Le Patriote Français* (16 March 1789); this prospectus appears in Gilchrist and Murray, 46–47. Dena Goodman notes that the *Mercure Universel* similarly "proclaimed itself a 'central point of correspondence'"; see Goodman, *Republic of Letters*, 293.

26. AP 28:243 (13 July 1791).

27. Ibid., 266 (14 July 1791), 247 (13 July 1791).

28. Goupil-Prefeln, AP 28:317 (15 July 1791).

29. Ferrières, AP 28:247 (13 July 1791).

30. AP 29:276 (8 August 1791).

31. AP 28:266 (14 July 1791).

32. Quoted in Lucien Jaume, "Les Jacobins et l'opinion publique," in *Le modèle républicain,* ed. Serge Berstein and Odile Rudelle (Paris: Presses Universitaires de France, 1992), 59.

33. Ibid.

34. AP 25:690 (10 May 1791).

35. Timothy Tackett, "Nobles and the Third Estate in the Revolutionary Dynamic of the National Assembly, 1789–1790," *American Historical Review* 94 (April 1989): 324–25.

36. Lynn Hunt, *Politics, Culture, and Class in the French Revolution* (Berkeley and Los Angeles: University of California Press, 1984), 44; see also Lucien Jaume, "Les Jacobins: une organisation dans le processus de la Révolution, 1789–1794," in *Les Révolutions Françaises. Les phénomènes révolutionnaires en France du Moyen Age à nos jours*, ed. Frederic Bluche and Stephane Rials (Paris: Fayard, 1989), 245–46.

37. AP 25:678–9 (9 May 1791).

38. Emmanuel Joseph Sieyès, *Qu'est-ce que le tiers état?* in *Ecrits politiques,* ed. Roberto Zapperi (Paris: Editions des Archives Contemporaires, 1985), 179.

39. Ibid., 134.

40. D'André, AP 29:622 (29 September 1791).

41. AP 31:617 (29 September 1791).

42. Billaud-Varenne, quoted in Jaume, "Les Jacobins: une organisation," 245.

43. Gunn, 392.

44. Muguet de Nanthon, AP 28:234, 242 (13 July 1791).

45. AP 47:641 (10 August 1792).

46. Ibid.

47. Stewart, 219; Lamarque, AP 45:435 (21 June 1792).

48. Furet and Halévi, 1027 (7 September 1789).

49. Sieyès, *Tiers état*, 118–21.

50. Anthoine, in Aulard, *Jacobins*, 4:157; *Le Patriote Français*, 1 July 1792.

51. AP 45:653 (28 June 1792).

52. François Furet, *Interpreting the French Revolution*, trans. Elborg Forster (Cambridge: Cambridge University Press, 1981), 184.

53. Patrice Gueniffey, "Elections," in *Critical Dictionary*, 37.

54. See, for example, AP 45:435 (21 June 1792).

55. AP 23:388–89 (21 February 1791).

56. Lamarque, AP 45:435 (21 June 1792).

57. Ibid., 629 (27 June 1792); Isnard, AP 47:129 (25 July 1792).

58. *Le Patriote Français*, 9 June 1792; *L'Ami des Patriotes*, 1 January 1791.

59. *L'Ami des Patriotes*, 18 December 1790.

60. AP 29:276 (8 August 1791).

61. Jaume, "Les Jacobins et l'opinion publique," 58.

62. *L'Ami des Patriotes*, 1 January 1791.

63. AP 28:316 (15 July 1791).

64. Ibid., 271 (14 July 1791).

65. Jeremy Popkin, *Revolutionary News: The Press in France, 1789–1799* (Durham, N.C.: Duke University Press, 1990), 3; Jaume, "Les Jacobins et l'opinion publique," 59.

66. Mona Ozouf, "'Public Opinion' at the End of the Old Regime," *Journal of Modern History* 60 (September 1988): 1; see also Lucien Jaume, *L'échec au libéralisme: Les Jacobins et l'état* (Paris: Editions Kimé, 1990), 46.

67. AP 8:283 (23 July 1789).

68. Popkin, *Revolutionary News*, 4.

69. Ibid., 5.

70. *Le Journal de Paris*, 16 July 1791.

71. *Révolutions de Paris*, 14 July 1792.

72. Gary Kates, *The Cercle Social, the Girondins, and the French Revolution* (Princeton, N.J.: Princeton University Press, 1985), 56; see also Marcel Dorigny, "Le Cercle social ou les écrivains au cirque," in *La carmagnole des muses*, ed. Jean-Claude Bonnet (Paris: Armand Colin, 1988), 49–66.

73. Quoted in Maurice Genty, *Paris, 1789–1795: L'apprentissage de la citoyenneté* (Paris: Messidor/Editions Sociales, 1987), 133.

74. Quoted in Genty, 134.

75. See R. B. Rose, *The Making of the Sans-Culottes: Democratic Ideas and Institutions in Paris 1789–92* (Manchester: Manchester University Press, 1983), 90–96.

76. Raymonde Monnier, *L'espace public démocratique. Essai sur l'opinion à Paris de la Révolution au Directoire* (Paris: Editions Kimé, 1994).

77. *L'Ami du Roi*, 17 July 1791, 2 May 1791; *La Gazette Universelle*, 31 July 1791. On conservative opposition to the Jacobins, see William James Murray, *The Right-Wing Press in the French Revolution: 1789–92* (Suffolk: The Boydell Press, 1986), 113–16; Paul R. Hanson, "Monarchist Clubs and the Pamphlet Debate over Political Legitimacy in the Early Years of the French Revolution," *French Historical Studies* 21 (spring 1998): 299–324.

78. *Le Journal de Paris*, 21 June 1792.

79. AP 31:617 (29 September 1791).

80. Tackett, *Becoming a Revolutionary*, 141; see also Furet, *Interpreting*, 52; George Rudé, *The Crowd in the French Revolution* (Oxford: Oxford University Press, 1959), 61.

81. AP 8:166 (27 June 1789).

82. Tallien, Aulard, *Jacobins*, 4:109.

83. Etienne Dumont, *Souvenirs sur Mirabeau* (Paris: C. Gosselin, 1832), 78.

84. *L'Ami du Roi*, 11 October 1790. At least one historian doubts whether the spectators really influenced the deputies of the right; see Patrick Brasart, *Paroles de la Révolution: Les assemblées parlementaires, 1789–1794* (Paris: Minerve, 1988), 71.

85. Dumont, 181.

86. Goupil-Prefeln, AP 28:317 (15 July 1791); Deusy, AP 47:46 (22 July 1792); *Le Patriote Français*, 10 October 1789. Brasart cites a report by some German observers that the galleries were mostly filled with women from the lower classes; see Brasart, 112.

87. Tackett, *Becoming a Revolutionary*, 197.

88. Some of the documents from the investigation appear in Philip Dawson, ed., *The French Revolution* (Englewood Cliffs, N.J.: Prentice-Hall, 1967), 59, 62, 66; see also Rudé, 74–75.

89. *L'Ami du Roi*, 6 May 1791.

90. *Le Patriote Français*, 9 October 1789.

91. AP 46:397 (12 July 1792).

92. *La Gazette Universelle*, 26 June 1792.

93. AP 45:628 (27 June 1792).

94. Aulard, *Jacobins*, 4:101–2 (13 July 1792).

95. De la Rochefoucauld-Liancourt, AP 26:202 (18 May 1791).

96. Chabot, in Aulard, *Jacobins*, 4:183.

97. Lamarque, AP 45:435 (21 June 1792); De la Rochefoucauld-Liancourt, AP 26:203 (18 May 1791).

98. Briois-Beaumetz, AP 25:689 (10 May 1791).

99. *Révolutions de Paris*, 14 July 1792.

100. *La Gazette Universelle*, 19 July 1791.

101. AP 45:629 (27 June 1792); see also AP 45:645.

102. AP 47:553 (8 August 1792).

103. *Révolutions de Paris*, 14 July 1792; Delacroix, AP 46:164 (6 July 1792).

104. *Révolutions de Paris*, 23 June 1792; *L'Ami du Roi*, 31 August 1791.

105. John Hall Stewart, ed., *A Documentary Survey of the French Revolution* (New York: MacMillan, 1951), 218–19.

106. *La Gazette Universelle*, 19 July 1791.

107. *L'Ami du Roi*, 31 August 1791.

108. Quoted in Genty, 91.

109. Quoted in Genty, 189.

110. Rose, 173.

111. AP 45:627 (27 June 1792).

112. AP 46:397 (12 July 1792); *L'Ami du Roi*, 23 June 1791.

113. Prugnons, AP 26:119 (16 May 1791).

114. Quoted in Rudé, 223.

115. Furet, *Interpreting*, 49; Gueniffey, "Elections," 34. Furet, of course, knew that the revolutionaries' claims regarding public opinion were fictitious, but the language he chose to use here was unfortunate, as it risked perpetuating an all-too-common misperception about public opinion in the Revolution.

116. Gueniffey, "Elections," 34.

117. Dumont, 72.

118. Tackett, *Becoming a Revolutionary*, 197.

119. Dumont, 184; see also Tackett, *Becoming a Revolutionary*, 199.

120. Robespierre, quoted in Albert Mathiez, *Le dix août, 1792* (Paris: Hachette, 1931), 84; see Mathiez's account, 70–90; see also Frédéric Braesch, *La commune du 10 Août 1792. Etude sur l'histoire de Paris du 20 juin au 2 décembre 1792* (Paris: Hachette, 1911).

121. Note Dena Goodman's statement that the philosophes sought to expand their Republic of Letters and "saw virtue in numbers"; see Goodman, *Republic of Letters*, 146.

122. *L'Ami du Roi*, 23 June 1791.

123. M.-J.-A.-N. Caritat, marquis de Condorcet, *Oeuvres*, ed. A. Condorcet O'Connor and M. F. Arago, 12 vols. (Paris: F. Didot frères, 1847–1849), 10:194.

124. Grégoire, AP 25:687 (10 May 1791); Robespierre, AP 29:360 (11 August 1791); see also Rose, 38.

125. Rosanvallon, 186; see also Genty, 20, 117.

126. *Révolutions de Paris*, 6 December 1789.

127. AP 46:383–84 (12 July 1792).

128. Salle, AP 28:323 (10 August 1791).

129. AP 46:385 (12 July 1792).

130. Dumont, 339.

131. *Le Patriote Français*, 25 August 1789.

132. Sieyès, *Tiers état*, 159.

133. *Révolutions de Paris*, 14 November 1789; *Les Révolutions de l'Europe*, quoted in Genty, 88.

134. *L'Ami du Peuple* 458 (14 May 1791), in *Oeuvres politiques* 5:2870; *L'Ami du Peuple* 493 (18 June 1791), in *Oeuvres politiques* 5:3047.

135. *L'Ami du Roi*, 25 September 1790.

136. See, for example, Robespierre, AP 26:125 (16 May 1791); de Montlosier, ibid., 209 (18 May 1791); Barrère de Vieuzac, ibid., 226 (18 May 1791).

137. Quoted in Gueniffey, *Le nombre*, 129.

138. Dumont, 345, 372.

139. AP 47:598 (9 August 1792).

140. See, for example, Grégoire's comments, AP 28:319 (15 July 1791).

Chapter IV: The Beginnings of the Republic, 1792–1793

1. *Moniteur* 15:415.

2. Ibid., 417.

3. On the use of the terms "Gironde" and "Mountain," and the question of the existence of these two groups, see M. J. Sydenham, *The Girondins* (London: Athlone, 1961); Alison Patrick, *The Men of the First French Republic: Political Alignments in the National Convention of 1792* (Baltimore, MD.: Johns Hopkins University Press, 1972); Gary Kates, The Cercle Social, *the Girondins, and the French Revolution* (Princeton, N.J.: Princeton University Press, 1985), 269; Michael L. Kennedy, *The Jacobin Clubs: The Middle Years* (Princeton, N.J.: Princeton University Press, 1988), 297.

4. See, for example, the petition of the Quinze-Vingts section, AP 48:285 (16 August 1792); Rabaut Saint-Etienne, AP 56:9 (28 December 1792).

5. Pétion, AP 56:177 (3 January 1793); Danton, AP 61:347 (5 April 1793).

6. Isnard, AP 64:336 (8 May 1793).

7. Robespierre, in Aulard, *Jacobins*, 5:44 (25 February 1793); Pons, AP 57:47 (14 January 1793).

8. Chabot, in Aulard, *Jacobins*, 4:601.

9. AP 64:549 (11 May 1793); Robespierre, 5:18.

10. AP 56:20 (28 December 1792).

11. AP 61:532 (10 April 1793). Furet's statement that the people were "defined by their aspirations" rather than their socioeconomic status or opinions is a useful point if one keeps in mind that this was only one definition and that these were aspirations that orators imputed to them; see François Furet, *Interpreting the French Revolution*, trans. Elborg Forster (Cambridge: Cambridge University Press, 1981), 27.

12. AP 56:18, 20 (28 December 1792).

13. Choudieu, AP 60:132 (12 March 1793).

14. See Maurice Genty, *Paris, 1789–1795. L'apprentissage de la citoyenneté* (Paris: Messidor/Editions Sociales, 1987), 192; Saint-Just said it resided in the communes; AP 63:205 (24 April 1793).

15. AP 58:586 (15 February 1793).

16. AP 63:194 (24 April 1793).

17. On the Rennes Jacobin club, see Kennedy, 324. On 6 April 1793 a committee of the National Convention declared that "sovereignty resides in the national representation"; AP 61:360.

18. See, for example, Prost, AP 56:52 (29 December 1792); Isnard, AP 61:277 (3 April 1793); Lanjuinais, AP 64:626 (13 May 1793).

19. *Révolutions de Paris*, 11 August 1792.

20. On Caron, see George Rudé, *The Crowd in the French Revolution* (Oxford: Oxford University Press, 1959), 227; see also Albert Soboul, *Les sans-culottes parisiens en l'an II. Mouvement populaire et gouvernement révolutionnaire* (Paris: Editions du Seuil, 1968), 101–2.

21. AP 54:352 (4 December 1792). For Merlin's reply to Robespierre, see Aulard, *Jacobins*, 4:562 (8 December 1792).

22. AP 53:42 (29 October 1792); AP 60:165 (13 March 1793).

23. Barère, AP 56:206, 208, 209 (4 January 1793).

24. *Le Père Duchesne* #189, #167.

25. AP 48:285 (16 August 1792).

26. Salle, AP 63:113 (22 April 1793).

27. AP 56:205 (4 January 1793).

28. Ibid., 20 (28 December 1792); Philippeaux, AP 62:198 (16 April 1793); see also Robert, AP 63:386 (26 April 1793).

29. Moreau, AP 56:96 (31 December 1792); for similar comments, see Lequinio, AP 56:7 (28 December 1792); Barère, AP 56:205 (4 January 1793); *Le Patriote Français*, 24 September 1792.

30. AP 64:430 (10 May 1793); Robespierre, 5:16; see also 4:360.

31. AP 63:108, 113 (22 April 1793).

32. AP 55:716 (27 December 1792).

33. Vergniaud, AP 56:91 (31 December 1792).

34. Gros, in Aulard, *Jacobins*, 4:215–16 (17 August 1792).

35. See Genty, 189; Patrick, 158, 174; Furet says even the sections showed less interest in binding mandates than in the recall of representatives, but some did favor them; see François Furet, *Revolutionary France: 1770–1880*, trans. Antonia Nevill (Oxford: Blackwell, 1992), 131; see also Soboul, 112–13.

36. Aulard, *Jacobins*, 4:241 (27 August 1792); Chabot, ibid., 329 (24 September 1792).

37. AP 62:134 (15 April 1793).

38. AP 60:420 (21 March 1793).

39. *Le Père Duchesne* #168.

40. Robespierre, 5:169.

41. Delacroix, AP 52:388 (7 October 1792).

42. AP 60:425 (21 March 1793).

43. One deputy who favored letting a department recall its own representative was Moras; see Aulard, *Jacobins*, 4:253. For contrary views, see Dufriche-Valazé, AP 64:206; Delaunay, AP 63:18–19; Jeanbon, in Aulard, *Jacobins*, 5:30.

44. AP 53:161 (5 November 1792).

45. AP 60:164 (13 March 1793).

46. Gensonné, AP 56:149 (2 January 1793); see also Rabaut, AP 56:7 (28 December 1792); Fockedey, AP 56:55 (29 December 1792).

47. *Révolutions de Paris*, 20 October 1792; for Condorcet's views, see AP 58:585; Michel Pertué, "La censure du peuple dans le projet de Constitution de Condorcet," in *Condorcet, mathématicien, économiste, philosophe, homme politique: colloque international*, ed. Pierre Crépel and Christian Gilain (Paris: Minerve, 1989), 322–32.

48. Aulard, *Jacobins*, 4:323 (23 September 1792).

49. Dufriche-Valazé, AP 64:206 (6 May 1793); Vergniaud, AP 56:95 (31 December 1793).

50. AP 55:716 (27 December 1792).

51. Ibid., 715.

52. Chambon, ibid., 724 (27 December 1792); Birotteau, AP 56:46 (29 December 1792).

53. AP 55:715 (27 December 1792).

54. AP 56:19, 16 (29 December 1792).

55. Lequinio, AP 55:723 (27 December 1792).

56. See the comments of Robespierre, AP 56:20 (28 December 1792); also Jeanbon AP 56:120 (31 December 1792).

57. Carra, AP 56:157 (2 January 1793); see also Fabre, in Aulard, *Jacobins*, 4:645 (4 January 1793).

58. Jeanbon, AP 56:120 (31 December 1792).

59. Ibid., 151 (2 January 1793).

60. Ibid., 128 (31 December 1792).

61. David P. Jordan, *The King's Trial: Louis XVI vs. the French Revolution* (Berkeley and Los Angeles: University of California Press, 1979), 177, 158.

62. Mailhe, AP 53:277 (7 November 1792). The people's perpetual right to change the constitution was included as Article 30 of the new draft of the Declaration of Rights; see AP 63:116.

63. See Robespierre's statement quoted on page 94.

64. *Révolutions de Paris*, 18 August 1792.

65. AP 60:56–57 (10 March 1793); Collot d'Herbois, ibid., 434 (27 October 1792). Robespierre recommended a division but not a balance of powers; see AP 64:430–32 (8 May 1793).

66. AP 52:70 (21 September 1792).

67. *Le Père Duchesne* #170.

68. Augustin Cochin, "La crise de l'histoire révolutionnaire: Taine et M. Aulard," in *L'esprit du jacobinisme: Une interprétation sociologique de la Révolution française*, ed. J. Baechler (Paris: Presses Universitaires de France, 1979), 113–14.

69. On the events of 31 May–2 June 1793, see Morris Slavin, *The Making of an Insurrection: Parisian Sections and the Gironde* (Cambridge, Mass.: Harvard University Press, 1986).

70. J. A. W. Gunn, *Queen of the World: Opinion in the Public Life of France from the Renaissance to the Revolution* (Oxford: Voltaire Foundation, 1995), 329. Later, Gunn does add that "the revolutionary Left never discarded talk of public opinion" (p. 360). For another example of this argument, see Patrice Higonnet, *Goodness beyond Virtue: Jacobins during the French Revolution* (Cambridge, Mass.: Harvard University Press, 1998), 127.

71. Mona Ozouf, "Public Spirit," in *A Critical Dictionary of the French Revolution*, ed. François Furet and Mona Ozouf, trans. Arthur Goldhammer (Cambridge, Mass.: Belknap Press of Harvard University Press, 1989), 774. She also writes: "The terms *opinion publique* and *esprit public* competed for favor during the entire second half of the eighteenth century. The Revolution tended to opt for *esprit public* and even for *conscience publique*"; see Mona Ozouf, "'Public Opinion' at the End of the Old Regime," *Journal of Modern History* 60 (September 1988): 1.

72. AP 56:199 (4 January 1793); Aulard, *Jacobins*, 4:604 (21 December 1792).

73. AP 56:20 (28 December 1792).

74. See, for example, Pétion, AP 56:178 (3 January 1793); also the letter from officials in the Charente, AP 61:462 (9 April 1793).

75. AP 56:698 (9 January 1793).

76. AP 58:583 (15 February 1793); *Révolutions de Paris*, 22 December 1792.

77. Gunn, 357. For examples of references to the public spirit having become corrupted, see Barère, AP 60:426 (21 March 1793); Bonconseil Section, AP 61:456 (8 April 1793); Robespierre, ibid., 534 (10 April 1793); L'Eveque de Nevers, in Aulard, *Jacobins*, 4:497 (20 November 1792); Robert, ibid., 612 (23 December 1792); Paris Jacobins' message to the affiliates, ibid., 657 (7 January 1793); *Révolutions de Paris*, 24 November 1792.

78. AP 56:16 (28 December 1792), 246 (6 January 1793).

79. Robespierre, in Aulard, *Jacobins*, 5:47 (27 February 1793).

80. *Révolutions de Paris*, 6 October 1792; AP 61:541 (10 April 1793).

81. *Le Père Duchesne* #178; *Le Patriote Français*, 22 September 1792.

82. Lamarque, AP 60:698 (29 March 1793).

83. In Aulard, *Jacobins*, 5:171 (1 May 1793); Danton, ibid., 116 (31 March 1793).

84. AP 62:706 (19 April 1793); AP 57:531 (21 January 1793).

85. AP 52:127 (24 September 1792); AP 56:14 (28 December 1792).

86. *Révolutions de Paris*, 24 November 1792.

87. *Le Père Duchesne* #189; AP 56:20 (28 December 1792).

88. AP 56:7 (28 December 1792).

89. Dubois-Crancé, ibid., 98 (31 December 1792); Lequinio, ibid., 7 (28 December 1792).

90. Robespierre, 5:75.

91. Barrère de Vieuzac, AP 26:225 (19 May 1791); Jeanbon, AP 56:119 (31 December 1792); *Le Patriote Français*, 21 September 1792.

92. AP 56:698 (9 January 1793).

93. Vergniaud, AP 63:26 (20 April 1793); Prieur de la Marne, AP 59:719 (8 March 1793).

94. Delaunay, AP 63:20 (20 April 1793); Aulard, *Jacobins*, 4:634 (1 January 1793).

95. Quinze-Vingts Section, AP 48:285 (16 August 1792).

96. AP 54:362ff (5 December 1792).

97. Gerbet, in Aulard, *Jacobins*, 4:204 (13 August 1792).

98. *Le Patriote Français*, 21 September 1792.

99. AP 64:426 (10 May 1793).

100. Gamon, AP 54:74 (3 December 1792); Thuriot, AP 57:442 (19 January 1793).

101. See, for example, the petition in AP 62:134 (15 April 1793).

102. Lucien Jaume, *Le discours Jacobin et la democratie* (Paris: Fayard, 1989), 322.

103. Quoted in Genty, 207.

104. AP 62:124 (15 April 1793); Chasset, AP 63:684 (1 May 1793).

105. AP 63:689 (1 May 1793).

106. Chabot, in Aulard, *Jacobins*, 4:340 (28 September 1792).

107. *Le Patriote Français*, 4 December 1792; *Le Père Duchesne* #182.

108. Barère, AP 61:343 (5 April 1793); Cochin, *L'esprit*, 99.

109. AP 61:453–54 (8 April 1793).

110. On the physiocrats' outlook on this point, see Keith Michael Baker, "The Idea of a Declaration of Rights," in *The French Idea of Freedom: The Old Regime and the Declaration of Rights of 1789*, ed. Dale K. Van Kley (Stanford, Calif.: Stanford University Press, 1994), 166.

111. AP 63:682 (1 May 1793).

112. AP 61:530 (10 April 1793).

113. AP 52:400 (8 October 1792).

114. Chales, in Aulard, *Jacobins*, 4:495 (20 November 1792); ibid., 323 (23 September 1792).

115. Guyomar, AP 56:146 (2 January 1793).

116. AP 52:525, 526 (16 October 1792).

117. Chabot, in Aulard, *Jacobins*, 4:262 (7 September 1792).

118. Ibid., 5:218 (31 May 1793).

119. Soboul, 131.

120. Robespierre, 4:359.

121. AP 65:643 (31 May 1793); Aulard, *Jacobins*, 4:261 (7 September 1792).

122. AP 56:119 (31 December 1792); AP 62:133 (15 April 1793).

123. *Le Père Duchesne* #238.

124. Paris Commune, AP 65:653 (31 May 1793); Robespierre, *Oeuvres*, 5:197.

125. AP 52:130 (25 September 1792).

126. AP 65:53 (19 May 1793).

127. AP 61:527 (10 April 1793).

128. AP 56:44 (29 December 1792).

129. Ibid., 14 (28 December 1792).

130. AP 55:725 (27 December 1792).

131. Birotteau, AP 56:44 (29 December 1792); *Le Patriote Français*, 15 December 1792.

132. *Révolutions de Paris*, 27 October 1792.

133. Gamon, AP 65:44 (18 May 1793).

134. AP 64:431 (10 May 1793).

135. Thuriot and Lanjuinais, AP 65:36 (18 May 1793).

136. AP 62:134 (15 April 1793); see also Higonnet, 160.

137. AP 53:159 (5 November 1792); Chales, in Aulard, *Jacobins*, 4:605 (21 December 1792).

138. Kennedy, 323.

139. Aulard, *Jacobins*, 5:125 (5 April 1793).

140. AP 65:352 (26 May 1793).

141. AP 56:9 (28 December 1792).

142. AP 60:426 (21 March 1793); AP 65:314 (25 May 1793).

143. See Bonconseil Section, AP 64:153–54 (5 May 1793); Buzot, AP 62:124 (15 April 1793); Vergniaud, AP 63:26–27 (20 April 1793); Thuriot, AP 64:214 (6 May 1793); Paris Commune, AP 65:688 (1 June 1793).

144. AP 56:119 (31 December 1792).

145. On the turnout, see Malcolm Crook, *Elections in the French Revolution: An Apprenticeship in Democracy, 1789–1799* (Cambridge: Cambridge University Press, 1996), 85. The low turnout bothered the deputies enough to provoke discussion of making voting mandatory; see AP 64:205.

146. AP 56:176 (3 January 1793), 207 (4 January 1793).

147. Robespierre, AP 64:433 (10 May 1793); Louvet, AP 53:57 (29 October 1792); Dufriche-Valazé, AP 64:208 (6 May 1793). On problems in the holding of elections, see Patrice Gueniffey, *Le nombre et la raison: La Révolution française et les élections* (Paris: Editions de l'Ecole des Hautes Etudes en Sciences Sociales, 1993), 313; Crook, 93.

148. AP 56:203–5 (4 January 1793).

149. AP 62:137 (15 April 1793).

150. AP 56:205, 210 (4 January 1793).

151. Mailhe, AP 53:281 (7 November 1792); Fonfrède, AP 61:528 (10 April 1793).

152. Aulard, *Jacobins*, 4:323 (23 September 1792).

153. Ibid., 558 (7 December 1792).

154. AP 48:316 (17 August 1792).

155. Jordan, *King's Trial*, 202; see also 158–59, 196. Jordan holds that the lack of actual attacks disproves claims that intimidation affected the trial's outcome, but rumored violence did not have to happen to be intimidating.

156. AP 65:314 (25 May 1793).

157. Patrick, 150, 168.

158. Crook, 4–6; Gueniffey, *Le nombre*, 469, 392; see also Kennedy, 45; both Crook and Gueniffey note that the Vendée voted republican; see Crook, 5; Gueniffey, *Le nombre*, 411.

159. Gueniffey, *Le nombre*, 464.

160. AP 61:83 (2 April 1793).

161. See, for example, Jordan, *King's Trial*, 98–99.

162. Crook, 93.

163. Aulard, *Jacobins*, 4:240 (27 August 1792).

164. Ibid., 485 (17 November 1792), 497 (20 November 1792), 565 (9 December 1792), 369 (9 October 1792).

165. AP 60:55 (10 March 1793); AP 65:29 (18 May 1793).

166. Chales, in Aulard, *Jacobins*, 4:478 (16 November 1792); L'Eveque de Nevers, ibid., 497 (20 November 1792); Thuriot, ibid., 607 (24 December 1792).

167. Kennedy, 25, 179, 184, 300, 378; on hatred for Marat boosting the Girondins' support, see 180, 357; see also Gueniffey, *Le nombre*, 452–53; Paul R. Hanson, *Provincial Politics in the French Revolution: Caen and Limoges, 1789–1794* (Baton Rouge: Louisiana State University Press, 1989), 98.

168. Kennedy, 326–27, 379, 343–47, 362; see also Albert Mathiez, *La Révolution Française*, vol. 2, *La Gironde et la Montagne*, 3d ed. (Paris: Armand Colin, 1929), 112.

169. Kennedy, 357.

170. AP 65:134 (21 May 1793).

171. Ibid., 293 (25 May 1793).

172. Ibid., 294, 295 (25 May 1793).

173. Kennedy, 327, 330, 381.

174. AP 63:26 (20 April 1793).

175. Such divisions appear within each class, socioeconomic category, and region. On dissent within regions, see, for example, Alan Forrest, *The Revolution in Provincial France: Aquitaine, 1789–1799* (Oxford: Oxford University Press, 1996), 149; on the presence of many bourgeois among the sans-culottes, see Soboul, 53, 55.

176. See Manuel's proposal and the discussion of it; AP 52:69 (21 September 1792).

177. AP 53:53–54 (29 October 1792); *Le Père Duchesne* #186. Ironically, despite the many complaints about the masses' personalist tendencies, no one had a more personalist outlook than those leaders themselves, whose debates often seem to be nothing more than a series of ad hominem arguments.

178. Marcel Gauchet, *La révolution des pouvoirs. La souveraineté, le peuple et la représentation, 1789–1799* (Paris: Gallimard, 1995), 16.

179. Aulard, *Jacobins*, 5:126 (5 April 1793).

180. See, for example, Jaume, *Discours Jacobin*, 155; Gueniffey, "Robespierre," in *Critical Dictionary*, 306; Furet, *Revolutionary France*, 145.

181. Patrick, 132.

182. Deperret, in Aulard, *Jacobins*, 4:303 (17 September 1792).

183. AP 53:42 (29 October 1792).

184. AP 55:724 (27 December 1792).

185. Rabaut, AP 56:9 (28 December 1792); Philippeaux, AP 62:200 (16 April 1793).

186. Bourdon, in Aulard, *Jacobins*, 4:352 (30 September 1792).

187. AP 60:426 (21 March 1793).

188. Fonfrède, AP 59:720 (8 March 1793); Chabot, in Aulard, *Jacobins*, 4:515 (25 November 1792).

189. AP 60:23 (9 March 1793).

190. AP 62:199–200 (16 April 1793); AP 65:302 (25 May 1793).

191. Ibid., 302–3 (25 May 1793).

192. Aulard, *Jacobins*, 5:180 (8 May 1793); *Le Père Duchesne* #214.

193. Aulard, *Jacobins*, 4:458 (4 November 1792); AP 59:721 (8 March 1793).

194. Desfieux, in Aulard, *Jacobins*, 5:74 (8 March 1793); AP 61:539 (10 April 1793).

195. Robespierre, AP 56:22 (28 December 1792); Aulard, *Jacobins*, 4:637 (1 January 1793). Aulard questions whether this comment was really made, but he notes that it did appear in the *Journal de la Montagne*'s account of that session; see his footnote, 637.

196. Moreau, AP 56:96 (31 December 1792).

197. Merlin, in Aulard, *Jacobins*, 4:183 (5 August 1792).

198. Mathiez, *Gironde*, 119; *Le Père Duchesne* #211.

199. On "third-person effects," see W. Phillips Davison, "The Third-Person Effect in Communication," *Public Opinion Quarterly* 47 (1983): 1–15.

200. AP 53:39, 42 (29 October 1792).

201. Ibid., 160 (5 November 1792).

202. See Gueniffey, *Le nombre*, 247; Kennedy, 288.

203. AP 53:42 (29 October 1792).

204. AP 63:24 (20 April 1793).

205. On this problem, see Patrick, 143; Kennedy, 175.

206. AP 64:669 (14 May 1793). Modern opinion researchers have noted a *fait accompli* phenomenon, in which the number of survey respondents expressing approval for a policy already enacted tends to be higher than the number approving the same idea when framed as a theoretical proposal.

207. For a discussion of this issue in the Aquitaine, see Forrest, 4ff.

208. Cochin, 114.

Chapter V: The Terror

1. AP 75:661. The written protests, mostly undated, appear in an annex to the *Archives Parlementaires* for 3 October 1793.

2. AP 66:21 (3 June 1793).

3. AP 75:650.

4. Raymond Carré de Malberg, *Contribution à la théorie générale de l'état*, 2 vols. (Paris: Sirey, 1920–1922); Guillaume Bacot, *Carré de Malberg et l'origine de la distinction entre souveraineté du peuple et souveraineté nationale* (Paris: Editions du CNRS, 1985), 10–15.

5. Bacot, 19.

6. See Lucien Jaume, *Le discours Jacobin et la démocratie* (Paris: Fayard, 1989), 108, 149; David P. Jordan, *The Revolutionary Career of Maximilien Robespierre* (Chicago: University of Chicago Press, 1985), 10, 226; Pierre Rosanvallon, *Le sacre du citoyen. Histoire du suffrage universel en France* (Paris: Gallimard, 1992), 176.

7. R. R. Palmer, *Twelve Who Ruled: The Year of the Terror in the French Revolution* (New York: Atheneum, 1969), 277; Lucien Jaume, *L'échec au libéralisme: Les Jacobins et l'etat* (Paris: Editions Kimé, 1990), 54; Annie Geoffroy, "Le peuple selon Saint-Just," in *Actes du colloque Saint-Just (Sorbonne, 25 juin 1967)* (Paris: Société des Etudes Robespierristes, 1968), 237.

8. AP 76:313 (10 October 1793).

9. Ibid., 314 (10 October 1793).

10. Aulard, *Jacobins*, 6:82 (18 April 1794), 286 (26 July 1794).

11. Albert Soboul, *Les sans-culottes parisiens en l'an II. Mouvement populaire et gouvernement révolutionnaire* (Paris: Edtions du Seuil, 1968), 109.

12. Camille Desmoulins, *Le Vieux Cordelier*, ed. Pierre Pachet (Paris: Belin, 1987), 96.

13. AP 75:557 (Annex #5).

14. Aulard, *Jacobins*, 5:583 (26 December 1793); see also Lucien Jaume, "Les Jacobins et l'opinion publique," in *Le modèle républicain,* ed. Serge Berstein and Odile Rudelle (Paris: Presses Universitaires de France, 1992), 62–63.

15. *Moniteur* 19:629 (7 March 1794).

16. *Le Père Duchesne* #297, #272.

17. Ibid., #244, #275.

18. *Moniteur* 20:115 (3 April 1794).

19. Ibid., 19:633 (7 March 1794).

20. Aulard, *Jacobins*, 5:311 (24 July 1793).

21. Ibid., 596 (7 January 1794).

22. AP 75:132 (25 September 1793).

23. *Moniteur* 20:19 (23 March 1794).

24. Ibid., 21:333 (27 July 1794).

25. AP 75:650 (Annex #9).

26. Renaudin, in Aulard, *Jacobins*, 5:508 (11 November 1793).

27. Ibid., 415 (21 September 1793).

28. Danton, ibid., 113 (31 March 1793); Thuriot, ibid., 181 (8 May 1793).

29. Jaume, *Discours Jacobin*, 258.

30. AP 78:704 (10 November 1793).

31. Aulard, *Jacobins*, 6:67 (12 April 1794), 300 (29 July 1794).

32. Ibid., 5:248 (10 June 1793).

33. AP 80:360 (29 November 1793).

34. *Moniteur* 19:688 (14 March 1794).

35. Soboul, 117.

36. *Moniteur* 20:221 (16 April 1794); see also Françoise Theuriot, "Saint-Just: esprit et conscience publique," in *Actes du Colloque Saint Just*, 218; Mona Ozouf, "'Public Opinion' at the End of the Old Regime," *Journal of Modern History* 60 (September 1988): 21.

37. Geoffroy, 231.

38. *Moniteur* 21:277 (23 July 1794).

39. Aulard, *Jacobins*, 5:509 (13 November 1793); *Moniteur* 19:586 (1 March 1794).

40. *Moniteur*, 20:697 (11 June 1794).

41. Bronislaw Baczko, "The Terror before the Terror? Conditions of Possibility, Logic of Realization," in *The Terror*, vol. 4 of *The French Revolution and the Creation of Modern Political Culture*, ed. Keith Michael Baker (Oxford: Pergamon Press, 1994), 34.

42. *Moniteur* 20:103 (1 April 1794).

43. Desmoulins, 107; AP 75:132 (25 September 1793); Drouet, AP 73:423 (5 September 1793).

44. *Le Père Duchesne* #312; *Moniteur* 20:109 (2 April 1794).

45. See, for example, *Moniteur* 20:13 (22 March 1794); Aulard, *Jacobins*, 6:286 (26 July 1794).

46. AP 75:698 (Annex #33).

47. Desmoulins, 129; *Le Père Duchesne* #249, #270.

48. *Le Père Duchesne* #250.

49. See, for example, Barère, *Moniteur* 21:334 (29 July 1794); Desmoulins, 95; "La Convention au peuple français," *Moniteur* 21:341 (30 July 1794).

50. Aulard, *Jacobins*, 5:272 (23 June 1793); *Moniteur* 21:334 (29 July 1794).

51. Simond, in Aulard, *Jacobins*, 5:327 (4 August 1793).

52. Ibid., 504 (9 November 1793).

53. Ibid., 6:296 (29 July 1794).

54. *Moniteur* 19:707 (16 March 1794).

55. AP 70:295 (5 August 1793).

56. *Moniteur* 20:154 (8 April 1794).

57. Desmoulins, 87; among those calling the crowd "the people" was *Le Père Duchesne* #282.

58. Dumas, in Aulard, *Jacobins*, 6:20 (26 March 1794).

59. Ibid., 5:254 (14 June 1793).

60. *Le Père Duchesne* #261.

61. *Moniteur* 21:341 (30 July 1794).

62. Aulard, *Jacobins*, 5:582 (26 December 1793); *Le Père Duchesne* #284.

63. In Jaume, *L'échec*, 53.

64. Duquesnoy, *Moniteur* 19:586 (1 March 1794); Fabre, in Aulard, *Jacobins* 5:643 (7 February 1794).

65. Terrasson, in Aulard, *Jacobins*, 5:230 (5 June 1793).

66. Ibid., 580 (26 December 1793).

67. Maure, ibid., 621 (27 January 1794); *Moniteur* 19:688 (14 March 1794).

68. Aulard, *Jacobins*, 6:141 (18 May 1794).

69. Desfieux, ibid., 5:414 (20 September 1793); La Chevardière, ibid., 647 (9 February 1794).

70. Robespierre, ibid., 6:220 (14 July 1794).

71. *Le Père Duchesne* #248.

72. AP 75:556 (Annex #5).

73. See, for example, the comment by the convention's president that "the National Convention is happy and proud of the approval of France"; AP 72:32 (11 August 1793).

74. Ibid., 33 (11 August 1793).

75. Rosanvallon, 192.

76. Theuriot, 224.

77. R. R. Palmer, 128.

78. Aulard, *Jacobins*, 5:343 (11 August 1793).

79. Unnamed, AP 80:636 (4 December 1793).

80. Ibid., 629 (4 December 1793).

81. R. R. Palmer, 128.

82. Aulard, *Jacobins*, 5:533 (26 November 1793); Briart, ibid., 6:10 (23 March 1794).

83. *Moniteur* 20:43 (26 March 1794).

84. *Le Père Duchesne* #245.

85. AP 78:704 (10 November 1793); Vadier, *Moniteur* 20:142 (6 April 1794).

86. AP 77:504 (24 October 1793).

87. Aulard, *Jacobins*, 5:532 (23 November 1793), 297 (10 July 1793).

88. *Moniteur* 19:629 (7 March 1794); Dufourny, in Aulard, *Jacobins*, 5:263 (16 June 1793).

89. *Moniteur* 19:692 (14 March 1794).

90. Habermas, *Structural Transformation*, 7–10.

91. *Moniteur* 21:279 (21 July 1794).

92. Aulard, *Jacobins*, 5:240, 235 (7 June 1793).

93. Ibid., 701 (18 March 1794), 576 (23 December 1793).

94. Renaudin, in ibid., 507 (11 November 1793); AP 75:133 (25 September 1793).

95. On the scene in Paris, see Frédéric Bluche, *Danton* (Paris, 1984), 481; on similar patterns in Aquitaine, see Forrest, 313.

96. Gueniffey, *Le nombre*, 250, 251, 254; see also Crook, 148.

97. Crook, 106; Gueniffey, *Le nombre*, 250.

98. Albert Mathiez, *La Révolution Française*, vol. 3, *La Terreur*, 2d ed. (Paris, 1928), 34; see also Crook, 113.

99. R. R. Palmer, 137.

100. AP 70:290 (5 August 1793).

101. Dartigoeyte, in Aulard, *Jacobins*, 5:260 (16 June 1793).

102. Jaume, *Discours Jacobin*, 20.

103. *Le Père Duchesne* #320.

104. Aulard, *Jacobins*, 6:25–26 (28 March 1794).

105. Garnier, in ibid., 47 (5 April 1794).

106. *Moniteur* 20:221 (16 April 1794).

107. *Le Père Duchesne* #322.

108. See *Moniteur* 19:671 (12 March 1794).

109. Mathiez, *Terreur*, 173; Rudé, 137; see also Isser Woloch, *Jacobin Legacy: The Democratic Movement under the Directory* (Princeton, N.J.: Princeton University Press, 1970), 11; Higonnet, 57; Martin Lyons, *France under the Directory* (Cambridge: Cambridge University Press, 1975), 8–9.

110. Rudé, 140.

111. Hanson, *Provincial Politics*, 9.

112. AP 75:546 (Annex #3).

113. Ibid., 697 (Annex #33).

114. Ibid., 557 (Annex #5).

115. *Moniteur* 20:131 (5 April 1794).

116. Ibid., 143 (6 April 1794).

117. Garnier, ibid.

118. *Le Père Duchesne* #250.

119. Aulard, *Jacobins*, 5:248 (10 June 1793).

120. Ibid., 464 (17 October 1793).

121. Ibid., 468 (19 October 1793); ibid., 6:18 (26 March 1794).

122. Ibid., 5:520 (16 November 1793), 641 (6 February 1794).

123. Ibid., 5:647 (9 February 1794); the report on Vannes is in R. R. Palmer, 210.

124. Mathiez, *Terreur*, 34, 13.

125. R. R. Palmer, 277.

126. Albert Mathiez, *La Révolution Française*, vol. 3, *La Terreur*, 2d ed. (Paris: Armand Colin, 1928), 175; see also George Rudé, *The Crowd in the French Revolution* (Oxford: Oxford University Press, 1959), 133.

127. See, for example, Rudé, 136–37; Alan Forrest, *The Revolution in Provincial France: Aquitaine, 1789–1799* (Oxford: Oxford University Press, 1996), 258.

128. *Le Père Duchesne* #282.

129. Ibid., #291.

130. Paul R. Hanson, *Provincial Politics in the French Revolution: Caen and Limoges, 1789–1794* (Baton Rouge: Louisiana State University Press, 1989), 6, 30, 245; see also Maurice Genty, *Paris, 1789–1795: L'apprentissage de la citoyenneté* (Paris: Messidor/Editions Sociales, 1987), 238; Soboul, 110, 125.

131. *Le Père Duchesne* #289.

132. Aulard, *Jacobins*, 5:329 (5 August 1793).

133. Duval, *Moniteur* 21:335 (29 July 1794); Barère, ibid., 334, 345.

134. Ibid., 336 (29 July 1794).

135. Ibid., 338, 344 (29 July 1794).

136. Jaume, *L'échec*, 7–10.

137. Aulard, *Jacobins*, 5:492 (1 November 1793).

138. AP 70:295–96 (5 August 1793).

139. Desmoulins, 39, 112.

140. Ibid., 113, 62.

141. AP 78:704 (10 November 1793).

142. Coupé, in Aulard, *Jacobins*, 5:412 (18 September 1793).

143. AP 78:704 (10 November 1793).

144. Rosanvallon, 177.

145. On this point, see Jaume, *Discours Jacobin*, 416; H. Kelsen, *La Démocratie. Sa nature, sa valeur*, ed. M. Troper, trans. Charles Eisenmann (Paris: Sirey, 1932).

146. See Frédéric Bluche, *Danton* (Paris: Librairie Academique Perrin, 1984), 480.

147. AP 76:313 (10 October 1793); *Le Père Duchesne* #315.

Chapter VI: From Thermidor to Brumaire

1. *Moniteur* 21:369–70 (1 August 1794).

2. Dubois-Crancé, in Aulard, *Jacobins*, 6:316 (3 August 1794); Lequinio, ibid., 361 (20 August 1794).

3. *Moniteur* 21:441 (11 August 1794).

4. F.-A. Aulard, ed., "Réponse de Barère, Billaud-Varenne, Collot d'Herbois et Vadier aux imputations de Laurent Le Cointre," *Révolution Française* 34 (1898): 71–72.

5. Gamon, *Moniteur* 25:428 (6 August 1795).

6. Joseph de Maistre, *De la souveraineté du peuple: Un anti-contrat social*, ed. Jean-Louis Darcel (Paris: Presses Universitaires de France, 1992).

7. *Moniteur* 25:292–93 (20 July 1795).

8. *La Quotidienne* 170 (7 August 1795); Madame de Staël, *Des circonstances actuelles qui peuvent terminer la révolution* (Paris: Fishbacher, 1906), 33.

9. *L'Orateur du Peuple* 10 (9 vendémiaire III) [30 September 1795]; *La Quotidienne* 61 (20 April 1795).

10. *Moniteur* 25:109 (23 June 1795); Godechot, 82, 102.

11. *La Quotidienne* 61 (20 April 1795); Pierre-Louis Roederer, "Théorie de l'opinion publique," in Lucien Jaume, *L'échec au libéralisme: Les Jacobins et l'état* (Paris: Editions Kimé, 1990), 100.

12. *Moniteur* 23:661 (11 March 1795).

13. *L'Orateur du Peuple* 89 (21 ventose III) [11 March 1795].

14. Daunou, *Moniteur* 25:214 (11 July 1795).

15. *Le Journal des Hommes Libres* 33 (18 messidor III) [6 July 1795].

16. Jacques-Pierre Imbert-Colomès, "Imbert-Colomès, député du Rhône au Conseil des 500, à ses commetans et au peuple français sur la journée du 18 fructidor" (Frankfurt, 1797) [FRRC6.2/1854]; *La Quotidienne* 458 (29 July 1797), 449 (20 July 1797). On right-wing papers invoking revolutionary concepts, see Jeremy D. Popkin, *The Right-Wing Press in France, 1792–1800* (Chapel Hill: University of North Carolina Press, 1980), 122, 127.

17. Camille Jordan, "Camille Jordan, député du Rhône. A ses commettans. Sur la révolution du 18 fructidor" (Paris, 1797) [FRRC7/484.119].

18. *Moniteur* 21:362 (29 July 1794).

19. Aulard, *Jacobins*, 6:319 (3 August 1794), 324 (5 August 1794).

20. *Moniteur* 25:92 (23 June 1795).

21. Ibid., 21:727 (10 September 1794).

22. Ibid., 688 (30 August 1794).

23. Ibid., 22:153 (4 October 1794).

24. Delahaye, ibid., 25:535–36 (19 August 1795); Boudin, ibid. 24:92–93 (29 March 1795).

25. *Moniteur* 25:91 (23 June 1795).

26. Camille Jordan, 46, 118 [FRRC7/484].

27. Jeanbon, *Moniteur* 24:116 (1 April 1795).

28. Garrand, *Moniteur* 25:383 (31 July 1795).

29. *Moniteur* 25:92 (23 June 1795).

30. Ibid., 292 (20 July 1795).

31. *L'Orateur du Peuple* 129 (27 prairial III) [15 June 1795]; 10 (9 vendémiaire III) [30 September 1794].

32. Echasseriaux, *Moniteur* 25:335 (25 July 1795); ibid., 100 (23 June 1795).

33. *L'Orateur du Peuple* 127 (23 prairial III) [11 June 1795]; *Moniteur* 25:100 (23 June 1795).

34. *Moniteur* 25: 519 (17 August 1795).

35. See Pierre Rosanvallon, *Le sacre du citoyen: Histoire du suffrage universel en France* (Paris: Gallimard, 1992), 192–94; Patrice Gueniffey, *Le nombre et la raison: La Révolution française et les élections* (Paris: Editions de l'Ecole des Hautes Etudes en Sciences Sociales, 1993), 289.

36. Jeremy Popkin has taken issue with Ozouf's claim that the term "public opinion" disappeared in this period; see "The Concept of Public Opinion in the Historiography of the French Revolution: A Critique," *Storia della Storiografia* 20 (1991): 89.

37. "P.N.," *Le Journal des Hommes Libres* 78 (3 fructidor III) [20 August 1795]; de Staël, 89.

38. *L'Orateur du Peuple* 11 (12 vendémiaire III) [3 October 1794].

39. F.-A. Aulard, *Paris pendant la réaction thermidorienne et sous le Directoire*, vol. 4 (Paris: L. Cerf, 1900), 608–33.

40. Pierre-Louis Roederer, "Théorie de 'opinion publique," in Jaume, *Echéc*, 104.

41. *Gazette Nationale* 352 (8 September 1797); also note Fayau's comment that "the public spirit of the departments is always energetic," in Aulard, *Jacobins*, 6:561 (10 October 1794).

42. Audoin, in Aulard, *Jacobins*, 6:526 (28 September 1794); *L'Orateur du Peuple* 29 (21 brumaire III) [11 November 1794].

43. Chénier, *Moniteur* 23:637 (8 March 1795).

44. De Staël, 11.

45. Reprinted in *Le Journal des Hommes Libres* 38 (8 brumaire III) [29 October 1794].

46. Tallien, quoted in Bronislaw Baczko, *Ending the Terror: The French Revolution after Robespierre*, trans. Michel Petheram (Cambridge: Cambridge University Press, 1994), 84; *L'Orateur du Peuple* 26 (15 brumaire III) [5 November 1794].

47. *L'Orateur du Peuple* 20 (3 brumaire III) [24 October 1794]; Echasseriaux, *Moniteur* 25:554 (21 August 1795).

48. For Jaume's comments on the essay, see *L'échec*, 55–57. See also Jeremy D. Popkin, "The Newspaper Press in French Political Thought, 1789–1799," *Studies in Eighteenth-Century Culture* 10 (1981): 120.

49. Roederer, 100.

50. Jaume, *L'échec*, 55.

51. Roederer, 104.

52. Chénier, *Moniteur* 23:637 (8 March 1795); Duplantier, *Gazette Nationale* 266 (26 prairial VII) [14 June 1799].

53. *L'Orateur du Peuple* 7 (3 vendémiaire III) [24 September 1794], 8 (5 vendémiaire III) [26 September 1794], 20 (3 brumaire III) [24 October 1794].

54. Laugier, in Aulard, *Jacobins*, 6:363 (20 August 1794).

55. Dedelay-Dagier, *Gazette Nationale* 224 (14 floréal VI) [3 May 1798].

56. *La Quotidienne* 129 (27 June 1795).

57. *Moniteur* 25:562 (22 August 1795), 24:358 (1 May 1795).

58. Ibid., 22:476 (10 November 1794). For the decision to ban women, see 24:515.

59. *Le Journal des Hommes Libres* 78 (3 fructidor III) [20 August 1795].

60. Dumont, *Moniteur* 24:499 (20 May 1795); *La Quotidienne* 176 (13 August 1795).

61. Aulard, *Jacobins*, 6:620 (30 October 1794).

62. *La Quotidienne* 121 (19 June 1795). On the regime's educational plans and philosophy, see Daniel Hollander Colman, "The Foundation of the French Liberal Republic: Politics, Culture and Economy after the Terror" (Ph.D. diss., Stanford University, 1997).

63. *Moniteur* 25:527 (18 August 1795).

64. *La Quotidienne* 129 (27 June 1795).

65. Camille Jordan, 125 [FRRC7/484]; Albert Mathiez, *After Robespierre: The Thermidorian Reaction*, trans. Catherine Alison Phillips (New York: Alfred A. Knopf, 1931), 247.

66. De Staël, 89, 91, 90.

67. Jean-Pierre Gallais, "Dix-huit fructidor, ses causes et ses effets" (Hamburg, 1799), 211 [FRRC7/793].

68. *Moniteur* 21:558 (24 November 1794), 486 (13 August 1794).

69. Goujon, ibid., 24:108 (31 March 1795).

70. Ibid., 358 (1 May 1795).

71. Ibid., 25:109–10 (23 June 1795).

72. *Gazette Nationale* 329 (29 thermidor VII) [16 August 1799].

73. Camille Jordan, 46 [FRRC7/484].

74. *Moniteur* 24:108 (31 March 1795); ibid., 22:6 (19 September 1794).

75. *Gazette Nationale* 329 (29 thermidor VII) [16 August 1799].

76. *Moniteur* 21:379 (2 August 1794).

77. See, for example, Barère, ibid., 379 (2 August 1794).

78. *L'Orateur du Peuple* 92 (27 ventôse III) [17 March 1795]; *Moniteur* 21:604 (26 August 1794).

79. Roederer, 105.

80. D'Outrepont, *Gazette Nationale* 270 (30 prairial VII) [18 June 1799].

81. Darracq, ibid.

82. *Moniteur* 24:358 (1 May 1795).

83. Aulard, *Jacobins*, 6:360.

84. Crassous, ibid., 567 (12 October 1794); Fayau, ibid., 594 (18 October 1794); *Le Journal des Hommes Libres* 69 (9 thermidor V) [27 July 1797].

85. Mailhe, *Moniteur* 25:564, 580 (23 August 1795).

86. *L'Orateur du Peuple* 17 (26 vendémiaire III) [17 October 1794].

87. *Gazette Nationale* 329 (29 thermidor VII) [16 August 1799].

88. Goupilleau, ibid., 21:582 (24 August 1794); Chales, in Aulard, *Jacobins*, 6:337 (13 August 1794).

89. *Moniteur* 24:498 (20 May 1795).

90. *La Quotidienne* 61 (20 April 1795).

91. Title III, Article 29; see Godechot, 106.

92. Larévellière-Lépaux, *Moniteur* 24:89 (28 March 1795).

93. Ibid., 497 (20 May 1795).

94. Ibid., 111–14 (1 April 1795); ibid., 143–44 (4 April 1795), 117 (1 April 1795).

95. Ibid., 502 (20 May 1795).

96. Creuzé-Latouche, ibid., 25:299 (20 July 1795); Reubell, ibid., 22:476 (10 November 1794).

97. *L'Orateur du Peuple* 29 (21 brumaire III) [11 November 1794].

98. Ibid., 133 (5 messidor III) [23 June 1795].

99. *Moniteur* 24:531 (23 May 1795), 25:99 (23 June 1795).

100. See ibid., 26:351 (5 November 1795).

101. See ibid., 24:114 (1 April 1795), 498 (20 May 1795).

102. *L'Orateur du Peuple* 23 (9 brumaire III) [30 October 1794].

103. Duhem, Maure, in Aulard, *Jacobins*, 6:605 (22 October 1794).

104. Aréna, ibid., 635 (5 November 1794).

105. *L'Orateur du Peuple* 29 (21 brumaire III) [11 November 1794]; *Le Journal des Hommes Libres* 53 (n.d.); *Moniteur* 22:474 (10 November 1794).

106. Collombel, *Moniteur* 25:555 (21 August 1795); ibid., 26:17 (24 September 1795).

107. Thibaudeau, ibid., 647 (5 December 1795).

108. *La Quotidienne* 61 (20 April 1795); *Moniteur* 25:92 (23 June 1795).

109. Baudin, *Moniteur* 25:527 (18 August 1795).

110. See Martin Lyons, *France under the Directory* (Cambridge: Cambridge University Press, 1975), 35.

111. *Moniteur* 26:50 (25 September 1795); see also Anonymous, "Vérités terribles sur notre situation actuelle" (Paris, n.d.) [FRRC7/163].

112. *Moniteur* 25:252 (15 July 1795).

113. Roederer, 99.

114. Halle-aux-Blés Section, *Moniteur* 26:50 (25 September 1795).

115. Rouchen, *Gazette Nationale* 231 (21 floréal VI) [10 May 1797].

116. Eure, Administration départementale, "Aux vrais républicains" (Evreux, n.d.) [New York Public Library, French Revolution pamphlets, *KVR 10285].

117. *Gazette Nationale* 186 (6 germinal VI) [26 March 1798].

118. Merlin de Thionville, *Moniteur* 21:611 (30 August 1794).

119. Ibid., 687 (5 September 1794).

120. Guyomard, ibid., 734 (11 September 1794).

121. Ibid., 604 (26 August 1794).

122. *L'Orateur du Peuple* 140 (20 messidor III) [8 July 1795], 139 (18 messidor III) [6 July 1795].

123. Reprinted in *Le Journal des Hommes Libres* 38 (8 brumaire III) [29 October 1795].

124. Baczko, *Ending the Terror*, 135.

125. F.-A. Aulard, *The French Revolution: A Political History, 1789–1804*, vol. 3, *The Revolutionary Government, 1793–1797*, trans. Bernard Miall (London: T. F. Unwin, 1910), 387.

126. See Malcolm Crook, *Elections in the French Revolution: An Apprenticeship in Democracy, 1789–1799* (Cambridge: Cambridge University Press, 1996), 4, 144; Aulard, *Revolutionary Government*, 329.

127. See F.-A. Aulard, *The French Revolution: A Political History, 1789–1804*, vol. 4, *The Bourgeois Republic and the Consulate, 1797–1804*, trans. Bernard Miall (London: T. F. Unwin, 1910), 31; Georges Lefebvre, *The Thermidorians and the Directory: Two Phases of the French Revolution*, trans. Robert Baldick (New York: Random House, 1964), 199.

128. François Furet, *Revolutionary France, 1770–1880*, trans. Antonia Nevill (Oxford: Blackwell, 1992), 181, 213. Mathiez wrote that the Thermidorians "had nobody behind them but the purchasers of national property and the army-contractors"; see Mathiez, *After Robespierre*, 260.

129. De Staël, 91; Furet, *Revolutionary France*, 168, 196; Crook, 125; Isser Woloch, *The New Regime: Transformations of the French Civic Order, 1789–1820s* (New York: W. W. Norton, 1994), 46.

130. Bernard Saint-Afrique, *Moniteur* 25:547 (20 August 1795).

131. See, for example, Aulard, *Bourgeois Republic*, 141–43; A. Goodwin, "The French Executive Directory—A Reevaluation," *History* 22 (December 1937): 217; Lyons, 160.

132. Lynn Hunt, David Lansky, and Paul R. Hanson, "The Failure of the Liberal Republic in France, 1795–1799: The Road to Brumaire," *Journal of Modern History* 51 (December 1979): 755, 735.

133. Isser Woloch, *Jacobin Legacy: The Democratic Movement under the Directory* (Princeton, N.J.: Princeton University Press, 1970), 242.

134. For a statement of the case for excluding the poor, see Boissy d'Anglas, *Moniteur* 25:92 (23 June 1795); Paine, ibid., 25:171 (7 July 1795).

135. Lefebvre, *Thermidorians*, 453, 447.

136. Aulard, *Revolutionary Government*, 221; Rosanvallon, 195.

137. See Goodwin, 216; Hunt, Lansky, and Hanson, 755.

138. Saint-Martin, *Moniteur* 25:341 (25 July 1795).

139. See *Moniteur* 25:100 (23 June 1795).

140. Regarding Sieyès's proposal, see ibid., 293 (20 July 1795).

141. Roederer, 105.

142. *La Quotidienne* 449 (20 July 1797).

143. Goupilleau, *Moniteur* 21:582 (24 August 1795); ibid., 25:637 (31 August 1795).

144. Richer-Serisy, "Richer-Serisy au Directoire" (Rouen, 1798) [FRRC 6.2/1862].

145. See, for example, Hunt, Lansky, and Hanson, 737.

146. *Le Journal des Hommes Libres* 123 (2 prairial III) [21 May 1795].

147. Quoted in Aulard, *Bourgeois Republic*, 52.

148. Lefebvre, *Thermidorians*, 303.

149. Aulard, *Bourgeois Republic*, 121; Woloch, *Jacobin Legacy*, 252, 287; see also Hunt, Lansky, and Hanson, 754.

150. Thuriot, *Moniteur* 21:616 (30 August 1794); Fréron, ibid., 23:583 (1 March 1795).

151. Baczko, *Ending the Terror*, 110.

152. On this point, see Hunt, Lansky, and Hanson, 737, 740.

153. Lefebvre, *Thermidorians*, 250.

154. *Moniteur* 25:196 (9 July 1795).

155. Girod-Pouzol, ibid., 216 (11 July 1795).

156. Jourdan, *Gazette Nationale* 232 (22 floréal VI) [11 May 1798].

157. Desgraves, *Moniteur* 25:537 (19 August 1795).

158. *La Quotidienne* 57 (16 April 1795).

159. *Le Journal des Hommes Libres* 33 (18 messidor III) [6 July 1795].

160. See his statements in *Gazette Nationale* #49 (19 brumaire VIII) [9 November 1799], #51 (21 brumaire VIII) [11 November 1799], #53 (23 brumaire VIII) [13 November 1799].

Conclusion

1. That argument is perhaps the most important theme of *Revolutionary France*.

2. Godechot, 34.

3. Amar, AP 57:531 (21 January 1793); Barère, AP 61:96 (2 April 1793).

4. AP 60:65 (10 March 1793); AP 54:76 (3 December 1792); AP 64:431 (10 May 1793).

5. See AP 63:644–46 (30 April 1793); AP 65:134 (21 May 1793), 294 (25 May 1793).

6. Simon Schama, *Citizens: A Chronicle of the French Revolution* (New York: Vintage Books, 1989), 153–54.

7. AP 61:279 (3 April 1793).

8. Schama, 447.

9. Taking issue with those who have sought to explain revolutionary illiberalism by citing Rousseau's influence, Patrice Higonnet offers an alternative explanation by emphasizing France's "clerico-monarchic" past; see Patrice Higonnet, *Goodness Beyond Virtue: Jacobins during the French Revolution* (Cambridge, Mass.: Harvard University Press, 1998), 7, 11, 70. Yet as argued in chapter 2, although Rousseau certainly did not "cause" the Revolution, his influence grew enormously once the Revolution began. Even if they were only parroting ideas and phrases they had heard others cite, orators nonetheless invoked Rousseau's concepts ad infinitum, with references to his ideas appearing on countless pages of the constitutional debates. It seems undeniable that Rousseau's ideas and his overall utopianism had a profound influence on the Revolution, helping fuel the illiberal attitudes that led to political stalemate and violence, and also helping create visions of public opinion that proved a very poor basis for settling conflicts or endowing leaders with legitimacy. None of this is to deny the important legacy of France's "clerico-monarchic" past, but simply to reject the idea of treating France's absolutist heritage and Rousseau's influence as mutually exclusive.

10. For a discussion of this issue, see Dena Goodman, *The Republic of Letters: A Cultural History of the French Enlightenment* (Ithaca, N.Y.: Cornell University Press, 1994), 300–4.

Works Cited

Aulard, F.-A. *The French Revolution: A Political History, 1789–1804.* Vol. 3, *The Revolutionary Government, 1793–1797.* Translated by Bernard Miall. London: T. F. Unwin, 1910.

———. *The French Revolution: A Political History, 1789-1804.* Vol. 4, *The Bourgeois Republic and the Consulate, 1797–1804.* Translated by Bernard Miall. London: T. F. Unwin, 1910.

———. *Paris pendant la réaction thermidorienne et sous le Directoire.* Vol. 4. Paris: L. Cerf, 1900.

———, ed. "Réponse de Barère, Billaud-Varenne, Collot d'Herbois et Vadier aux imputations de Laurent le Cointre." *Révolution Française* 34 (1898): 57–80.

———, ed. *La Société des Jacobins. Recueil de documents pour l'histoire du Club des Jacobins de Paris.* 6 vols. Paris: Jouaust, 1889–1897.

Bacot, Guillaume. *Carré de Malberg et l'origine de la distinction entre souveraineté du peuple et souveraineté nationale.* Paris: Editions du CNRS, 1985.

Baczko, Bronislaw. *Ending the Terror: The French Revolution after Robespierre.* Translated by Michel Petheram. Cambridge: Cambridge University Press, 1994.

———. "The Terror before the Terror? Conditions of Possibility, Logic of Realization." In *The Terror.* Vol. 4 of *The French Revolution and the Creation of Modern Political Culture,* edited by Keith Michael Baker, 19–38. Oxford: Pergamon Press, 1994.

Baker, Keith Michael. "Constitution." In *A Critical Dictionary of the French Revolution,* edited by François Furet and Mona Ozouf, translated by Arthur Goldhammer, 479–93. Cambridge, Mass.: Belknap Press of Harvard University Press, 1989.

———. "Defining the Public Sphere in Eighteenth-Century France: Variations on a Theme by Habermas." In *Habermas and the Public Sphere,* edited by Craig Calhoun, 181–211. Cambridge, Mass.: MIT Press, 1992.

———. "The Idea of a Declaration of Rights." In *The French Idea of Freedom: The Old Regime and the Declaration of Rights of 1789,* edited by Dale K. Van Kley, 154–96. Stanford, Calif.: Stanford University Press, 1994.

———. *Inventing the French Revolution.* Cambridge: Cambridge University Press, 1990.

———. "Representation." In *The Political Culture of the Old Regime.* Vol. 1 of *The French Revolution and the Creation of Modern Political Culture,* edited by Keith Michael Baker, 469–92. Oxford: Pergamon Press, 1987.

———. "Sieyès." In *A Critical Dictionary of the French Revolution,* edited by François Furet and Mona Ozouf, translated by Arthur Goldhammer, 313–23. Cambridge, Mass.: Belknap Press of Harvard University Press, 1989.

———. "Sovereignty." In *A Critical Dictionary of the French Revolution,* edited by François Furet and Mona Ozouf, translated by Arthur Goldhammer, 844–59. Cambridge, Mass.: Belknap Press of Harvard University Press, 1989.

Baker, Keith Michael, and Anthea Waleson, trans. "Remonstrance of the *Cour des aides* (6 May 1775)." In *The Old Regime and the French Revolution,* edited by Keith Michael Baker, 51–70. Chicago: University of Chicago Press, 1987.

Barny, Roger. *L'éclatement révolutionnaire du Rousseauisme.* Paris: Les Belles Lettres, 1988.

———. *Rousseau dans la Révolution. Le personnage de Jean-Jacques et le début du culte révolutionnaire.* Oxford: Voltaire Foundation, 1986.

————. *Prélude idéologique à la Révolution française. Le Rousseauisme avant 1789.* Paris: Les Belles Lettres, 1985.

Bell, David A. *Lawyers and Citizens: The Making of a Political Elite in Old Regime France.* New York and Oxford: Oxford University Press, 1994.

————. "The 'Public Sphere,' the State, and the World of Law in Eighteenth-Century France." *French Historical Studies* 17 (fall 1992): 912–34.

Besterman, T., ed. *Voltaire's Correspondence.* Vol. 65. Geneva, 1953–1965.

Bickart, Roger. *Les parlements et la notion de la souveraineté nationale au XVIIIe siècle.* Paris: F. Alcan, 1932.

Bien, David D. "Offices, Corps, and a System of State Credit: The Uses of Privilege under the Ancien Régime." In *The Political Culture of the Old Regime.* Vol. 1 of *The French Revolution and the Creation of Modern Political Culture*, edited by Keith Michael Baker, 89–114. Oxford: Pergamon Press, 1987.

Biou, Jean. "Est-il utile de tromper le peuple?" In *Images du peuple au dix-huitième siècle. Colloque d'Aix-en-Provence, 25 et 26 octobre 1969*, 187–99. Paris: Armand Colin, 1973.

Bluche, Frédéric. *Danton.* Paris: Libairie Academique Perrin, 1984.

Bodin, Jean. *Les six livres de la république.* 3d ed. Paris: Chez Iacque de Puys, 1578.

Bossenga, Gail. "City and State: An Urban Perspective on the Origins of the French Revolution." In *The Political Culture of the Old Regime.* Vol. 1 of *The French Revolution and the Creation of Modern Political Culture*, edited by Keith Michael Baker, 115–40. Oxford: Pergamon Press, 1987.

Bossuet, Jacques-Bénigne. "Politique tirée des propres paroles de l'Ecriture sainte." In *Oeuvres choisies de Bossuet.* Vol. 2. Paris: Hachette, 1892.

Braesch, Frédéric. *La commune du 10 Août 1792. Etude sur l'histoire de Paris du 20 juin au 2 décembre 1792.* Paris: Hachette, 1911.

Brasart, Patrick. *Paroles de la Révolution. Les assemblées parlementaires, 1789–1794.* Paris: Minerve, 1988.

Buchez, Philippe-Joseph-Benjamin, and Prosper-Charles Roux, eds. *Histoire parlementaire de la Révolution Française.* 40 vols. Paris: Paulin, 1834–1838.

Carré de Malberg, Raymond. *Contribution à la théorie générale de l'état.* 2 vols. Paris: Sirey, 1920–1922.

Castaldo, André. *Les methodes de travail de la Constituante.* Paris: Presses Universitaires de France, 1989.

Chartier, Roger. *The Cultural Origins of the French Revolution.* Translated by Lydia G. Cochrane. Durham, N.C.: Duke University Press, 1991.

————. "Culture populaire et culture politique dans l'Ancien Régime: quelques réflexions." In *The Political Culture of the Old Regime.* Vol. 1 of *The French Revolution and the Birth of Modern Political Culture*, edited by Keith Michael Baker, 243–58. Oxford: Pergamon Press, 1987.

Chisick, Harvey. *The Limits of Reform in the Enlightenment: Attitudes toward the Education of the Lower Classes in Eighteenth-Century France.* Princeton, N.J.: Princeton University Press, 1981.

Clere, Jean-Jacques. "L'emploi des mots nation et peuple dans le langage politique de la Révolution Française (1789–1799)." In *Nation et république. Les éléments d'un débat. Actes du colloque de Dijon (6–7 April 1994)*, 51–65. Aix-en-Provence: Presses Universitaires d'Aix-Marseilles, 1995.

Cochin, Augustin. *L'esprit du jacobinisme. Une interprétation sociologique de la Révolution française*, edited by Jean Baechler. Paris: Presses Universitaires de France, 1979.

Colman, Daniel Hollander. "The Foundation of the French Liberal Republic: Politics, Culture and Economy after the Terror." Ph.D. diss., Stanford University, 1997.

Condorcet, M.-J.-A.-N. Caritat, marquis de. "Réflexions sur le commerce des blés." In *Oeuvres de Condorcet*, vol. 2, edited by A. Condorcet O'Connor and M. F. Arago. Paris: F. Didot Frères, 1847.

———. "Vie de M. Turgot." In *Oeuvres de Condorcet*, vol. 5, edited by A. Condorcet O'Connor and M. F. Arago. Paris: F. Didot Frères, 1847.

———. *Oeuvres*. 12 vols. Edited by A. Condorcet-O'Connor and M. F. Arago. Paris: F. Didot Frères, 1847–1849.

Cowans, Jon. "Habermas and French History: The Public Sphere and the Problem of Political Legitimacy." *French History* 13 (June 1999): 134–60.

———. "Wielding the People: Opinion Polls and the Problem of Legitimacy in France since 1944." Ph.D. diss., Stanford University, 1994.

Cranston, Maurice. "The Sovereignty of the Nation." In *The Political Culture of the French Revolution*. Vol. 2, *The French Revolution and the Creation of Modern Political Culture*, edited by Colin Lucas, 97–104. Oxford: Pergamon Press, 1988.

Crook, Malcolm. *Elections in the French Revolution: An Apprenticeship in Democracy, 1789–1799*. Cambridge: Cambridge University Press, 1996.

Crow, Thomas E. *Painters and Public Life in Eighteenth-Century Paris*. New Haven, Conn.: Yale University Press, 1985.

Davison, W. Phillips. "The Third-Person Effect in Communication." *Public Opinion Quaterly* 47 (1983): 1–15.

Dawson, Philip, ed. *The French Revolution*. Englewood Cliffs, N.J.: Prentice-Hall, 1967.

Desmoulins, Camille. *Le Vieux Cordelier*. Edited by Pierre Pachet. Paris: Belin, 1987.

Dictionnaire historique de la Révolution Française. Paris: Presses Universitaires de France, 1988.

Dorigny, Marcel. "Le Cercle social ou les écrivains au cirque." In *La carmagnole des muses*, edited by Jean-Claude Bonnet, 49–66. Paris: Armand Colin, 1988.

Dumont, Etienne. *Souvenirs sur Mirabeau*. Paris: C. Gosselin, 1832.

Fabre, Jean. "L'article 'Peuple' de l'"Encyclopédie' et le couple Coyer-Jaucourt." In *Images du peuple au dix-huitième siècle. Colloque d'Aix-en-Provence, 25 et 26 octobre 1969*, 11–24. Paris: Armand Colin, 1973.

Farge, Arlette. *Subversive Words: Public Opinion in Eighteenth-Century France*. Translated by Rosemary Morris. University Park: Pennsylvania State University Press, 1995.

Faÿ, Bernard. *Naissance d'un monstre: L'opinion publique*. Paris: Librairie Academique Perrin, 1965.

Fitzsimmons, Michael P. *The Remaking of France: The National Assembly and the Constitution of 1791*. Cambridge: Cambridge University Press, 1994.

Forrest, Alan. *The Revolution in Provincial France: Aquitaine, 1789–1799*. Oxford: Oxford University Press, 1996.

Fralin, Richard. *Rousseau and Representation: A Study of His Concept of Political Institutions*. New York: Columbia University Press, 1978.

Furet, François. *Interpreting the French Revolution*. Translated by Elborg Forster. Cambridge: Cambridge University Press, 1981.

———. *Revolutionary France, 1770–1880*. Translated by Antonia Nevill. Oxford: Blackwell, 1992.

Furet, François, and Mona Ozouf. "Deux legitimations historiques de la société française au dix-huitième siècle: Mably et Boulainvilliers." *Annales ESC* 34 (May–June 1979): 438–50.

Furet, François, and Ran Halévi, eds. *Orateurs de la Révolution Française*. Vol. 1, *Les constituants*. Paris: Gallimard, 1989.

Gauchet, Marcel. *La révolution des droits de l'homme*. Paris: Gallimard, 1989.

————— . *La révolution des pouvoirs. La souveraineté, le peuple et la représentation, 1789–1799.* Paris: Gallimard, 1995.

————— . "Rights of Man." In *A Critical Dictionary of the French Revolution*, edited by François Furet and Mona Ozouf, translated by Arthur Goldhammer, 818–28. Cambridge, Mass.: Belknap Press of Harvard University Press, 1989.

Genty, Maurice. *Paris, 1789–1795. L'apprentissage de la citoyenneté.* Paris: Messidor/Editions Sociales, 1987.

Geoffroy, Annie. "Le peuple selon Saint-Just." In *Actes du colloque Saint-Just (Sorbonne, 25 juin 1967)*, 231–37. Paris: Société des Etudes Robespierristes, 1968.

Gilchrist, J., and W. J. Murray, eds. *The Press in the French Revolution: A Selection of Documents Taken from the Press of the Revolution for the Years 1789–1794.* New York: St. Martin's Press, 1971.

Godechot, Jacques, ed. *Les constitutions de la France depuis 1789.* Paris: Garnier Flammarion, 1970.

Goodman, Dena. "Governing the Republic of Letters: The Politics of Culture in the French Enlightenment." *History of European Ideas* 13 (1991): 183–99.

————— . *The Republic of Letters: A Cultural History of the French Enlightenment.* Ithaca, N.Y.: Cornell University Press, 1994.

Goodwin, A. "The French Executive Directory—A Reevaluation." *History* 22 (December 1937): 201–18.

Gordon, Daniel. *Citizens without Sovereignty: Equality and Sociability in French Thought, 1670–1789.* Princeton, N.J.: Princeton University Press, 1994.

Graham, Lisa Jane. "Crimes of Opinion: Policing the Public in Eighteenth-Century Paris." In *Visions and Revisions of Eighteenth-Century France*, edited by Christine Adams, Jack R. Censer, and Lisa Jane Graham, 79–103. University Park: Pennsylvania State University Press, 1997.

Gruder, Vivian R. "Whither Revisionism? Political Perspectives on the Ancien Régime." *French Historical Studies* 20 (spring 1997): 245–85.

Gueniffey, Patrice. "Les assemblées et la représentation." In *The Political Culture of the French Revolution*. Vol. 2, *The French Revolution and the Creation of Modern Political Culture*, edited by Colin Lucas, 233–57. Oxford: Pergamon Press, 1988.

————— . "Elections." In *A Critical Dictionary of the French Revolution*, edited by François Furet and Mona Ozouf, translated by Arthur Goldhammer, 33–44. Cambridge, Mass.: Belknap Press of Harvard University Press, 1989.

————— . *Le nombre et la raison. La Révolution française et les élections.* Paris: Les Editions de l'Ecole des Hautes Etudes en Sciences Sociales, 1993.

————— . "Robespierre." In *A Critical Dictionary of the French Revolution*, edited by François Furet and Mona Ozouf, translated by Arthur Goldhammer. Cambridge, Mass.: Belknap Press of Harvard University Press, 1989.

Guiffrey, Jules. "Etude sur la collection publiée sous le titre de Archives Parlementaires." *La Révolution Française* 16 (1889): 5–29.

Gunn, J. A. W. *Queen of the World: Opinion in the Public Life of France from the Renaissance to the Revolution.* Oxford: Voltaire Foundation, 1995.

Habermas, Jürgen. "Concluding Remarks." In *Habermas and the Public Sphere*, edited by Craig Calhoun, 462–79. Cambridge, Mass.: MIT Press, 1992.

————— . *The Structural Transformation of the Public Sphere: An Inquiry into a Category of Bourgeois Society.* Translated by Thomas Burger and Frederick Lawrence. Cambridge, Mass.: MIT Press, 1989.

Hanson, Paul R. "Monarchist Clubs and the Pamphlet Debate over Political Legitimacy in the Early Years of the French Revolution." *French Historical Studies* 21 (spring 1998): 299–324.

——— . *Provincial Politics in the French Revolution: Caen and Limoges, 1789–1794.* Baton Rouge: Louisiana State University Press, 1989.

Higonnet, Patrice. *Goodness beyond Virtue: Jacobins during the French Revolution.* Cambridge, Mass.: Harvard University Press, 1998.

Hunt, Lynn. "The 'National Assembly.'" In *The Political Culture of the Old Regime.* Vol. 1 of *The French Revolution and the Creation of Modern Political Culture*, edited by Keith Michael Baker, 403–15. Oxford: Pergamon Press, 1987.

——— . *Politics, Culture, and Class in the French Revolution.* Berkeley and Los Angeles: University of California Press, 1984.

Hunt, Lynn, David Lansky, and Paul R. Hanson. "The Failure of the Liberal Republic in France, 1795–1799: The Road to Brumaire." *Journal of Modern History* 51 (December 1979): 734–59.

Jaucourt, Louis de. "Le Peuple." In *The Encyclopédie of Diderot and D'Alembert: Selected Articles*, edited by J. Lough, 172–77. Cambridge: Cambridge University Press, 1954.

Jaume, Lucien. *Le discours Jacobin et la démocratie.* Paris: Fayard, 1989.

——— . *L'échec au libéralisme: Les Jacobins et l'état.* Paris: Editions Kimé, 1990.

——— . "Les Jacobins et l'opinion publique." In *Le modèle républicain.* Edited by Serge Berstein and Odile Rudelle, 57–69. Paris: Presses Universitaires de France, 1992.

——— . "Les Jacobins: une organisation dans le processus de la Révolution, 1789–1794." In *Les Révolutions Françaises. Les phénomènes révolutionnaires en France du Moyen Age à nos jours*, edited by Frederic Bluche and Stephane Rials, 244–53. Paris: Fayard, 1989.

Jordan, David. *The King's Trial: Louis XVI vs. the French Revolution.* Berkeley and Los Angeles: University of California Press, 1979.

——— . *The Revolutionary Career of Maximilien Robespierre.* Chicago: University of Chicago Press, 1985.

Julliard, Jacques. *La faute à Rousseau. Essai sur les conséquences historiques de l'idée de souveraineté populaire.* Paris: Editions du Seuil, 1985.

Kates, Gary. *The Cercle Social, the Girondins, and the French Revolution.* Princeton, N.J.: Princeton University Press, 1985.

Kelsen, H. *La Démocratie. Sa nature, sa valeur.* Edited by M. Troper. Translated by Charles Eisenmann. Paris: Sirey, 1932.

Kennedy, Michael L. *The Jacobin Clubs: The Middle Years.* Princeton, N.J.: Princeton University Press, 1988.

Klaits, Joseph. *Absolute Monarchy and Public Opinion: Printed Propaganda under Louis XIV.* Princeton, N.J.: Princeton University Press, 1976.

Koselleck, Reinhardt. *Critique and Crisis: Enlightenment and the Pathogenesis of Modern Society.* Cambridge, Mass.: MIT Press, 1988.

La Vopa, Anthony J. "Conceiving a Public: Ideas and Society in Eighteenth-Century Europe." *Journal of Modern History* 64 (March 1992): 79–116.

Lefebvre, Georges. *The Thermidorians and the Directory: Two Phases of the French Revolution.* Translated by Robert Baldick. New York: Random House, 1964.

Levy, Darline Gay. *The Ideas and Careers of Simon-Nicolas-Henri Linguet: A Study in Eighteenth-Century French Politics.* Urbana: University of Illinois Press, 1980.

Loyseau, Charles. "A Treatise on Orders." In *The Old Regime and the French Revolution*, edited by Keith Michael Baker, translated by Sheldon Mossberg and William H. Sewell, Jr., 13–31. Chicago: University of Chicago Press, 1987.

Lucas, Colin. "The Crowd and Politics." In *The Political Culture of the French Revolution*. Vol. 2, *The French Revolution and the Creation of Modern Political Culture*, edited by Colin Lucas, 259–85. Oxford: Pergamon Press, 1988.

———. "Revolutionary Violence, the People, and the Terror." In *The Terror*. Vol. 4 of *The French Revolution and the Creation of Modern Political Culture*, edited by Keith Michael Baker. Oxford: Pergamon Press, 1994.

Lyons, Martin. *France under the Directory*. Cambridge: Cambridge University Press, 1975.

Maistre, Joseph de. *De la souveraineté du peuple: Un anti-contrat social*. Edited by Jean-Louis Darcel. Paris: Presses Universitaires de France, 1992.

Manin, Bernard. "Volonté générale ou délibération? Esquisse d'une théorie de la délibération politique." *Le débat* 33 (January 1985): 72–93.

Marat, Jean-Paul. *Oeuvres politiques, 1789–1793*. Vol. 1. Edited by Jacques de Cock and Charlotte Goëtz. Brussels: Pole Nord, 1989.

Margerison, Kenneth. *Pamphlets and Public Opinion: The Campaign for a Union of Orders in the Early French Revolution*. West Lafayette, Ind.: Purdue University Press, 1998.

Mathiez, Albert. *After Robespierre: The Thermidorian Reaction*. Translated by Catherine Alison Phillips. New York: Alfred A. Knopf, 1931.

———. *Le dix août, 1792*. Paris: Hachette, 1931.

———. *La Révolution Française*. Vol. 2. *La Gironde et la Montagne*. 3d ed. Paris: Armand Colin, 1929.

———. *La Révolution Française*. Vol. 3. *La Terreur*. 2d ed. Paris: Armand Colin, 1928.

Maza, Sarah. *Private Lives and Public Affairs: The Causes Célèbres of Prerevolutionary France*. Berkeley and Los Angeles: University of California Press, 1993.

McCloy, Shelby. *The Humanitarian Movement in Eighteenth-Century France*. Lexington: University of Kentucky Press, 1957.

McDonald, Joan. *Rousseau and the French Revolution*. London: Athlone, 1965.

Merrick, Jeffrey. *The Desacralization of the French Monarchy in the Eighteenth Century*. Baton Rouge: Louisiana State University Press, 1990.

Monnier, Raymonde. *L'espace public démocratique. Essai sur l'opinion à Paris de la Révolution au Directoire*. Paris: Editions Kimé, 1994.

Mornet, Daniel. *Les origines intellectuelles de la Révolution française (1715–1787)*. Paris: Armand Colin, 1933.

Mortier, Roland. "Diderot et la notion de 'peuple.'" *Europe* 405–6 (January–February 1963): 78–88.

Murray, William James. *The Right-Wing Press in the French Revolution: 1789–92*. Suffolk: The Boydell Press, 1986.

Nathans, Benjamin. "Habermas's 'Public Sphere' in the Era of the French Revolution." *French Historical Studies* 16 (1990): 620–44.

Necker, Jacques. "De l'administration des finances de la France." In *Oeuvres complètes*, vol. 4, edited by Auguste Louis de Staël-Holstein. Darmstadt: Scientia Verlag Aalen, 1970.

Noelle-Neumann, Elisabeth. *The Spiral of Silence: Public Opinion—Our Social Skin*. Chicago: University of Chicago Press, 1984.

Ozouf, Mona. "Equality." In *A Critical Dictionary of the French Revolution*, edited by François Furet and Mona Ozouf, translated by Arthur Goldhammer. Cambridge, Mass.: Belknap Press of Harvard University Press.

———. "'Public Opinion' at the End of the Old Regime." *Journal of Modern History* 60 (September 1988): S1–S21.

———. "Public Spirit." In *A Critical Dictionary of the French Revolution*, edited by François Furet and Mona Ozouf, translated by Arthur Goldhammer, 771–80. Cambridge, Mass.: Belknap Press of Harvard University Press, 1989.

Palmer, Paul A. "The Concept of Public Opinion in Political Theory." In *Essays in History and Political Theory: In Honor of Charles Howard McIlwain*, edited by Carl Wittke, 230–57. Cambridge, Mass.: Harvard University Press, 1936.

Palmer, R. R. *Twelve Who Ruled: The Year of the Terror in the French Revolution*. New York: Atheneum, 1969.

Patrick, Alison. *The Men of the First French Republic: Political Alignments in the National Convention of 1792*. Baltimore, Md.: Johns Hopkins University Press, 1972.

Payne, Harry C. *The Philosophes and the People*. New Haven, Conn.: Yale University Press, 1976.

Pertué, Michel. "La censure du peuple dans le projet de Constitution de Condorcet." In *Condorcet, mathématicien, économiste, philosophe, homme politique: colloque international*, edited by Pierre Crépel and Christian Gilain, 322–32. Paris: Minerve, 1989.

Peuchet, Jacques. "Discours préliminaire." In *Encyclopédie méthodique: Jurisprudence*. Vol. 9, *La police et les municipalités*. Paris: Chez Panckoucke, 1789.

Popkin, Jeremy D. "The Concept of Public Opinion in the Historiography of the French Revolution: A Critique." *Storia della Storiografia* 20 (1991): 77–92.

———. "The Newspaper Press in French Political Thought, 1789–1799." *Studies in Eighteenth-Century Culture* 10 (1981): 113–33.

———. *Revolutionary News: The Press in France, 1789–1799*. Durham, N.C.: Duke University Press, 1990.

———. *The Right-Wing Press in France, 1792–1800*. Chapel Hill: University of North Carolina Press, 1980.

Richet, Denis. "Revolutionary Assemblies." In *A Critical Dictionary of the French Revolution*, edited by François Furet and Mona Ozouf, translated by Arthur Goldhammer, 529–37. Cambridge, Mass.: Belknap Press of Harvard University Press, 1989.

Robespierre, Maximilien. *Oeuvres complètes*. Vol. 4. Edited by Gustave Laurent. Paris: Société des Etudes Robespierristes, 1939.

Roche, Daniel. *The People of Paris: An Essay in Popular Culture in the Eighteenth Century*. Translated by Marie Evans and Gwynne Lewis. Berkeley and Los Angeles: University of California Press, 1987.

Roederer, Pierre-Louis. "Théorie de l'opinion publique," in Lucien Jaume, *L'échec au libéralisme: Les Jacobins et l'état*. Paris: Editions Kimé, 1990.

Roels, Jean. *Le concept de représentation politique aux dix-huitième siècle français*. Louvain: Editions Nauwelaerts, 1969.

Rosanvallon, Pierre. *Le sacre du citoyen. Histoire du suffrage universel en France*. Paris: Gallimard, 1992.

Rose, R. B. *The Making of the Sans-Culottes: Democratic Ideas and Institutions in Paris, 1789–92*. Manchester: Manchester University Press, 1983.

Rosso, Corrado. *Mythe de l'egalité et rayonnement des Lumières*. Pisa: Editrice Libreria Golliardica, 1980.

Rousseau, Jean-Jacques. *The Social Contract*. Translated by Maurice Cranston. Harmondsworth: Penguin Books, 1968.

Rudé, George. *The Crowd in the French Revolution*. Oxford: Oxford University Press, 1959.

Schama, Simon. *Citizens: A Chronicle of the French Revolution*. New York: Vintage Books, 1989.

Sewell Jr., William H. *A Rhetoric of Bourgeois Revolution: The Abbé Sieyes and* What Is the Third Estate? Durham, N.C., Duke University Press, 1994.

Shklar, Judith N. "General Will." In vol. 2 of *Dictionary of the History of Ideas*, edited by Philip P. Wiener, 275–81. New York: Scribner, 1973.

Sieyès, Emmanuel-Joseph. *Dire sur la question du veto royal*. In *Ecrits politiques*, edited by Roberto Zapperi. Paris: Editions des Archives Contemporaines, 1985.

———. *Qu'est-ce que le tiers état?* In *Ecrits politiques*, edited by Roberto Zapperi. Paris: Editions des Archives Contemporaines, 1985.

Slavin, Morris. *The Making of an Insurrection: Parisian Sections and the Gironde*. Cambridge, Mass.: Harvard University Press, 1986.

Soboul, Albert. *Les sans-culottes parisiens en l'an II. Mouvement populaire et gouvernement révolutionnaire*. Paris: Editions de Seuil, 1968.

Solé, Jacques. "Lecture et classes populaires à Grenoble au dix–huitième siècle: le témoignage des inventaires après décès." In *Images du peuple au dix-huitième siècle. Colloque d'Aix-en-Provence, 25 et 26 octobre 1969*, 95–102. Paris: Presses Universitaires d'Aix-Marseilles, 1973.

Staël, Madame de. *Des circonstances actuelles qui peuvent terminer la révolution*. Paris: Fishbacher, 1906.

Stewart, John Hall, ed. *A Documentary Survey of the French Revolution*. New York: MacMillan, 1951.

Sydenham, M. J. *The Girondins*. London: Athlone, 1961.

Tackett, Timothy. *Becoming a Revolutionary: The Deputies of the French National Assembly and the Emergence of a Revolutionary Culture (1789–1790)*. Princeton, N.J.: Princeton University Press, 1996.

———. "The Constituent Assembly and the Terror." In *The Terror*. Vol. 4 of *The French Revolution and the Creation of Modern Political Culture*, edited by Keith Michael Baker, 39–54. Oxford: Pergamon Press, 1994.

———. "Nobles and the Third Estate in the Revolutionary Dynamic of the National Assembly, 1789–1790." *American Historical Review* 94 (April 1989): 271–301.

Theuriot, Françoise. "Saint-Just: esprit et conscience publique." In *Actes du Colloque Saint-Just (Sorbonne, 25 juin 1967)*. Paris: Société des Etudes Robespierristes, 1968.

Tocqueville, Alexis de. *The Old Régime and the Revolution*. Translated by Stuart Gilbert. Garden City, N.Y.: Doubleday, 1955.

Van Kley, Dale K. *The Damiens Affair and the Unraveling of the Old Regime, 1750–1770*. Princeton, N.J.: Princeton University Press, 1984.

———. "In Search of Eighteenth-Century Parisian Public Opinion." *French Historical Studies* 19 (Spring 1995): 215–26.

Vissière, Isabelle. "L'émancipation du peuple selon Condorcet." In *Images du peuple au dix-huitième siècle. Colloque d'Aix-en-Provence, 25 et 26 octobre 1969*, 201–13. Paris, 1973.

Weil, Françoise. "La notion de 'peuple' et ses synonymes de 1715 à 1755 dans les textes non littéraires." In *Images du peuple au dix-huitième siècle. Colloque d'Aix-en-Provence, 25 et 26 octobre 1969*, 25–33. Paris: Armand Colin, 1973.

Wiener, Philip P., ed. *Dictionary of the History of Ideas*. New York: Scribner, 1973.

Woloch, Isser. *Jacobin Legacy: The Democratic Movement under the Directory*. Princeton, N.J.: Princeton University Press, 1970.

———. *The New Regime: Transformations of the French Civic Order, 1789–1820s*. New York: W. W. Norton, 1994.

Wright, J. K. "National Sovereignty and the General Will: The Political Program of the Declaration of Rights." In *The French Idea of Freedom: The Old Regime and the Declaration of Rights of 1789*, edited by Dale K. Van Kley, 200–210. Stanford, Calif.: Stanford University Press, 1994.

Index